Effective Revenue Writing

A basic course designed to give a brief,
practical review of writing principles,
grammar, and punctuation

U.S. TREASURY DEPARTMENT
Internal Revenue Service

Training No. 82–0 (Rev. 5–61)

This book is the text of an in-service training course prepared for Internal Revenue Service employees as part of the IRS Writing-Improvement Program. The course, conducted by the correspondence method, is intended primarily as a means of self-development. In addition to the text, it consists of a workbook containing 10 objective-type quizzes, a set of solution sheets, and templates for quick grading.

Only the text itself is for sale by the Superintendent of Documents.

For sale by the Superintendent of Documents, U.S. Government Printing Office
Washington 25, D.C. - Price $1.00

EFFECTIVE REVENUE WRITING 1

Table of Contents

Foreword   *Page*
Text	1	Sentence Sense	1
Text	2	Naming Words—Case	19
Text	3	Agreement and Reference	41
Text	4	Tense of Verbs and Verbals	61
Text	5	Mood and Voice	81
Text	6	Modifiers	95
Text	7	Connectives	119
Text	8	Punctuation and Good Sentences	141
Text	9	Watch Your Words	165
Text	10	The Effective Sentence	189
Writer's Guide to Current Usage			217
Index			251

This course and its companion course, Effective Revenue Writing 2, are part of the continuing writing-improvement program of the Internal Revenue Service.

Effective Revenue Writing 1, the basic course, was prepared by Lucile B. Spurlock and Luthera B. Dawson, employee development officers in the Training Division.

Effective Revenue Writing 2, the advanced course, was written for the Service by Dr. Calvin D. Linton, dean of Columbian College, George Washington University, Washington, D.C.

Foreword...

THIS BASIC COURSE and its companion course, Effective Revenue Writing 2, give writers an opportunity for self-development—an opportunity for brushing up on the basic elements of good writing which all writers must know if they are to communicate ideas clearly and effectively.

They supplement and complement the IRS Writing-Improvement Workshops and the GSA Plain Letters Workshops that many Revenue writers have attended. Writers tell us that these Workshops made them realize that their writing is an essential part of the work they do; that it is, in fact, often the *only* evidence of the work they have done. They tell us, too, that the Workshops stimulated them to look critically at their own writing, to try to diagnose its weaknesses, and to do something about improving it.

These two courses, then, are for those writers who want an intensive review of both basic and advanced writing principles.

Effective Revenue Writing 1 gives a review of the *functions* that various parts of the English language perform. This functional approach may differ from the approach you took in your earlier study of grammar, when you learned the names of the eight parts of speech and memorized a set of unalterable rules governing their use. We have tried to present grammar in a practical way, one that you can use in your work, by showing the function of words, *how* they are used—that is, whether they name something, describe it, tell about an action, or connect one thing with another.

Effective Revenue Writing 2 is an advanced course which, though it also stresses writing principles, builds on the foundation laid by this basic course. It is not a course on grammatical theory; instead, it is a course designed to guide the experienced writer in his efforts to make his writing more effective.

Both courses (unlike other IRS correspondence courses) are printed in book form, so that they may be used not only as correspondence courses but also as desk reference books.

TEXT 1

Sentence Sense

1	Introduction	4c	Verb
		4d	Adjective
2	The language of grammar	4e	Adverb
2a	Diagnosing sentences	4f	Preposition
2b	Relating rules to principles	4g	Conjunction
3	Eight writing principles	5	Clauses
3a	All the units of a sentence must fit together.	5a	Phrases
3b	Keep the time-order of events straight.	6	Sentence classification
		6a	Simple sentence
3c	Prefer the active voice	6b	Compound sentence
3d	Keep related words together	6c	Complex sentence
3e	Show relationship between ideas.	6d	Compound-complex sentence
3f	Punctuate for meaning	7	Functional classification
3g	Make words do your bidding	7a	Subject
3h	Strive for effective writing	7b	Verb
		7c	Complement
4	Glossary of terms	7d	Modifiers
4a	Noun	7e	Connectives
4b	Pronoun	7f	Verbals.

1

TEXT 1

Sentence Sense

1 Introduction

"A basic course designed to give a brief, practical review of writing principles, grammar, and punctuation." Thus the title page of Effective Revenue Writing 1 describes the course. What do you expect the course to be like? What can it do for you? How can it help you on the job?

You will find that this course follows the definition on its title page. It does not attempt, like Sir Francis Bacon, to take all knowledge for its province; neither does it skim so lightly over the subject that it touches on only the high points.

To most Revenue writers, English is the mother tongue. All our lives we have been speaking, reading, and writing English in a more or less acceptable fashion. This course, then, will present nothing new, nothing startling. It will recall grammatical terms which we once knew but which have lately become rusty from lack of use; in daily conversation, for example, we discuss predicates far less than such topics as tax revision or power steering. You may find the arrangement or grouping of topics we discuss is unlike the way you studied grammar, but you will find the basic material unchanged. In this course we use the functional method to present the subject; and "functional" is only another way of saying "in a practical way."

2 The Language of Grammar

This course is concerned primarily with sentences, which are the basic parts of larger units, paragraphs, letters, or reports. In this first text we review the names of the words and groups of words that together form sentences. Like the language of taxation, English grammar has technical terms. It is possible, we admit, to discuss tax matters without using technical terms; but how much more difficult (and how unnecessary, we often think) it is to do so! The technical terms of English grammar which we use in this course are no more incomprehensible than tax terms; they give us a common language for the subject we are discussing. The first step in Effective Revenue Writing 1, then, is to recognize these names of sentence parts.

2a   Diagnosing sentences

Knowing only the names of sentence components is not enough. It may give us a smug feeling of superiority if we can glibly recite the names of the eight parts of speech—but can we use this knowledge to help us communicate more effectively? We need to understand first how these parts function within the sentence, how they combine to form clear, effective sentences. Next we need to learn how to diagnose our sentences—tell exactly what their ailments are—so that we can cure their ills by revising or rewriting them.

You may belong to that large (but ever-shrinking) group of writers who think such grammatical scrutiny is highly unnecessary, who rewrite sentences "by feel" or by a vague sensing that something is wrong. We agree that it is possible to do an adequate job of revising by ear. Would we, however, sanction a revenue agent's basing his judgment in a tax case on a particular section of the Code just because he "felt" that the section covered the facts? Would we choose a doctor, for example, who did not diagnose his patients' ailments, but who instead prescribed medicine he "felt" might cure them? The agent's case might stand up in court, and the patients might survive the doctor's prescription. But how much more secure would you feel if the agent or the doctor based his action upon exact knowledge instead of on guesswork? This course takes the guesswork out of grammar; by explaining the relationship between grammar and writing principles, it can help you to follow rules of grammar to make your writing correct and to apply principles of writing to make it more effective.

2b   Relating rules to principles

Effective writing depends upon a knowledge of both principles and rules, not upon a slavish following of either one to the exclusion of the other. Writing principles are generally recognized guidelines, the large framework from which grammar rules have been formulated. Grammar is, after all, based upon commonsense. It is true that the rules of grammar have their roots in many sources and, for that reason, may trail cobwebs from an earlier time. It

Sentence Sense 5

is also true that many rules of grammar are somewhat arbitrary, but so are traffic rules. A red traffic light could just as sensibly mean "go" instead of "stop"; but if we are to have any kind of order on our public roads, we must expect our drivers to accept the "rule" that says, "Red means stop; green means go." So with grammar. The rules that govern the use of English words serve us best because they provide a pattern that everyone can follow with the assurance that everyone else who uses the language has the same set of rules.

Our primary concern is with writing principles that we can follow in getting our ideas across through writing. But undergirding every writing principle are one or more rules of grammar that support it and give it strength. To apply the principle, we need to understand and observe the rule of grammar on which it depends.

3 Eight Writing Principles

In this course we have selected a few of the most important writing principles and have built around each a text which explains the supporting rules of grammar. There is, of course, no magic number of writing principles. Some writing texts lump them into a few general categories; other subdivide them into a bewildering number of smaller parts. We have selected eight:

1. Make the units of a sentence fit together—agree with each other.
2. Keep the time-order of events straight.
3. Prefer the active voice to the passive.
4. Keep related words close together.
5. Show clearly the relationship between ideas.
6. Punctuate for meaning.
7. Make words do your bidding.
8. Strive for effective writing.

3a All the units of a sentence must fit together

Texts 2 and 3 show how to apply the principle, "All the units of a sentence must fit together." Why, for instance, do we say, "He is the man *whom* we thought to be best qualified," but "He is the man *who* was best qualified"? Why is it correct to say, "They selected *him and me*," but *"He and I* were selected"? All these words—*who, whom, he, him, me, I*—are good words when properly used; the question is how to select the one that works harmoniously with the other words in your sentence pattern. Whether we select the right word depends upon our ability to recognize subjects and objects. Text 2 helps us with this problem by explaining case as a means of showing the function of nouns and pronouns in a sentence.

Case problems concern chiefly pronouns, which change form to show nominative, possessive, and objective cases—that is, whether they are subjects or objects, or whether they indicate possession.

The concept of agreement, the subject of Text 3, underlies our basic principle of parts in a sentence fitting together. Subjects and verbs must match if they are to work together; a singular subject coupled with a plural verb results in a sentence that splits and goes in opposite directions. Here again, the problem narrows to a question of recognition: is the subject singular or plural?

Pronouns, even more than nouns, need a firm guiding hand to keep them from straying—often to keep them from saying things we never meant to say. Unless a pronoun refers clearly to its logical referent, its meaning may be ambiguous. The pronoun may get too far away from its referent; other nouns may slip in between the parent noun and its pronoun offspring. If the parts of a sentence are to fit together tightly, there must be no confusion arising from mismated subjects and verbs or from wandering pronouns.

36   Keep the time-order of events straight

"Tense means time," Text 4 says. This is the basis underlying the writing principle, "Keep the time-order of events straight." A study of tense can do more than enable you to conjugate verbs; it can show you how to express logically the time relationship of several actions to one another. This statement is, you realize, an oversimplification of a complicated problem. All actions do not fit into neat compartments of time slots; some actions are continuing or progressive, and a sentence may refer to several actions occurring at different times. Tense is a means of fitting these seeming contradictions into a logical pattern. By our choice of tense in the main verb in a sentence we select a point of view; from that point we can show by the tense of other verbs whether we are looking forward in time, backward at something that took place at an earlier time, or seeing something occurring at the same time.

Sentence Sense 7

You can express yourself more exactly and much more concisely if you know how to use tense correctly. Have you ever found yourself hopelessly twisted up in a sentence like, "If he had wanted to have gone, he would have said so." How much simpler (and shorter) the sentence becomes when we straighten out the sequence of tenses: "If he had wanted (in the past) to go (at that same time in the past), he would have said so."

3c Prefer the active voice

Text 5 also discusses verbs, but from the viewpoint of voice. It illustrates the old saying, "It isn't *what* you say, but *how* you say it." If we say, "The memorandum was written by Agent Jones," we have a grammatically *correct* statement. But if we say, "Agent Jones wrote the memorandum," we have a more *effective* sentence. The difference lies in our choice of the voice of the verb, a passive verb in the first illustration, an active verb in the second.

Text 5 explains the basis for the writing principle, "Prefer the active voice." This voice emphasizes the doer of the action, not the act itself. The active verb is direct, concise, and vigorous; its use can strengthen your writing.

We do not mean that the passive voice should never be used. If we want to tell the reader that the important point was the action, not who did it, we properly use the passive voice. Unfortunately, this voice has become almost a trademark of government writing. We use it too often, not realizing that it is a factor in making our writing long, roundabout, stilted—even old fashioned. Use the passive voice when it expresses what you want to say. Our plea is that you use the active voice instead of the passive *when either will serve your purpose.*

Text 5 will help you recognize active and passive verbs. Learn to spot them in your writing. Turn some of the passive verbs into active verbs occasionally and see your writing come to life.

3d Keep related words together

Text 6 on Modifiers illustrates the principle, "Keep related words close together." It shows, perhaps better than any other text in this course, that grammar boils down to three things—word choice, word order, and word relationships. We have, first of all, a wide choice of modifiers. They are available in a variety of forms: they may be single words, either adjectives or adverbs (*long* form, file *early*); groups of words such as phrases or clauses (the source *of the income*, or a return *that shows the source of the income*); or combinations of words (*well-arranged* and *up-to-date* office).

Modifiers are willing to work wherever we put them. They attach themselves to the nearest substantive, no matter whether the resulting statement makes sense; their meaning is dependent upon the word order we select. We often string modifier after modifier, creating rambling monsters of sentences, not realizing that a more skillful use of modifiers would align neatly the complex relationship of our ideas.

Any sentence will pull apart at the seams if the subject and verb are widely separated. We remember Mark Twain's description of a sentence in a foreign language going on for several pages before "it comes up at the end with the verb in its mouth." The many categories of modifiers, like subjects and verbs, must be watched to be sure they stay close to their related words if they are to do the work they can to make sentences both clear and effective.

3e Show clearly the relationship between ideas

Text 7 gives the "how to" behind the principle, "Show clearly the relationship between ideas." Don't sell your ideas short. Let your knowledge of connectives—those little miscellaneous words, prepositions, conjunctions, and relative pronouns—help you show how the ideas are related to each other. Don't rely on only short simple sentences to get your ideas across to the reader; he often needs either signals to point to the direction the sentence is taking, or bridges for the gaps in thought between sentences. Connectives can tie thoughts together, subordinate one thought while emphasizing another, contrast or balance ideas, or show cause and effect.

The writer of a paragraph may see no need for connectives. He sees his ideas as succinctly expressed, his sentences as reasonably short, his language simple. Unfortunately, he often reads into his sentences words that are not actually present; he mentally supplies links that connect his thoughts and show the relationships between them. But his reader, dependent upon only what is before him, may see unexplained gaps between the sentences and no obvious relationships between ideas. Be kind to your reader. Guide him from the beginning of the paragraph to the end by choosing and using the right connectives. In doing so, you are being kind to yourself, too. For you run much less risk of having your ideas misunderstood or misinterpreted when you supply the connecting words instead of leaving it to your reader to supply the ones he thinks you had in mind.

3f Punctuate for meaning

Text 8 describes punctuation as a functional tool—a tool which the writer should be familiar with and should use. The reader, too, should be equally familiar with this tool if he is to interpret correctly the signal the writer is sending.

Functional punctuation differs from conventional in that it has a greater effect on meaning. It is more flexible than conventional punctuation, for it rests on principles rather than on hard-and-fast rules. In using functional punctuation, the writer considers the meaning he wants to convey and the effect he wants to have on the reader; then he applies those principles of functional punctuation that he knows will accomplish his purpose.

Conventional punctuation, on the other hand, has its greatest effect on style. It is somewhat more rigid and therefore rests on rules. One of the principal requirements of effective conventional punctuation is that the writer (or his secretary) be consistent in following agreed-upon rules.

Bad writing cannot be well punctuated. Indeed, careful punctuation simply shows up basic sentence deficiencies if they exist. But the principles of punctuation, if kept in mind as we write and as we edit our writing, can help us build clear sentences.

3g Make words do your bidding

Texts 9 and 10 depart from the solid ground of established rules of grammar set out by earlier texts; with the last two texts in the course we enter that shadowy land of writing style, where the criterion of effectiveness takes on more importance.

Text 9 explains the problem the writer faces in choosing the words that will make his writing clear and effective. We need to look at words objectively and to acknowledge the fact that they may mean one thing to our readers and another to us. We must guard against using overly technical terms or words carrying hidden emotional brickbats; we also need to know how to economize with words to make our writing concise. Words can be your best ally or your worst enemy. Learn how to make them work for and with you.

3h Strive for effective writing

Text 10 reviews briefly and summarizes the writing principles listed in this text, and shows how to apply these principles in writing sentences that are well-organized, clear, concise, and appropriately expressed.

4 *Glossary of Grammatical Terms*

The last part of Text 1 is a glossary of the grammatical terms we shall use throughout this course. Succeeding texts will develop these terms more fully; this section is included as a refresher now and as a reference later.

The conventional classification of parts of speech is by form: noun, pronoun, verb, adjective, adverb, preposition, conjunction. The functional classification, which we use in this course, groups parts of speech by use: subject, verb, complement, modifier, connective. In this section we define these terms and illustrate them.

4a Noun

A noun is a word used to name a person, place, thing, or quality.

John, Washington, desk, truth

4b Pronoun

A pronoun is a word used in place of a noun. Pronouns are classified as:

Personal: *I, we, you, she, him, it*
Relative: *who, which, that*

Sentence Sense 11

       Interrogative: *who, which, what*
       Demonstrative: *this, that, these, those*
       Indefinite: *one, any, each, somebody*
       Intensive and
          Reflexive: *myself, yourself, himself*

4c   Verb

A verb is a word or group of words that expresses being of the subject or action to or by the subject. The verb, together with any words that complete or modify its meaning, forms the predicate of the sentence.

4d   Adjective

An adjective is a word that describes or limits (modifies) the meaning of a noun or pronoun.

    higher morale, *adjusted net* income, *rolling* stone

4e   Adverb

An adverb is a word that modifies a verb, an adjective, or another adverb. It answers the questions where, how or how much, when.

    write *legibly*, long *enough*, *very* high production

4f   Preposition

A preposition is a word used to relate a noun or pronoun to some other word in the sentence.

    at, in, by, from, toward

4g   Conjunction

A conjunction is a word used to join words, phrases, or clauses.

    and, but, nor

5   *Clause*

A clause is a group of related words containing a subject and a predicate.

An *independent* (or main) clause makes a complete statement and is not introduced by any subordinating word. When it stands alone, it is a simple sentence.

We shall print and *distribute* the report by the end of the month.

A *dependent* (or subordinate) clause cannot stand alone as a complete sentence; it depends upon some word in the independent clause to complete its meaning. Dependent clauses are classified as:

    Adjective: This is the man *who wrote to us for information.*
                    I have the report *he is looking for.* ("that" understood)

    Adverb: *As soon as you have finished the letter,* bring it to my office.

    Noun: *Whoever conducts the meeting* will be able to answer your questions.
                    Can you tell me *what the meeting will be about?*

5a Phrase

A phrase is a group of related words *without a subject and predicate* used as a noun, adjective, adverb, or verb. Phrases are classified as:

    Prepositional: Put the finished letter *on my desk.*
    Participial: The man *giving the speech* works in my office.
                      The report *submitted by the committee* was discussed at the October meeting.
    Gerund: *Writing this report* has been a long and difficult task.
    Infinitive: Our purpose is *to make the report as useful as possible.*

6 Sentence Classification

To construct sentences which will effectively convey our meaning to our readers, we must be able to recognize sentence classification and to know what kind of sentence best does each writing job. There are four types of sentences:

6a Simple sentence

A simple sentence contains only one clause (an independent clause). This does not mean, however, that it must be short. It may include many phrases, a compound subject or predicate, and a number of modifiers.

    A return was filed.
    You should set forth your proposal in writing and enclose the latest balance sheets of the corporation.

6b Compound sentence

A compound sentence has two or more independent clauses. Each of these clauses could be written as a simple sentence. There are no dependent clauses in a compound sentence.

> You may discuss this problem with our representative in the Baltimore office, or you may mail your return to this office.

6c Complex sentence

A complex sentence contains one independent clause and one or more dependent clauses.

> When we were reviewing the evaluation reports for February and March, we noted a number of inconsistencies.

6d Compound-complex sentence

A compound-complex sentence contains at least two independent clauses and one or more dependent clauses.

> Since that letter appears to answer your needs, we are enclosing a copy; we hope that it will answer all your questions fully.

7 Functional Classification of Sentence Parts

The parts of speech defined in this text are basic to a study of grammar. We can now group these parts according to their *use* and classify them by function as we discuss them in later texts.

The basic parts of the sentence are the subject, verb, and complement. Modifiers and connectives support this basic sentence, modifiers by making the meaning more exact and connectives by showing the relationship between parts.

7a Subject

The subject of a sentence is the word or group of words which names the thing, person, place, or idea about which the sentence makes a statement. The single words most often used as subjects are nouns and pronouns.

> The *Director* called the meeting for 3 o'clock. (noun)
> *He* wants everybody to attend. (personal pronoun)

Two verbals—the gerund and, less often, the infinitive—may also be the subject of a sentence.

>*Walking* is good exercise. (gerund)
>*To run* is more tiring than to walk. (infinitive)

The demonstrative, interrogative, and indefinite pronouns are among the other parts of speech used as subjects.

>*That* is going to be a difficult task. (demonstrative)
>*What* are your plans for doing it? (interrogative)
>*Everyone* is eager to have you succeed. (indefinite)

A phrase serving as a noun may be the subject of a sentence.

>*Writing that letter* was the smartest thing he did.
>*To make this report as comprehensive as possible* is our objective.

An entire dependent clause may be used as the subject.

>*Whoever answers the telephone* will be able to give you the information.
>*Whether the report has been released or not* will determine our action.

NOTE: In the texts that follow and in Effective Revenue Writing 2, you may find these five elements referred to generally as "substantives." A substantive is a noun or a word or group of words used as a noun.

7b Verb

The verb tells what the subject itself does (active verb), what something else does to the subject (passive verb), or what the subject is (linking verb). Every sentence must contain a verb. Verbals, although they come from verbs, cannot serve as verbs in the predicate of a sentence.

The properties of a verb are *number, person, tense, mood,* and *voice*. To indicate these properties we either change the form of the verb itself or add, to the main verb, other verb forms called *auxiliary verbs—be, have, can, may, might, shall, will, should, would, could, must, do.*

Number tells whether the verb is singular or plural; *person* tells whether the first person (*I*), second person (*you*), or third person (*he, it, they*) is performing the action. A verb and its subject must

Sentence Sense 15

agree in number and person. This problem of agreement—so essential to the writing of clear sentences—is discussed in Text 3.

Tense is the means by which we show the time of an action—whether it happened in the past, is happening in the present, or will happen in the future. *Mood* (indicative, imperative, subjunctive) indicates the manner of assertion—statement, command, wish, or condition.

Voice is the property of a verb that indicates whether the subject is performing or receiving the action of the verb. A verb in the *active voice* tells what the subject is doing; a verb in the *passive voice* tells what is being done to the subject.

> The *technician completed* the report on time.
> (The verb *completed*, in the active voice, tells what the subject, *technician*, did.)
>
> The *report was completed* on time.
> The verb *was completed*, in the passive voice, tells what was done to the subject, *report*.)

7c   Complement

The complement is the word or group of words that comes after the verb and completes its meaning. A complement may be (1) a direct object of the verb, (2) an indirect object of the verb, (3) a predicate nominative, or (4) a predicate adjective.

(1) Direct object:

> He gave the *report* to his secretary.
> (*Report* is the direct object of the verb.)
>
> We are trying *to find a solution to this problem.*
> (The infinitive phrase is the direct object of the verb.)
>
> Give me *whatever information you have.*
> (The noun clause is the direct object of the verb.)

(2) Indirect object:

> He gave (to) *her* the report.
> (*Her* is the indirect object of the verb; *report* is the direct object.)
>
> Give (to) *whoever answers the door* this letter.
> (The noun clause is the indirect object of the verb.)

(3) Predicate nominative:

The predicate nominative is also called the predicate noun, predicate complement, or subjective complement. The predicate nominative follows the linking verbs and renames the subject. It may be a noun, a pronoun, a verbal, a phrase, or a clause.

>   Noun: He is *chairman* of the committee.
>   Pronoun: They thought the author was *he*.
>   Gerund: My favorite exercise is *swimming*.
>   Infinitive phrase: The purpose of this memorandum is *to clarify the matter*.
>   Noun clause: The conference leader should be *whoever is best qualified*.

(4) Predicate adjective:

A predicate adjective is an adjective (or adjective phrase) appearing in the predicate and modifying the subject. A predicate adjective occurs only after the linking verbs and sense verbs.

>   The flower smells *sweet*.
>   The meeting we are planning for Tuesday will be *on that subject*.
>   This material is *over my head*.

7d   Modifiers

Modifiers—single words, phrases, or clauses—are used to limit, describe, or define some element of the sentence. They must attach to a sentence element which is both clear and expressed. A modifier is said to dangle when it cannot attach both logically and grammatically to a definite element in the sentence.

Adjectives describe or limit the meaning of nouns or pronouns.

>   The *new* employee has been assigned the *difficult* task of analyzing the *statistical* reports on *income* tax.
>
>   The report *of the Audit committee* is being studied.
>   (Prepositional phrase used as an adjective.)
>
>   The report *submitted by the Audit committee* is being studied.
>   (Participial phrase used as an adjective.)

Adverbs modify verbs, verbals, adjectives, or other adverbs. They answer the questions where, how or how much, when, why.

>   We will hold the meeting *here*.
>   She types *rapidly*.
>   The meeting is scheduled *for 3 o'clock*.
>   Bring me the letter *as soon as it is finished*.

Sentence Sense

7e Connectives

Connectives join one part of a sentence with another and show the relationship between the parts they connect. Conjunctions and prepositions are the most important connectives.

(1) Connectives joining elements of equal rank—

> coordinate conjunctions, correlative conjunctions, conjunctive adverbs

Coordinate conjunctions are perhaps the most used, and the most overused, connectives. They join sentence elements of equal grammatical importance—words with words, phrases with phrases, independent clauses with independent clauses. The coordinate conjunctions are:

> *and, but, or, nor, for, yet*

Correlative conjunctions work in pairs to connect sentence elements of equal rank. Each member of a pair of correlative conjunctions must be followed by the same part of speech. Examples of these conjunctions are:

> *either . . . or, neither . . . nor, not only . . . but also, both . . . and*

Conjunctive adverbs connect independent clauses and show a relation between them. Although the clause introduced by the conjunctive adverb is grammatically independent, it is logically dependent upon the preceding clause for its *complete* meaning. These are some conjunctive adverbs:

> *therefore, however, consequently, accordingly, furthermore, moreover, nevertheless*

(2) Connectives joining elements of unequal rank—

> subordinate conjunctions, relative pronouns, relative adverbs

Subordinate conjunctions introduce dependent adverb clauses and join them to independent clauses. Some of these conjunctions are:

> *before, since, after, as, because, if, unless, until, although*

Relative pronouns not only introduce noun and adjective clauses but also act as pronouns within their own clauses. These pronouns include:

> *that, which, who, whom, whatever, whichever, whoever*
>
> The man *who called for an appointment* has just arrived.
>   (Adjective clause)
> When he calls, tell him *that I had to leave for a meeting.*
>   (Noun clause)

Relative adverbs introduce subordinate clauses. The most common of these connectives are:

> *how, where, when, while*

(3) Prepositions

A preposition connects its object with the word in the main clause that the prepositional phrase modifies; it shows the relationship between that word and the object of the preposition. Some prepositions are:

> *to, of, by, from, between, in, over, under, for*

7f Verbals

Verbals are words formed from verbs; however, they can never act as verbs. They may serve as subject, complement, and modifier. The three kinds of verbals are gerunds, participles, and infinitives.

Infinitive (may or may not be preceded by *to*):

> *To screen* these applications will take a long time.   (subject)
> Can you suggest someone *to speak* at the meeting?   (complement)
> I will be happy *to send* you the copy.   (modifier)

Participle:

> The outline, *covering* the main points of the discussion, has been prepared.
> The main points of the discussion, *covered* by the outline, are these.
> *Having covered* the main points of the discussion, the speaker ended his talk.

Gerund (the *ing* form of the verb used as a noun):

> *Creating* machinery to put the law into effect was an enormous task.
> We will appreciate your *furnishing* this information.

TEXT **2**

Naming Words—Case

8	Naming words	12c	Subject of clause introduced by *than* or *as*
9	Characteristics of nouns and pronouns	12d	Words following forms of *be*
9a	Gender	12e	Direct address
9b	Case	12f	Nominative absolute
9c	Number	13	Objective case
10	Recognizing nouns	13a	Direct object of a verb or verbal
10a	Proper noun	13b	Indirect object of a verb or verbal
10b	Common noun	13c	Object of a preposition
10c	Collective noun	13d	Subject of an infinitive
10d	Concrete noun	13e	Word following infinitive *to be*
10e	Abstract noun	13f	Subject of a participle
11	Recognizing pronouns	14	Possessive case
11a	Personal pronoun	14a	Possessive of singular words
11b	Relative pronoun	14b	Possessive of plural words
11c	Interrogative pronoun	14c	Use of the *of* phrase to form possessive
11d	Indefinite pronoun	14d	Possessive of compound words
11e	Demonstrative pronoun	14e	Joint, separate, and alternative possession
11f	Intensive and reflexive pronouns	14f	Possessive of abbreviations
12	Nominative case	14g	Parallel possessives
12a	Subject of a verb	14h	Possessive with a gerund
12b	Subject of a relative clause		

19

TEXT 2

Naming Words—Case

8 Naming Words

Nouns are the principal "naming" words; certain kinds of pronouns also name things and persons. Both nouns and pronouns serve as *subject* and as *complements*.

If the writer is to use them effectively, he should refresh his knowledge of the kinds or classes of nouns and pronouns and of the peculiar characteristics that may cause them to be troublesome.

Let us consider, first, the characteristics (the grammatical properties) that nouns and pronouns have in common.

9 Characteristics of Nouns and Pronouns

Both nouns and pronouns have three properties: gender, case, and number.

9a **Gender** states the sex of the object being named. In English there are three genders: masculine, feminine, and neuter. Since the problem of gender is not very troublesome to the writer (except as he faces the need for being consistent), very little emphasis will be placed on it in this course.

9b **Case** is the property of a noun or pronoun which shows, either by inflection (change in the form of the noun or pronoun) or by position, the relation of the noun or pronoun to other parts of the sentence. English has three cases: nominative, objective, and possessive.

The latter half of this text gives and illustrates principles that the writer can follow in insuring the use of the appropriate case.

9c **Number** is the property by which we indicate whether one thing or more than one is being named. In English, we recognize two numbers: singular and plural.

The writer faces two problems in connection with the number of nouns and pronouns. The first is how to change a singular noun to a proper plural form. The second is how to accurately determine the number of the noun that is serving as a subject (or of the pronoun, which may depend on its antecedent for its number), so that he can make the verb agree with its subject in number. Text 3 gives and illustrates principles that the writer can follow in solving both these problems.

10 Recognizing Nouns

Nouns are the principal naming words. To use them effectively, the writer needs background information about (1) the kinds or classes of nouns and (2) the grammatical properties of nouns.

A noun names a person, thing, idea, place, or quality. There are five classes of nouns: proper, common, collective, concrete, and abstract.

10a A **proper** noun names a particular place, person, or thing. The writer's chief problem with proper nouns is recognizing them so that he can capitalize them. The IRS Correspondence Style Handbook will help the writer determine which of the terms used in Revenue writing are considered to be proper nouns so that he can be consistent in capitalizing them.

Atlanta, Mr. Jones, the Commissioner of Internal Revenue, Form 1040

10b A **common** noun names a class or group of persons, places, or things. The writer has two problems with common nouns: having enough of them at his command so that he can be selective in choosing nouns that will be familiar to his reader.

return, agency, budget, tax

10c A **collective** noun, singular in form, names a group or collection of individuals. The writer's chief problem with collective nouns is determining the number of the verb to use with the collective

Naming Words—Case

noun. For this reason, it is discussed at length in Text 3, under agreement of subject and verb.

committee, jury, council, task force

10d A **concrete** noun names a particular or specific member of a class or group.

apple, not *fruit; typist,* not *personnel*

10e An **abstract** noun names a quality, state, or idea.

justice, truth, objectivity

Concrete and abstract words are discussed at some length in Text 9. Recognizing these two types of nouns and deciding which will better serve his purpose presents the writer with a serious problem, for the overuse of abstract words can make his writing difficult to understand.

11 Recognizing Pronouns

Pronouns are the second line of naming words. They stand in place of nouns. The six classes of pronouns are: personal, relative, interrogative, indefinite, demonstrative, and intensive and reflexive.

11a The **personal** pronoun shows which person (first, second, or third) is the subject. Personal pronouns are troublesome to the writer because of their many forms; they change form to indicate number, person, and case.

First person: *I, we, me, us, my, mine, our, ours*
Second person: *you, your, yours*
Third person: *he, she, it, they, his, hers, its, theirs, him, her, them, their*

Because of their role in indicating case, personal pronouns are discussed extensively in the latter half of this text.

11b The **relative** pronoun serves two purposes: (1) it takes the place of a noun in the clause it introduces, and (2) like a conjunction, it connects its clause with the rest of the sentence.

who, whom, which, that, whoever, whomever, whichever, whatever

The relative pronoun, like the personal pronoun, changes form to indicate number, person, and case. The number and the person of relative pronouns are discussed in Text 3; this text discusses their function in indicating case.

11c The **interrogative** pronoun is the same in form as the relative pronoun, but different in function. The interrogative pronoun asks a question.

who, whom, which, what

11d The **indefinite** pronouns listed here are singular, as are most indefinites. Their chief problem, that of number, is discussed in detail in Text 3.

another, anyone, each, either, everyone, no one, nothing . . .

11e The **demonstrative** pronouns point out or refer to a substantive which has been clearly expressed or just as clearly implied. They may be used as pronouns

These are the letters he wants.

or as adjectives.

Bring me *those* letters.

NOTE: Do not use the personal pronoun *them* as an adjective. Use either of the demonstratives *these* or *those*, instead.

Not: Give *them* letters to the messenger.
But: Give *those* letters to the messenger.
or: Give *them* to the messenger.

11f Both **intensive** and **reflexive** pronouns are compound personal pronouns:

myself, yourself, himself, themselves, ourselves, herself

An intensive pronoun emphasizes or intensifies a meaning. It is not set off by commas.

I *myself* will see that it is done.
The director *himself* gave the order.
I will take it to him *myself*.

A reflexive pronoun appears as the direct object of a verb; its antecedent, as the subject of the verb.

I taught *myself* how to type.
He hurt *himself* when he fell.

It can, however, be the object of a preposition,

He finished the assignment by *himself*.
He was beside *himself* with joy.

the indirect object of a verb,

I bought *myself* a new suit yesterday.

or a predicate nominative.

I am just not *myself* today.

In formal usage, the reflexive pronoun is not used where the shorter personal pronoun can be substituted for it with no change in meaning.

Not: Both the Director and *myself* endorse the policy.
But: Both the Director and *I* endorse the policy.

NOTE: Most errors (usually in oral communication) in the use of these pronouns are such careless errors as:

The use of *hisself* for *himself*.
The use of *theirselves* for *themselves*.
The use of *myself* instead of the personal pronoun *me* or *I* in such constructions as "The secretary and *myself* were assigned to do this work."

CASE

Case is the property of a noun or pronoun which shows, either by inflection (change in form) or by position, the relation of the word to other parts of the sentence.

English has three cases: nominative, objective, and possessive.

All nouns and a few pronouns keep the same form in the nominative and in the objective cases. Consequently, we must depend on the position of these words in the sentence to indicate their function. Since nouns don't change form to indicate nominative and objective case, our only real difficulty with them comes in the formation and use of the possessive.

On the other hand, some pronouns are inflected (change form) in the nominative and objective cases, as well as in the possessive. Because of this, the case of pronouns causes us more trouble than does the case of nouns, and pronouns are more frequently misused.

12 *Nominative Case*

The nominative (or subjective) case is used primarily to name the subject of a verb or the predicate complement after a linking verb (such as *seem, appear,* or any form of *be*).

If either the subject or predicate complement is compound, both members must be in the nominative case.

>   Not: Either *she* or *me* will be responsible.
>   But: Either *she* or *I* will be responsible.
>   (Either *she* will be . . . or *I* will be . . . .)

NOTE: An appositive, which is a word or group of words standing next to another word and denoting the same person or thing, is always in the same case as its antecedent (the word it stands in apposition to). Therefore, *if the antecedent is in the nominative case,* the appositive must also be in the nominative case. If the antecedent is in the objective case, the appositive is also in the objective case.

>   Not: The representatives, *John and me*, are to meet on Friday.
>   But: The representatives, *John and I*, are to meet on Friday.
>   (*John and I* are to meet . . . .)

12a Subject of a verb in a main clause.

A noun or pronoun serving as the subject of a verb (except the subject of an infinitive) is in the nominative case.

>   *I* was late for work this morning.
>   (*I* is in the nominative case.)
>
>   *He* is planning to finish his report this week.
>
>   *He* and *I* have been assigned a new case.
>   (Both words joined by the coordinate conjunction are in the nominative case.)
>
>   Neither *he* nor *I* had heard of this before.
>
>   The culprits, *she and I*, were reprimanded.
>   (The appositive, *she and I*, is in the nominative case because its antecedent, *culprits*, is the subject of the sentence.)

The pronoun *who* used as the subject of a verb is not affected by a parenthetical expression such as *I think, he believes, they say* intervening between the subject and the verb.

> He is the person *who* I think *is* best qualified.
> (Disregard "I think"; *who* is the subject of the clause.)

> We asked Susan, *who* we knew *had always been* a student of English.
> (Ignore "we knew"; *who* is the subject of the clause.)

> Mr. Jones is the attorney *who* we suppose *will prepare* the brief.
> ("We suppose" is a parenthetical expression; *who* is the subject of the clause.)

The interrogative pronouns (*who, which, what*), which introduce questions, appear to require the nominative case because they usually come first in the sentence. In informal writing and speaking we may put these pronouns in the nominative case; in other types of writing the interrogative pronoun takes the case called for by its function in the sentence.

> Informal: *Who* did you send the information to?
> Formal: *Whom* did you send the information to?
> (or: To *whom* did you send the information?)

12b Subject of a relative clause

A relative pronoun (*who, whoever, which, whichever*) used as the subject of a clause is in the nominative case.

> Give the letter to *whoever answers the door.*

The clause itself may be a subject or, as in this example, an object; however, the case of the relative pronoun depends upon its use *within the clause.*

> The award will go to him *who completes the course with the highest score.*
> (The antecedent of the relative pronoun—*him*—is in the objective case, but *who* is in the nominative case because it is the subject of the clause.)

> *Whoever is selected* must report on Monday.
> (The clause is the subject of the sentence; the relative pronoun is in the nominative case because it is the subject of the clause.)

12c Subject of clause introduced by *than* or *as*

If the word following *than* or *as* introduces a clause, even if part of the clause is understood, that word must be in the nominative case. But if the word following *than* or *as* does not introduce a clause, it must be in the objective case. To test whether the word should be in the nominative or objective case, complete the clause.

> He has been here longer than *she*. (than *she has*)
> Mary is a better stenographer than *I*. (than *I am*)
>
> They were as late as *we* in filing the report. (as *we were*)
> We were told as promptly as *they*. (as *they were*)

In the following examples, the word following *than* or *as* may be in either the nominative or the objective case, depending on the intended meaning. If there is any chance your meaning might be misunderstood, complete the clause.

> She likes this work better than I. (than *I like it*)
> She likes this work better than *me*. (than *she likes me*)
>
> I have known John as long as *she*. (as *she has*)
> I have known John as long as *her*. (as *I have known her*)

12d Words following forms of *be* (predicate nominative)

A noun or pronoun following a form of the verb *be* (except for the infinitive if it has its own subject) must be in the nominative case. (This word is called the *predicate nominative*—or, if a noun, the *predicate noun*.) The general rule applying to this construction is that the word following the verb *be* must be in the same case as the word before the verb. Imagine that the verb *be* has the same meaning as the equals sign (=) in mathematics.

> Not: They thought I was *him*.
> But: They thought I was *he*. (*I* = *he*)
>
> Not: I am expecting my secretary to call. Is that *her?*
> But: I am expecting my secretary to call. Is that *she?*

A noun or pronoun following the infinitive *to be* is in the nominative case if the infinitive has no subject. For a discussion of the case of the noun or pronoun following an infinitive when the infinitive has a subject, see section 13e.

> He was thought to be *I*.
> My brother was taken to be *I*.

Naming Words—Case

NOTE: Writers frequently have trouble when one or both of the members of the compound subject or predicate nominative are pronouns. Try this simple test: Decide which case would be appropriate if *one* pronoun were the simple subject or predicate nominative, and then use the same case for both.

Example:
   The new *chairmen* are *he and I*.
Reverse positions:
   He and I are the new *chairmen*.

Example:
   If any one of the agents is chosen, *it* should be *he*.
Reverse positions:
   If any one of the agents is chosen, *he* should be *it*.

Example:
   The *author* was thought to be *I*.
Reverse positions:
   I was thought to be the *author*.

12e Direct address

Direct address is a construction used parenthetically to direct a speech to some particular person. Nouns or pronouns in direct address are in the nominative case and are set off by commas. This construction will cause little trouble, since proper names, which are the main examples of direct address, do not change form to indicate case.

   James, come here for a minute.
   It is true, *sir*, that I made that remark.
   Tell me, *Doctor*, is he showing much improvement?

12f Nominative absolute

The nominative absolute is a phrase that consists of a noun or a pronoun and a participle. It modifies the whole sentence but is grammatically independent of the rest of the sentence. The noun or pronoun in a nominative absolute construction is in the nominative case.

   We left the office together, HE *having finished his work*.
   (The phrase beginning *he having finished* . . . is a nominative absolute phrase modifying the main clause. The pronoun *he* is the subject of the *action implied* by the participle *having finished;* it is in the nominative case.)
   HE *having been elected chairman*, I am sure the meeting will have outstanding results.

13   *Objective Case*

The objective (or accusative) case is used chiefly to name the receiver or object of the action of a verb, or to name the object of a preposition.

When one part of a compound expression (joined by a coordinate conjunction) is in the objective case, all other parts of the same expression must also be in the objective case.

> When you reach the station call either *him* or *me*.
>   (*Call him . . . or call me*)
> The work was given to *you* and *me*.
>   (*To you . . . to me*.)

When the antecedent of an appositive is in the objective case because it is serving a function that requires that case, the appositive must also be in the objective case.

> The director has appointed *us, you and me*, to the committee.
>   (*has appointed you . . . has appointed me*)
> He gave *us auditors* a copy of the report.
>   (*he gave us . . .*)
> That principle is basic to *us Americans*.
>   (*is basic* to *us*)

13a   Direct object of a verb or verbal

A noun or pronoun serving as the direct object of a verb or verbal is in the objective case.

> The driver returned *him* to his home.
>   (*Him* is the object of the verb *returned*.)
> My supervisor called *him* and *me* to his office.
>   (The compound object *him and me* is the object of the verb *called*.)
> They will invite *us secretaries* to the meeting.
>   (*Us*, as well as its appositive *secretaries*, is the object of the verb *invite*.)
> *Whomever* you called before the meeting might like a copy of this report.
>   (The relative pronoun *whomever* is the object of the verb *called* in the relative clause; the entire clause is the subject of *might like*.)
> But: Call *whoever* is responsible before the meeting.
>   (The whole relative clause *whoever is responsible* is the object of the verb *call*; but *whoever* is in the nominative case because it is the subject of its clause.)
> I enjoyed meeting *him*.
>   (*Him* is the object of the gerund *meeting*.)
> I didn't intend to ask *them* again.
>   (*Them* is the direct object of the infinitive *to ask*.)

Naming Words—Case

Having called *him* and told *him* of our plan, we left the office.
(The first *him* is the direct object of the participle *having called*; the second *him* is the object of the participle *having told*.)

We have a letter from his company thanking *us* for our courtesy.
(*Us* is the direct object of the participle *thanking*.)

13b Indirect object of a verb or verbal

A word used as the indirect object of a verb or verbal is in the objective case.

The supervisor gave *me* the report.
(*Me* is the indirect object of the verb *gave*.)

The supervisor assigned *him* and *me* the task of reviewing the study.
(The compound object *him and me* is the indirect object of the verb *assigned*.)

The representative showed *us secretaries* the operation of the new typewriter.
(*Us*, as well as its appositive *secretaries*, is the indirect object of the verb *showed*.)

A letter giving *him* authority to represent the company is being prepared.
(*Him* is the indirect object of the participle *giving*.)

To tell *us* the latest developments, the Director held a staff meeting.
(*Us* is the indirect object of the infinitive *to tell*.)

13c Object of a preposition

A noun or pronoun serving as the object of a preposition is in the objective case.

Be sure to give the report to *him*.
(*Him* is the object of the preposition *to*.)

Several of *us* are concerned about the situation.
(*Us* is the object of the preposition *of*.)

He assigned the task of reviewing the report to *him* and *me*.
(*Him and me* is the compound object of the preposition *to*.)

The supervisor addressed his remarks to *us auditors*.
(*Us*, and its appositive *auditors*, is the object of the preposition *to*.)

Whom did you give the letter to?
(The interrogative pronoun *whom* is the object of the preposition *to*.)

The person to *whom* this letter is addressed has left the office.
(The relative pronoun *whom* is the object of the preposition *to* in the relative clause.)

But: Give this letter to *whoever* answers the door.
(Although the clause *whoever answers the door* is the object of the preposition *to*, the relative pronoun *whoever* is in the nominative case because it is the subject of its own clause.)

NOTE: *But* is a preposition when *except* may be substituted for it with no change in meaning.

>Everyone is going BUT *me*.
>(Everyone is going EXCEPT *me*.)

A special troublemaker is the compound object *you and me* after the preposition *between*. Do not say *between you and I;* say *between you and me*.

13d Subject of an infinitive

A noun or pronoun used as the subject of an infinitive is in the objective case.

>I want *him* to have this copy.
>(*Him* is the subject of the infinitive *to have*.)

>We expect *him* to be elected.
>(*Him* is the subject of the infinitive *to be elected*.)

>Please let *us* know if you are coming.
>(*Us* is the subject of the infinitive (*to*) *know*.)
>They invited *him and me* to attend the reception.
>(*Him and me* is the compound subject of the infinitive *to attend*.)

>The Director asked *us secretaries* to attend the meeting.
>(*Us*, and its appositive *secretaries*, is the subject of the infinitive *to attend*.)

>*Whom* do they expect to be the next chairman?
>(*Whom* is the subject of the infinitive *to be*.)

>*Whom* will we invite to speak at the convention?
>(In natural order—*we will invite* WHOM *to speak*. . . . *Whom* is the subject of the infinitive *to speak*.)

13e Word following infinitive *to be*

In section 12d we saw that the verb *to be* takes the same case after it as before it. Since the subject of an infinitive is in the objective case, a word following the infinitive is also in the objective case.

>I believe *him* to be honest.
>(*Him* is the subject of *to be*.)

>They thought him to be *me*.
>(Reverse, to test choice of case: They thought *me* to be *him*.)

>We assumed the author of the letter to be *him*.
>(Reverse: We assumed *him* to be the *author*. . . .)

>They did not expect the representatives to be *him and me*.
>(Reverse: They did not expect *him and me* to be the *representatives*.)

>We had expected the group selected to be *us secretaries*.
>(Reverse: We had expected *us secretaries* to be the *group selected*.)

Naming Words—Case

13f Subject of a participle

The subject of a participle is in the objective case. The writer's problem comes in determining whether a verbal is a participle or a gerund. Both may have the same form (the *ing* form of the verb), but only the subject of the *participle* is in the objective case. The subject of the *gerund* is in the possessive case. This technique may help you choose the correct case: When the *doer* of the action is stressed, the verbal is a participle performing its adjective function as a modifier of its subject; when the *action itself* is the important thing, the verbal is a gerund—a verbal noun.

> Imagine *him flying* an airplane.
> (The element being stressed here is the pronoun *him*; therefore the verbal *flying* is a participle modifying *him*, and the pronoun *him* is in the objective case.)
>
> Imagine *his flying* to Paris.
> (Here we are stressing not *him* but his *flying*; therefore the verbal *flying* is a gerund, and the pronoun *his* is in the possessive case.)
>
> *His rushing* to catch the plane was in vain.
> (We are talking about his *rushing*, not the person himself; therefore *rushing* is a gerund, and its subject must be in the possessive case.)
>
> We watched *him rushing* to catch the plane.
> (Here we are stressing *him*. The verbal *rushing* is a participle modifying *him*; therefore, the subject, *him*, is in the objective case.)

14 Possessive Case

The possessive (or genitive) case is used to indicate possession.

14a Possessive of singular words

To form the possessive of singular words not ending in *s* (including the indefinite pronouns), add the apostrophe and *s*.

> the *agent's* report; the *Director's* office; the *secretary's* desk; *anyone's* guess; *somebody's* coat

NOTE: When *else* is used with an indefinite pronoun, form the possessive by adding the apostrophe and *s* to *else*, rather than to the indefinite pronoun.

> *somebody's* coat   but: somebody *else's* coat
> *anyone's* idea   but: anyone *else's* idea

To form the possessive of a singular word ending in *s* or an *s*-sound, add the apostrophe alone if the possessive and the regular forms of the word are pronounced alike. If the possessive form is pronounced with an additional *s*-sound, add both the apostrophe and *s*. (In material prepared for printing by the Government Printing Office, use the apostrophe alone to form the possessive of any word ending in *s* or an *s*-sound.)

Singular form	*Possessive form*
boss	boss's (pronounced *boss-es*)
hostess	hostess' (pronounced *hostess*) or hostess's (pronounced *hostess-es*)

NOTE: To form the possessive of a proper name ending in *s* or an *s*-sound, follow this same method. If the possessive form is pronounced with an additional *s*-sound, add both the apostrophe and *s*. If the regular and the possessive forms of the proper name are pronounced alike, add the apostrophe alone to form the possessive. (In material prepared for printing by the Government Printing Office, use the apostrophe alone to form the possessive of any word ending in *s* or an *s*-sound.)

Either:	Charles'	or:	Charles's
Either:	James'	or:	James's
Either:	Mr. Simmons'	or:	Mr. Simmons's
But:	Roberts'	not:	Roberts's

The apostrophe is omitted in some organizational or geographical names that contain a possessive thought. Follow the form used by the organization itself.

Harpers Ferry   Pikes Peak
Governors Island   Citizens National Bank

Do not use the apostrophe in forming the possessive of the personal and relative pronouns. The possessive forms of these pronouns are:

Relative: *whose*

Personal: *her, hers* (not *her's*), *his, their, theirs, our, ours, my, mine, your, yours, its*

NOTE: *Its* is the possessive form of the personal pronoun *it*; *it's* is a contraction of *it is*. Similarly, *whose* is the possessive form of the relative pronoun *who*, and *who's* is a contraction of *who is*. The examples below illustrate the correct use of these words.

Its operation is simple.
It's (*it is*) simple to operate.

Naming Words—Case

> Don't use that typewriter; *its* ribbon needs changing.
> Don't use that typewriter; *it's* in need of a new ribbon.
>
> *Whose* typewriter is that?
> *Who's* (*who is*) going with me?
>
> *Whose* office is the meeting in?
> *Who's* conducting the meeting?

14b Possessive of plural words

To form the possessive of a plural word not ending in *s*, add the apostrophe and *s*.

> *men's, children's, women's, people's*

To form the possessive of a plural word ending in *s*, add the apostrophe only.

> All of the *District Directors'* reports have been received.

NOTE: Avoid placing the apostrophe before the final *s* of a word if the *s* is actually a part of the singular or plural form. To test, first form the plural; then add the correct possessive sign.

> Not: *Ladie's*   But: *Ladies'*
>
> (*Ladies* is the plural form; since the word ends in *s*, add the apostrophe alone to form the possessive, *ladies'*.)

14c Use of the *of* phrase to form possessive

Use an *of* phrase instead of an apostrophe or an apostrophe and *s* to form the possessive of inanimate things.

> Not: A corporation's long-term capital gain is taxed. . . .
> But: The long-term capital gain of a corporation is taxed. . . .
>
> Not: The *bill's passage* will no doubt mean higher taxes.
> But: The *passage of the bill* will no doubt mean higher taxes.

EXCEPTION: The apostrophe and *s* is used to form the possessive of inanimate objects denoting time, measure, or space. The illustrations below are examples of this idiomatic usage. Notice the placement of the apostrophe to indicate singular or plural.

> a day's work   two weeks' notice
> five days' pay   six months' course
> a dollar's worth   a stone's throw
> two dollars' worth   his money's worth
> an arm's length   a snail's pace

Use the *of* phrase in forming the possessive to avoid the "piling up" of possessives.

    Not: The *taxpayer's wife's income* must be reported.
    But: The *income of the taxpayer's wife* must be reported.

    Not: The *committee's treasurer's report* was read.
    But: The *report of the committee's treasurer* was read.

Use the *of* phrase to form the possessive of names consisting of several words, in order to avoid an awkward construction.

    Not: The local chapter of the National Association of Radio and Television Broadcasters' first meeting was held Thursday.
    But: The first meeting of the local chapter of the National Association of Radio and Television Broadcasters was held Thursday.

    Not: The Director of the Alcohol and Tobacco Tax Division's report . . . .
    But: The report of the Director of the Alcohol and Tobacco Tax Division . . . .

Sometimes both the *of* phrase and the possessive are needed to express meaning accurately.

    Not: This is the *Commissioner's picture.*
        (Could mean: This is a portrait of him.
            or: This is his property.)

    But: This is *a picture of the Commissioner.* (his portrait)
    or: This is *a picture of the Commissioner's.* (his property)

Use the *of* phrase to avoid adding a possessive to a pronoun that is already possessive.

    Not: We are going to a *friend of mine's house.*
    But: We are going to the *house of a friend of mine.*

14d   Possessive of compound words

Form the possessive on the last word of a compound word, whether or not the compound is hyphenated. A point to remember is that, even though the plural of a compound word is formed by adding "s" to the principal noun in the compound, the possessive is always formed by adding the *sign of the possessive* to the *last word in the compound.*

Singular possessive	*Plural*	*Plural possessive*
notary public's	notaries public	notaries public's
comptroller general's	comptrollers general	comptrollers general's
supervisor in charge's	supervisors in charge	supervisors in charge's

Naming Words—Case

If a possessive is followed by an appositive or an explanatory phrase, form the possessive on the explanatory word.

> That was *Mr. Smith the auditor's* idea.
> I was acting on my *attorney Mr. Brown's* advice.
> Have you read the *Senator from Arizona's* speech?

If the appositive or explanatory words are set off by commas, the possessive may be formed on both the main word and the explanatory word.

> Either: This is *Mary, my secretary's*, day off.
> Or: This is *Mary's, my secretary's*, day off.

> Either: I sent it to *Mr. Roberts, the collector's*, office.
> Or: I sent it to *Mr. Roberts', the collector's*, office.

NOTE: The methods just illustrated are grammatically correct ways to show possession; they do, however, sound awkward. To make your writing more effective (and just as correct), try using an *of* phrase to form the possessive of compound words.

> Not: This is the supervisor in charge's office.
> But: This is the office of the supervisor in charge.

> Not: I was acting on my attorney Mr. Brown's advice.
> But: I was acting on the advice of my attorney, Mr. Brown.

> Not: I sent it to Mr. Roberts', the collector's office.
> But: I sent it to the office of Mr. Roberts, the collector.

14e Joint, separate, and alternative possession

When two or more people possess the same thing jointly, form the possessive on the last word only.

> She is *Mr. Roberts and Miss Henry's* secretary.
>   (She is secretary to both people.)
> These pictures are from *John and Mary's* vacation trip.
> I bought my coat at *Woodward and Lothrop's* (*store* understood).

NOTE: When one of the words involved in the joint possession is a pronoun, each word must be in the possessive.

> This is *John's, Bob's,* and *my* office.
> Have you seen *Mary's* and *his* new home?

When it is intended that each of the words in a series possess something individually, form the possessive on each word.

> *Barbara's* and *Mary's* typing are certainly different.
> The *Secretaries'* and the *Accountants'* associations are meeting here this week.

When alternative possession is intended, each word must be in the possessive.

> I wouldn't want either *John's* or *Harry's* job.
> Is that the *author's* or the *editor's* opinion?

14f Possessive of abbreviations

Possessives of abbreviations are formed in the same way as are other possessives. Ordinarily the possessive sign is placed after the final period of the abbreviation.

Singular Possessive	*Plural*	*Plural Possessive*
M.D.'s	M.D.s	M.D.s'
Dr.'s	Drs.	Drs.'
Co.'s	Cos.	Cos.' or Cos'.
Bro.'s	Bros.	Bros.'

Enclosed is Johnson *Bros.'* bill for their work.
John Blank, *Jr.'s* account has been closed.
   (Note that there is no comma after *Jr.* when the possessive is used—GPO Style Manual preference.)

14g Parallel possessives

Be sure that a word standing parallel with a possessive is itself possessive in form.

> Not: *His* work, like an *accountant*, is exacting.
> But: *His* work, like an *accountant's*, is exacting.
>
> Not: The *agent's* job differs from the *auditor* in that . . . .
> But: The *agent's* job differs from the *auditor's* in that . . . .
>
> Not: *His* task is no more difficult than his *neighbor*.
> But: *His* task is no more difficult than his *neighbor's*.

14h Possessive with a gerund

A noun or pronoun immediately preceding a gerund is in the possessive case. A gerund is a verbal noun naming an action. A participle, which may have the same form as a gerund, functions as an adjective; its subject is in the objective case.

> *Our* being late delayed the meeting.
> *Mr. Jones'* being late delayed the meeting.
> You can always depend on *his* doing a good job.
> *Jim's* writing the letter made all the difference.
> *Washington's* being the capital makes it different from other cities.

Naming Words—Case

NOTE: There are three exceptions to this general rule:

(1) The possessive of an inanimate object is not usually formed by the apostrophe and *s*. When the subject of a gerund is a noun standing for an inanimate object, use the objective case, an *of* phrase, or a subordinate clause, whichever is most appropriate.

> Not: The *desk's refinishing* is almost complete.
> But: The *refinishing of the desk* is almost complete.
>   (*of*-phrase)
>
> Not: The possibility of the *meeting's ending* soon is doubtful.
> But: The possibility of the *meeting ending* soon is doubtful.
>   (objective case)
>
> Not: We missed our ride because of the *meeting's lasting so late.*
> But: We missed our ride because the *meeting lasted so late.*
>   (subordinate clause)

(2) Do not use the possessive case for the subject of a gerund unless the subject immediately precedes the gerund. If subject and gerund are separated by other words, the subject must be in the objective case.

> Not: I can see no reason for a *man's* with his background *failing* to pass the test.
> But: I can see no reason for a *man* with his background *failing* to pass the test.
>   (Without intervening words: I can see no reason for a *man's failing* to pass the test.)
>
> Not: I concede the difficulty of *his*, because of his interest, *being* completely fair.
> But: I concede the difficulty of *him*, because of his interest, *being* completely fair.

(3) There are no possessive forms for the demonstrative pronouns *that, this, these,* and *those.* Therefore, when these words are used as subjects of a gerund they do not change form.

> Not: We cannot be sure of *that's* being true.
> But: We cannot be sure of *that* being true.
>
> Not: What are the chances of *this'* being sold?
> But: What are the chances of *this* being sold?

TEXT 3

Agreement and Reference

15   Introduction
15a Agreement of subject and verb
15b Agreement of pronoun and antecedent
15c Agreement of both verb and pronoun with subject-antecedent

16   Subject problems
16a Collective words
16b Units of measure
16c Confusing singular and plural forms
16d Indefinite pronouns
16e Relative pronouns
16f Subjects joined by *and*
16g Subjects joined by *or* or *nor*
16h Subjects joined by *and/or*

17   Shifts in number or person

18   Structure problems
18a Verb precedes subject
18b Words intervene between subject and verb
18c Subject and predicate differ in number

19   Special problems of pronoun reference
19a Ambiguous antecedents
19b Antecedent in subordinate construction
19c Implied antecedents
19d Vague reference

TEXT 3

Agreement and Reference

15 Introduction

Agreement is the logical relationship between parts of speech in a sentence. There can be no good, clear sentences without agreement. Grammar starts here. For the parts of the sentence must be in harmony with one another (must *agree*) if they are to express a clear thought. In the first text we talked a little of the parts that make up a sentence. Now we will take a closer look at the way some of these parts fit together.

Agreement of subject and verb is the "heart" of the good sentence. For, stripped to its bare essentials, a sentence is simply a union of a *thing* (the subject) and an *action* (the verb). These two must agree; in fact, their agreement IS the sentence.

Other parts of the sentence, of course, must also be in agreement. Perhaps next in importance to the agreement of subject and verb is the agreement of a pronoun with its antecedent. It is these two areas that we will discuss in this text, since there is a relationship between the principles governing each.

15a Agreement of subject and verb

The verb must agree with the subject in number and in person. If the subject is singular, the verb form must also be singular; if the subject is in the third person—*it, he*—the verb must also be in the third person.

The chief problem for the writer is identifying the true subject of the sentence and determining whether it is singular or plural.

15b Agreement of pronoun and antecedent

The pronoun must agree with its antecedent (the word to which it refers—sometimes called its "referent") in number, in person, and in gender. Of the three, gender causes the writer the least difficulty.

The chief problem for the writer is identifying the antecedent and determining its number, person, and gender.

15c Agreement of both verb and pronoun with subject-antecedent

Often the subject of the verb is also the antecedent of the pronoun. One might think that this would greatly simplify things for the writer. And to some extent it does; for once he has determined that the subject-antecedent is singular, he knows where he stands—both verb and pronoun must likewise be singular. But here a word of caution: be consistent; don't confuse your reader by shifting from a singular verb (which properly agrees with its singular subject) to a plural pronoun later in the sentence.

16 **Subject Problems**

The first step in making the parts of a sentence agree is to identify the subject. No writer would have difficulty in identifying the *routine* subject of a sentence and in determining its number, person, and gender. In this section, therefore, we will discuss only those subjects that may present special problems.

16a Collective words

A collective names a group of people or things. Although usually singular in form, it is treated as either singular or plural according to the sense of the sentence:

Singular when members of the group act, or are considered, as a *unit:*

> The Survey Committee *is visiting* the X District this week. The National Office Evaluation Team *has* five trips scheduled for this quarter.

Plural when the members act, or are considered, *individually:*

> The jury *are* unable to agree on a verdict.

> The National Office Evaluation Team *pool* the data *they* gather and *prepare their* report.

Common collectives

assembly, association, audience, board, cabinet, class, commission, committee, company, corporation, council, counsel, couple, crowd, department, family, firm, group, jury, majority, minority, number, pair, press, public, staff, United States.

Company names as collectives

Company names also qualify as collectives and may be either singular or plural. Usually those ending with a singular sound are considered singular; those with a plural sound, plural.

> Flowers, Inc., *mails its* advertisements in envelopes with floral decorations.
> Jones Brothers *have sent their* representative to the conference.

A name ending in *Company* or *Corporation*, though usually considered singular, may—if the sense of the sentence requires—be used as a plural.

> The X Company *is* not on the list of tax-exempt organizations.
> The ABC Corporation *report* on the activities of *their* subsidiaries tomorrow morning.

(1) Short collectives

The following short words—though seldom listed as collectives—are governed by the rule for collectives. They are singular or plural according to the intended meaning of the sentence.

> *all, any, more, most, none, some, who, which*

When a prepositional phrase follows the word, the number of the noun in the phrase controls the number of the verb. When no such phrase follows, the writer signals his intended meaning by his choice of the singular or the plural verb.

> Some of the *work has been done.*
> Some of the *returns have been filed.*
> Most of the *correspondence is* routine.
> Most of the *letters are* acceptable.
> *Is* there *any* left? (any portion—any paper, any ink)
> *Are* there *any* left? (any individual items—any forms, any copies)
> *Which is* to be posted? (which one?)
> *Which are* to be posted? (which ones?)
> Either: None of the items *is* deductible.
> Or: None of the items *are* deductible.

NOTE: May writers treat *none* as singular in every instance, since it is a compound of *no one*. This usage is correct. It is equally correct, however, to treat *none* as plural (meaning *not any*) when it is followed by a prepositional phrase which has a plural object. Writers who want to emphasize the singular meaning often substitute *not one* for *none:*

    Not one of the applicants *is* eligible.

(2) Special collectives

Certain words—called "abstract collectives" by some grammarians—are also treated as collectives, even though they do not name a group of persons or things.

Their singular form is used when they refer to (1) qualities, emotions, or feelings common to a group of persons or things; or to (2) action common to such a group. Their plural form is used when this common or general idea is not present.

Use the singular under such circumstances as these:

attention	Supervisors have their *attention* called to the value of management training. (not *attentions*)
consent	Several gave their *consent* to the proposal.
failure	The taxpayers' *failure* to file amended returns delayed the processing of their claims for refund.
interest	Their *interest* was not so much in long-range self-development as in immediate advancement.
leaving	If the employees have legitimate reasons, the supervisor should not question their *leaving* the work area.
sense	Our interpretation is based on the *sense* of the amendment.
work	Attending the meeting will not interfere with their *work*.

Use either the singular or the plural:

opinion	The taxpayer and his counsel expressed their *opinion* (or *opinions*) on the matter.
time	The only *time* these restrictions are in order is when the taxpayer . . . . OR The only *times* these restrictions are in order are when the taxpayer . . . .
use	What *use* (or *uses*) can be made of the revised form?

166 Units of measure

When a number is used with a plural noun to indicate a unit of

Agreement and Reference 47

measurement (money, time, fractions, portions, distance, weight, quantity, etc.), a singular verb is used. When the term is thought of as individual parts, a plural verb is used.

> *Twenty dollars is* the amount of tax due.
> *Twenty dollars are* in this stack.
>
> *Ten years seems* like a long time.
> *Ten years have gone* by since I last saw him.
>
> *Twenty-one pages is* our quota for each day.
> *Twenty-one pages are* needed to finish the job.

When fractions and expressions such as *the rest of, the remainder of, a part of, percent of,* etc., are followed by a prepositional phrase, the noun or pronoun in that phrase governs the number of the verb.

> *Four-fifths* of the job *was* finished on time.
> *Four-fifths* of the letters *were* finished on time.
>
> The *rest* (or *remainder*) of the report *is* due Friday.
> The *rest* (or *remainder*) of the letters *were* mailed today.
>
> What *percent* of the information *is* available?
> What *percent* of the items *were* lost?

16c Confusing singular and plural forms

It is sometimes hard for us to tell by its form whether a word is singular or plural. Some words that end in *-s* may be singular, and some seemingly singular words may be plural.

These words are singular, though they are plural in form.

> *apparatus, news, summons, whereabouts*
>
> The *news is* disturbing.
> His *whereabouts has* not yet been determined.

These words are plural, though they are singular (or collective) in meaning.

> *assets, earnings, means* (income), *odds, premises, proceeds, quarters, savings, wages, winnings*
>
> His *assets are* listed on the attached statement.
> *Earnings are* up this quarter.
> The *odds are* against our settling this case swiftly.
> The *proceeds are* earmarked for the revolving fund.

These words may be either singular or plural, depending on their meaning, even though they are plural in form.

ethics, goods, gross, headquarters, mechanics, politics, series, species, statistics, tactics

Ethics is a subject on which he is well qualified to speak.
His business *ethics are* above question.

Statistics is the only course I failed in school.
The *statistics prove* that I am right.

A *gross* of pencils *is* not enough.
A *gross* of pencils *are* being sent.

A *series* of errors *has* marked our attempt.
A *series* of lucky breaks *are* about all that will save us now.

These nouns are plural, though they may appear to be singular because they have foreign or unusual plural forms.

The *analyses have* been completed.
  (*Analyses* is the plural of *analysis*.)
What *are* your *bases* for these conclusions?
  (*Bases* is the plural of *basis*.)
Some interesting *phenomena are* disclosed in this report.
  (*Phenomena* is the plural of *phenomenon*.)
His conclusion seems sound, but his *criteria are* not valid.
  (*Criteria* is the plural of *criterion*.)

NOTE: *Data* and *memoranda* require special mention. *Data* is the plural of *datum;* we must treat it as a plural when it refers to individual facts. But when *data* refers to a mass of facts as a unit, it more closely resembles a collective noun and may therefore be treated as a singular form.

The *data* from our last study *are* being analyzed.
This *data is* of the highest importance to our cause.

Memoranda is the Latin plural of *memorandum;* the English plural is *memorandums*. Either form is correct, though *memorandums* seems to be the more popular.

Either: These *memoranda* have been signed.
  or: These *memorandums* have been signed.

16d Indefinite pronouns

These indefinite pronouns are singular. When they are used as subjects, they require singular verbs; when used as antecedents, they require singular pronouns.

anybody, anyone, any one (any one of a group),
anything, each, either, every, everybody, everyone,
every one (every one of a group), *everything, neither,*

Agreement and Reference

    nobody, no one, nothing, one, somebody, someone, some one (some one of a group), *something*

    Anyone is welcome, as long as *he* (not *they*) behaves himself.
    *Any one of the men *is* capable of doing it.
    Each of us *is* obliged to sign *his* own name.
    Either of the alternatives *is* suitable.
    Everyone must buy *his* book for the course.
    *Every one of the employees *wishes* to sign the card.
    Everything seems to be going smoothly now.
    Neither of the plans *is* workable.
    No one believes that our plan will work.
    Someone has to finish this report.
    *Some one of you *has* to be responsible for it.

    *Written as two words when followed by a phrase.

Even when two indefinite pronouns are joined by *and*, they remain singular in meaning.

    Anyone and *everyone is* invited.
    Nothing and *no one escapes* her attention.

When *each* or *every* is used to modify a compound subject (subjects joined by *and*), the subject is considered singular.

    Every regional commissioner and *district director has sent* in *his* report.

When *each* is inserted (as a parenthetic or explanatory element) between a plural or a compound subject and its plural verb, neither the plural form of the verb nor the plural form of the pronoun is affected.

    Region A, Region B, and Region C *each expect* to increase *their* personnel ceilings.
    The Directors *each want* the requirements changed.
    The taxpayers *each have requested* permission to change *their* method of accounting.

Many a (unlike *many*) is singular in meaning and takes a singular verb and pronoun.

    Many a new employee feels insecure during *his* first few weeks on the job.
    But: *Many employees feel* insecure during *their* first few weeks on the job.

More than one, though its meaning is plural, is used in the singular.

    More than one vacation plan *was* changed because of the new requirement.
    More than one detail *is* needed to handle the additional workload.

These words are plural.

> both, few, many, several, others
>
> *Both* of us *have received* new assignments.
> *Few will be able* to finish their work on time.
> *Many plan* to work all weekend.
> *Several* of the divisions *have submitted* their reports.
> But *others have* not yet *finished theirs.*

16e Relative pronouns

The verb in a relative clause must agree in number and in person with the relative pronoun (*who, which, that*) serving as the subject of the clause. The relative pronoun, in turn, must agree with its antecedent. Therefore, before we can make the verb agree with the relative pronoun, we must find the antecedent and determine its person and number.

> Have you talked with the man *who was* waiting to see you?
> (*Man* is the antecedent of the relative pronoun *who*, and the verb *was* must agree with this antecedent in person and number.)
>
> Where are the books *that were* left on the table?
> (The verb in the relative clause—*were*—must agree with the relative pronoun—*that*—which must agree with its antecedent—*books*.)
>
> We *who have* met him do not doubt his ability.
> (The relative pronoun is *who*; the verb in the relative clause is *have*; the antecedent of the relative pronoun is *we*.)

In sentences that contain the phrases *one of the* or *one of those*, the antecedent of the relative pronoun is not *one*, but the plural words that follow.

> One of the letters *that were* on my desk has disappeared.
> (*One has disappeared*, or *One of the letters has disappeared*, is the main thought of the sentence. *That were on my desk* is a clause modifying *letters*, not *one*; thus the relative pronoun *that* must agree with *letters*, its antecedent, making the verb in the relative clause, *were*, plural.)
>
> Here is one of those men *who are* applying for the position.
> (The antecedent of the relative pronoun *who* is the plural noun *men*, not the singular *one*.)
>
> One of the men *who are* attending the meeting is wanted on the telephone.
> (The antecedent of the relative pronoun *who* is the plural noun *men*, not the singular *one*.)

NOTE: An easy way to find the antecedent of the relative pronoun in this type of sentence, is to shift the sentence elements thus:

Agreement and Reference 51

>Of the letters *that were* on my desk, one has disappeared.
>>(It now becomes obvious that the antecedent of the relative pronoun *that* is *letters*.)
>
>Of those men *who are* applying for the position, here is one.
>
>Of the men *who are* attending the meeting, one is wanted on the telephone.

But when the word *only* precedes *one* in this type of sentence, the singular pronoun *one* is considered to be the antecedent of the relative pronoun.

>He is *one* of the applicants *who are* eligible.
>
>He is the *only one* of the applicants *who is* eligible.
>>(Notice the difference in number of the relative pronoun *who*—and its verb—in these two sentences.)
>
>Robbins is the *only one* of the employees *who is* receiving an award.
>
>This is the *only one* of the letters *that has* not yet been answered.

(2) *Who, that,* or *which* may be used to refer to a collective noun. When the members of the group act, or are considered, as a unit, either *that* or *which* should be used—*that* is usually preferred if the group comprises persons rather than things. *Who* is used when the persons comprising a group act, or are considered, individually.

>He reports that there *is* a *group* of citizens *that* is critical of the city's long-range plan.
>>(Acting as a unit—*that* is used because the group is composed of persons, not things.)
>
>We have heard from an *association* of homeowners *who feel* strongly opposed to the present zoning regulations.
>>(Considered individually—*who* signals this point.)

16f   Subjects joined by *and*

When two or more subjects are joined by *and*, whether the subjects are singular or plural, they form a compound subject, which is considered plural.

>The *date and the time* of the meeting *have* not been decided.
>The *director and his assistants are* holding *their* weekly staff meeting.
>The *letters, reports, and other papers are* on the table where you left *them*.
>*He and I* will deliver *our* report in person.

Phrases or clauses serving as subjects follow the same rule: when two or more phrases or clauses serving as the subject of a sentence are joined by *and*, the resulting compound subject is considered plural.

> *Rising early in the morning* and *taking a walk before breakfast make* a person feel invigorated all day.
>
> *That your work is usually done satisfactorily* and *that you are usually prompt are* the factors I considered in excusing your recent conduct.

Exception: When the subjects joined by *and* refer to the same person or object or represent a single idea, the whole subject is considered singular.

> *Ham and eggs is* the traditional American breakfast.
> The *growth and development* of our country *is* described in this book.

We indicate to the reader, *by using the article or personal pronoun* before each member of the compound subject, whether we see the subject as a single idea or as different ideas.

> *My teacher and friend helps* me with my problems.
>   (one person)
> *My teacher* and *my friend help* me with my problems.
>   (two people)
> *The secretary and treasurer* of the committee *has* arrived.
> *The secretary* and *the treasurer* of the committee *have* arrived.

16g Subjects joined by *or* or *nor*

When singular subjects are joined by *or* or *nor*, the subject is considered singular.

> Neither the *director nor* the *assistant director knows* that *he* is scheduled to attend the meeting.
> *One or* the *other* of us has to go.
> Neither *love nor money is* sufficient to buy such devotion.
> Neither *heat nor cold nor sun nor wind affects* this material.

When one singular and one plural subject are joined by *or* or *nor*, the subject closer to the verb determines the number of the verb. Complications may arise, however, when the subject is also the antecedent of a pronoun. To avoid an awkward construction, rewrite the sentence.

> I believe that this *office or* the central *files have* the material you requested.
> I believe that the central *files or* this *office has* the material you requested.

Agreement and Reference

But:

> I don't think that the branch *chiefs or* the *director knows* that *he is* (*they are?*) scheduled to attend the meeting.
> Neither the *stenographer nor* the *typists have* finished *their* (*her?*) assignment.

Rewritten:

> I don't think that the branch *chiefs know* that *they are* scheduled to attend the meeting—or that the *director knows* that *he is.*
> The *stenographer has* not finished *her* assignment, nor *have* the *typists* finished *theirs.*

NOTE: Because your reader may be distracted by your use of a singular verb with a subject containing a plural element, place the plural element nearer the verb whenever possible.

> Ask him whether the *memorandum or* the *letters have* been signed.
> Neither the *equipment nor* the *employees are* capable of maintaining that pace.

When the subjects joined by *or* or *nor* are of different persons, the subject nearer the verb determines its person. This construction, though grammatically correct, will almost always result in awkward sentences which the careful writer would prefer to rewrite.

> I was told that *she or you were* to be responsible.
> I was told that *you or she was* to be responsible.

Rewritten:

> I was told that either *she was* to be responsible or *you were.*
>
> Do you think either *I or you are* being considered?
> Do you think either *you or I am* being considered?

Rewritten:

> Do you think that *you are* being considered, or that *I am?*
> Do you think that *either* of us *is* being considered?

16h Subjects joined by *and/or*

When both of the subjects joined by *and/or* are plural, the writer has no particular problem. The subject is considered plural, and all verbs and pronouns referring to it must be plural.

> The attorneys *and/or* their clients *were* present at the hearing.

It is when both subjects are singular, or when one subject is singular and the other plural, that the problem arises. The number of the subject depends upon the interpretation we give the connective

If we consider *and/or* to have the force of *and*, the subject is plural.

> The attorney *and/or* (*and*) his client *are* responsible for having the document signed.
> These forms *and/or* (*and*) any explanatory statement *are* due by April 15.

If we consider *and/or* to have the force of *or* (the usual interpretation), the subject nearer the verb controls.

> The attorney *and/or* (*or*) his client *is* required to be present in court when *his* case is called.
> These forms *and/or* (*or*) any explanatory statement *is* due by April 15.
> The taxpayer *and/or* (*or*) his representatives *are* required to file before the date set.

NOTE: Most grammarians discourage the use of *and/or* in letters not only because it is legalistic and overformal, but also because it is inexact. Our writing will be clearer if we substitute either *and* or *or* for *and/or*. Even if we need the whole of the idea expressed by *and/or*, we can say it more clearly: "the taxpayer or his attorney or both."

17 Shifts in Number or Person

Once you establish a word as either singular or plural, keep it the same throughout the sentence. Be sure that all verbs and all pronouns referring to that word agree with it in number

> Not: Because this *country* bases *its* economy on voluntary compliance with *its* tax laws, we must all pay our share if *they are* to carry out the necessary functions of government.
>   (The first two pronouns refer to *country* as a singular noun; later the reference changes to plural. Use either *it* or *they* throughout the sentence.)
> But: Because this *country* bases *its* economy on voluntary compliance with *its* tax laws, we must all pay our share if *it is* to carry out the necessary functions of government.
> Not: A *person needs* someone to turn to when *they are* in trouble.
>   (*Person* is singular; therefore, the use of the plural pronoun *they* is an incorrect shift.)
> But: A *person needs* someone to turn to when *he is* in trouble.
> Not: When *one* has had a hard day at the office, it is important that *they* be able to relax in the evening.

Agreement and Reference 55

        (*One* is singular; either of the singular pronouns *one* or *he* should be used to refer to it.)
    But: When *one* has had a hard day at the office, it is important that *one* (or *he*) be able to relax in the evening.

Be consistent. If you decide that a collective is singular, keep it singular throughout the sentence—use a singular verb to agree with it and a singular pronoun to refer to it. If you establish the collective as plural, see that both the verb and the pronoun are plural.

    The committee *has* announced *its* decision.
        (Singular—acting as a unit)
    The committee *have* adjourned and gone to *their* homes.
        (Plural—acting individually)
    Our staff *is* always glad to offer *its* advice and assistance.
        (Singular—acting as a unit)
    Our staff *are* assigned as liaison *officers* to the several operating divisions.
        (Plural—acting individually)
    The number of claims processed this year *is* larger than that processed last year.
        (Using "the" before "number" signals the reader that you consider the items as a unit.)
    A number of claims *have* been processed this month.
        (Using "a" before "number" signals that you are referring to the items individually.)

Most indefinite pronouns are singular and require singular verbs and pronouns.

    Not: Has *anyone* turned in *their* report?
        (The indefinite pronoun *anyone* takes both a singular verb and a singular pronoun.)
    But: Has *anyone* turned in *his* report?

Do not supply a verb form from one part of the sentence to another unless the same form is grammatically correct in both parts.

    Not: The *statistics were* checked and the report filed.
        (The *statistics were* checked and the *report* (*were*) filed.)
    But: The *statistics were* checked and the *report was* filed.

Avoid shifting the person of pronouns referring to the same antecedent.

    Not: When *one* is happy, it often seems as if everyone around *you* is happy, too.
        (*One* is third person; *you* is second person.)
    But: When *one* is happy, it often seems as if everyone around *one* (or *him*) is happy, too.

    Not: As the *ship* entered *her* berth, *its* huge gray shadow seemed to swallow us.

> But: As the *ship* entered *its* berth, *its* huge gray shadow seemed to swallow us.
>
> or: As the *ship* entered *her* berth, *her* huge gray shadow seemed to swallow us.

18 Structure Problems

Usually it's easy for us to identify the subject or antecedent and determine its number and person. But occasionally a puzzling sentence comes along. The subject is there, as clear as can be, but something in the structure of the sentence tries to make us believe that another word is the subject.

18a Verb precedes subject

When the verb precedes the subject in the sentence (either in a question or in a declarative sentence), locate the *true* subject and make the verb agree with it.

> *Are* the *file cabinet and the bookcase* in this room?
> (The *file cabinet and the bookcase are* . . . .)
> Walking down the hall *are* the *men* we are waiting for.
> Clearly visible on the desk *were* the *reports* he had asked us to file.
> From these books *come some* of our best *ideas*.
> To us *falls* the *task* of compiling the data.
> Among those attending *were* two former *presidents* of the organization.

Where, here, and *there,* when introducing a sentence, do not influence the number or person of the verb. In such sentences, find the real subject and make the verb agree with it.

> Where *are* the individual *sessions* to be held?
> Where *is* the *case* filed?
>
> Here *are* the *reports* for which we were waiting.
> Here *is* the *report* for which we were waiting.
>
> There *are* two *books* on the table.
> There *is* a *book* on the table.

What, who, which, the interrogative pronouns, do not affect the number of the verb. Again, find the subject of the sentence and make the verb agree with it.

> What *is* the *status* of the Adams case?
> What *are* your *recommendations* on this problem?
>
> Who *is* going to accompany you to the meeting?
> Who, in this group, *are* members of your staff?
>
> Which *is* the *report* that he means?
> Which *are* the *standards* that we are to apply?

Agreement and Reference

The expletive *it* or *there* introduces the verb and stands for the real subject, which comes later in the clause. The expletive *it* requires a singular verb, even when the real subject is plural. Following the expletive *there*, the verb is singular or plural according to the subject which follows it.

> It *is solutions* we are looking for, not problems.
> (Even though the real subject, *solutions*, is plural, the verb is singular to agree with the expletive.)
>
> It is doubtful that he will start today.
> (The clause *that he will start today* is the subject of the verb *is*.)
>
> There *are* enclosed five copies of the pamphlet you requested.
> There *is* attached a letter from District Director, Blankville, requesting additional copies of the book.
> (See sec. 86a, Text 10.)

NOTE: Avoid confusing your reader by using the expletive *it* and the personal pronoun *it* in the same sentence.

> Not: I haven't read the report yet; *it* has been hard for me to find time for *it*.
> (The first *it* is the expletive; the second *it* is a personal pronoun referring to *report*.)
>
> But: I haven't read the report yet; I haven't been able to find time for *it*.

18b Words intervene between subject and verb

The presence of explanatory or parenthetical phrases, or other modifiers, between the subject and verb does not change the number or person of the subject. Locate the real subject of the sentence and make the verb agree with it.

> His sworn *statement*, together with copies of the testimony and statements from others connected with the case, *was* made a part of the file.
> The *amount* shown, plus interest, *is* due within 30 days.
> The *letter* with its several attachments *was* received this morning.
> Our *letters*, like our speech, *are* indications of our knowledge of English.
> The *supervisor*, instead of the agents who had been assigned the case, *is* scheduled to visit the office.
> His *report*, including extensive notes on the furnishings of the office, *was* well received.
> That *fact*, in addition to our already large file on the case, *completes* the information we requested.
> *No one* but those present *knows* of this information.
> The *report*, accompanied by statements of the people involved, *is* being studied.

18c Subject and predicate differ in number

After forms of the verb *to be* we often find a construction (called the *predicate nominative*) that means the same thing as the subject. When the predicate nominative differs in number from the subject, the verb must agree with the element that precedes it (the subject).

> Our main *problem is* writing complete reports and keeping them short enough for fast reading.
> Writing complete reports and keeping them short enough for fast reading *are* our main problem.
> As always, the *question was* sufficient funds.
> As always, *sufficient funds were* the question.
> The director said that an increasing *problem is* the required statistical reports.
> The director said that the required statistical *reports are* an increasing problem.

19 Special Problems of Pronoun Reference

19a Ambiguous antecedents

Do not use forms of the same pronoun to refer to different antecedents.

> Not: The supervisor told Mr. Johnson that *he* thought *his* work was improving.
>> (Does the supervisor think that his own work is improving, or that Mr. Johnson's work is improving?)
> But: Mr. Johnson was told by his supervisor that his work was improving.

When it seems that the pronoun can logically refer to either of two antecedents, be sure that the reference is obvious.

> Not: The director told Mr. Roberts that *he* would have to make *his* proposed trip to Boston in June.
>> (The pronouns *he* and *his* can refer to either *director* or *Mr. Roberts*. The meaning may be apparent when this sentence is placed in context, but rewriting will insure clarity.)
> Could mean: Although Mr. Roberts had planned to travel to Boston in May, the director asked *him* to postpone the trip until June.
> or: Since the director is planning a trip to Boston in June, he was obliged to decline Mr. Roberts' invitation to speak at the June conference.

Place the pronoun as close as possible to its antecedent, to avoid ambiguity or confusion.

> Not: A young woman can readily find a job *that* is skilled in shorthand.
>> (Although the pronoun *that* refers to *woman*, its placement makes it appear to refer to *job*.)
> But: A young *woman that* is skilled in shorthand can readily find a job.

> Not: The letter is on the conference table *that* we received yesterday.
>> (If we assume that it was the letter that was received yesterday,

Agreement and Reference

not the conference table, this sentence should read:
The *letter that* we received yesterday is on the conference table.)

19b Antecedent in subordinate construction

If the antecedent of the pronoun is in a subordinate construction, the reference is likely to be vague. Be especially cautious of antecedents in the possessive case or in prepositional phrases. There may be a more prominent word in the sentence to which the pronoun may seem to refer.

> Not: The carbons of these letters were not initialled by the writers, so we are sending *them* back.
> > (What are we sending back? The carbons, the letters, or the writers?)
>
> But: We are sending back the carbons of the letters because *they* were not initialled by the writers.
>
> Not: When you have finished the last chapter of the book, please return *it* to the library.
> > (We can assume that the pronoun *it* refers to *book*. The more prominent noun "chapter" is the word to which *it* would grammatically refer, even though logically *it* refers to the noun in the subordinate construction.)
>
> But: Please return the *book* to the library when you have finished *its* (the) last chapter.

19c Implied antecedents

As a general rule, the antecedent of a pronoun must appear in the sentence—not merely be implied. And the antecedent should be a specific word, not an idea expressed in a phrase or clause. *It*, *which*, *this*, and *that* are the pronouns that most often lead our meaning astray. Any of these pronouns may refer to an idea expressed in a preceding passage if the idea and the reference are *unmistakably clear*. But too often the idea that is unmistakably clear to the writer is nowhere to be found when the reader looks for it.

> Not: Although the doctor operated at once, *it* was not a success and the patient died.
> > (The pronoun *it* refers to the idea of *operation*, which is implied but not expressed in the first part of the sentence.)
>
> But: Although the doctor performed the *operation* at once, *it* was not a success and the patient died.
>
> or: Although the doctor operated at once, the *operation* was not a success and the patient died.
>
> Not: This matter has also been taken up with the General Accounting Office, Washington, D.C., a copy of *which* is attached.

(In this sentence the antecedent of *which* is barely implied. We assume that the writer is attaching a copy of his letter to GAO, not a copy of GAO itself, as his sentence says.)

But: This matter has also been taken up with the General Accounting Office, Washington, D.C. A copy of our letter to them is attached.

Not: Mr. Roberts has recently been promoted. *This* brings him greater responsibility and will probably mean longer hours for him.
(Although it is pretty obvious that *this* refers to Mr. Roberts' promotion, the word *promotion* does not appear in the sentence.)

But: Mr. Roberts has recently received a *promotion*. *This* brings him greater responsibility and will probably mean longer hours for him.

Not: Miss Jones computed her tax liability under the premise that she was entitled to use rates applicable to the head of the household, *which* is in error.

But: Miss Jones computed her tax liability under the premise that she was entitled to use rates applicable to the head of the household. *This premise* is in error.

19d Vague reference

The usage illustrated below—the impersonal use of *it*, *they*, and *you*—is not incorrect. But using these impersonal pronouns tends to produce vague, wordy sentences.

Not: In the Manual *it* says to make three copies.
(Who says?)
But: The Manual says to make three copies.

Not: In the letter *it* says he will be here on Thursday.
But: The letter says he will be here on Thursday.
or: He says, in his letter, that he will be here on Thursday.

Not: *They* say we are in for a cold, wet winter.
But: The almanac predicts a cold, wet winter.

Not: From this report *you* can easily recognize the cause of the accident.
But: From this report *one* can easily recognize the cause of the accident.
(The first example is correct if the writer is addressing his remarks to a specific person.)
or: The cause of the accident can be easily recognized from this report.

TEXT **4**

Tense of Verbs and Verbals

20	Introduction	23	Sequence of tense
		23a	Tense of verbs in principal clauses
21	Tenses of verbs	23b	Tense of verbs in subordinate clauses
21a	Definition of tense		
21b	Formation of tenses		
21c	Principal parts of verbs	24	Tenses of verbals
		24a	Gerunds
		24b	Participles
22	Specific use of tenses	24c	Infinitives
22a	Present tense	24d	Verbals in sentence fragments
22b	Present perfect tense		
22c	Past tense	25	Tense sequence with verbals
22d	Past perfect tense	25a	Participles
22e	Future tense	25b	Infinitives
22f	Future perfect tense	25c	Gerunds
		25d	Timetable

TEXT 4

Tense of Verbs and Verbals

20 Introduction

The verb is the backbone of the sentence. It is the word that tells what action is taking place or what condition exists. The verb puts life into the sentence; without it, there *is* no sentence—just a group of words lined up with nothing to do, with no place to go. Give such words a verb, and they spring into action.

Since verbs are so important, it is to our advantage to get as much use from them as we can—make them do our bidding. To do this, we must get better acquainted with them. We must learn enough about verbs, for example, to know what happens when we use an *active* instead of a *passive* verb. For when a verb is *active* the whole sentence takes on life and vigor—the subject is busy *doing something;* when a verb is *passive*, the movement of the sentence slows down—the subject isn't *doing* anything, simply waiting passively while something is *being done to it by someone.*

And we must learn more about *verbals*, those interesting but confusing words that come from verbs. They are interesting (and valuable) because, in the hands of the experienced writer, they make writing more effective. They are confusing because, although they come from verbs and are like verbs in many ways, they can't do the work of verbs; instead, they function as other parts of speech—as nouns or as adjectives, for example.

Becoming more familiar with verbs and verbals will mean reviewing their peculiar characteristics (*properties*, the grammarians call them) and the way verbs change form to indicate these characteristics.

Two of the five properties of verbs—*number* and *person*—we discussed in the text on Agreement. Two others—*mood* and *voice*—we will discuss in the next text. In this text, we will discuss the most troublesome of all—*tense*.

21 Tenses of Verbs

21a Tense means time. We know that, as their main function, verbs describe an action or a state of being on the part of the subject. But verbs also tell *when* the action took place or *when* the state existed. This property of verbs is called tense.

Tense tells the time of the action from the point of view of the writer or speaker. Take the act of *walking* as an example.

If we say, "I AM WALKING to work," we are looking, from the standpoint of the *present* time, at an action that is taking place now.

If we say, "I WALKED to work last Tuesday," we are looking, again from the standpoint of the *present* time, at an action that happened in the past (last Tuesday).

If we say, "If I walk to work tomorrow, I SHALL HAVE WALKED to work every day this week," we are placing ourselves in the future (tomorrow) and speaking from that point of view.

If we say, "I told him yesterday that I HAD WALKED to work," we are speaking, from the point of view of some time in the past (yesterday), of an action that was completed even before that "past time."

21b English has six tenses: three simple tenses (*present*, *past*, and *future*) in which an action may be considered as simply occurring; and three compound—called *perfect*—tenses in which an action may be considered as completed. (To be *perfected* means to be *completed*.)

Present Tense:	I walk, he walks
Present Perfect Tense:	I have walked, he has walked
Past Tense:	I walked, he walked
Past Perfect Tense:	I had walked, he had walked
Future Tense:	I shall walk, he will walk
Future Perfect Tense:	I shall have walked, he will have walked

Each of the six tenses has a companion form—the *progressive* form. As its name indicates, the progressive says that the action named by the verb is a continued or progressive action. The progressive consists of the present participle (the *ing* form of the verb, that is, *walking*) plus the proper form of the verb *to be*. The progressive forms of the verb *to walk* are:

Present Tense:	I am walking, he is walking
Present Perfect Tense:	I have been walking, he has been walking

Tense of Verbs and Verbals

Past Tense: I was walking, he was walking
Past Perfect Tense: I had been walking, he had been walking

Future Tense: I shall be walking, he will be walking
Future Perfect Tense: I shall have been walking, he will have been walking

21c We indicate tense by changing the verb itself or by combining certain forms of the verb with auxiliary verbs. The verb forms that we use to indicate tense are called the *principal parts*. The principal parts of a verb are:

The infinitive or present tense: *talk, write*
The past tense: *talked, wrote*
The past participle: *talked, written*

The past participle is always used with an auxiliary verb, like *have, has,* or *had: they have talked, he has written*.

A fourth principal part, which is the same for all verbs, is the *present participle*. It consists of the present form plus *ing: talking, writing*.

Verbs are classified as *regular* (or *weak*) and *irregular* (or *strong*), according to the way in which their principal parts are formed. Regular verbs form their past tense and past participles by the addition of *ed* to the infinitive:

Infinitive	*Past Tense*	*Past Participle*
talk	talked	talked
help	helped	helped
tax	taxed	taxed

The principal parts of irregular verbs are formed by changes in the verb itself:

Infinitive	*Past Tense*	*Past Participle*
see	saw	seen
say	said	said
go	went	gone

Consult a standard dictionary when you are not sure of the principal parts of a verb. This area of usage is changing, and a verb that was irregular yesterday may be regular (or both regular and irregular) today.

The following verbs illustrate this change:

Infinitive	Past Tense	Past Participle
dive	dived (formerly dove)	dived
prove	proved	proved (formerly proven)

The principal parts of a verb are given in a dictionary at the beginning of the listing for that particular verb. If no entry is given, the past tense and the past participle are formed by the addition of *ed*. If the verb is irregular, or if it presents some difficulty of spelling, the past forms are given.

22 Specific Use of Tenses

22a Present tense

The present tense is used primarily to describe an action that is happening in the present—now—or a state that exists at the present time.

> I *am* a member of that club.
> I *am running* for the office of treasurer.

A special form of the present tense, called the *emphatic present*, uses *do* as an auxiliary verb. This tense form merely adds emphasis to a statement.

> Present: I may work slowly, but I *work* accurately.
> Emphatic: I may work slowly, but I *do work* accurately.

Some functions of the present tense used less frequently require special mention:

(1) The present tense is used to indicate habitual or customary action, regardless of the tense of other verbs in the same sentence.

> Whenever he *makes* a mistake, he *blames* his secretary.
> I always *eat* in the cafeteria.
> He *leaves* the office promptly at 4:30 every day.

(2) The present tense may express a universal or relatively permanent truth, such as scientific or historical fact.

> I was taught that two and two *are* four.
> He reported that his client *is* dead.
> He said that Atlanta *is* the capital of Georgia.
> The taxpayer said that his wife *is* blind.

Tense of Verbs and Verbals 67

(3) The present tense may be used to make more vivid the description of some past action. This usage is known as the *historical present*; it is more at home in narrative than in business writing.

> As Bob *is leaving* the house the telephone *rings*. He *turns* back into the house and *picks* up the receiver. It *is* his sister calling.

Either the historical present tense or the past tense may be used to restate or summarize the facts from a book, report, letter, or similar document.

> The author *describes* (or *described*) the events leading him to his conclusion. He *begins* (or *began*) with . . . .
> In his letter of January 24 Mr. Brown *states* (or *stated*) that he *is* (or *was*) unable to fill our order.

A word of caution: When you use the historical present, guard against unconsciously shifting to the past tense without cause.

> Not: The author *describes* the events leading him to his conclusion. He *began* with . . . .
> But: . . . He *begins* with . . . .

(4) The present tense is often used to express future time:
   (a) either with the help of a modifier fixing the time

> Tomorrow I *go* (or *shall go*) to Chicago.
> He *arrives* (or *will arrive*) Sunday for a week's visit.

(b) or in a subordinate clause introduced by *if, when, after, before, until, as soon as,* etc.

> As soon as he *arrives*, we shall begin the meeting.
> He will not be able to complete the report until I *give* him the figures.

22b Present perfect tense

The present perfect tense describes:

(1) an action just completed at the present time:

> The president *has* just *arrived* at the meeting.
> I *have worked* in the garden this afternoon.

(2) an action begun in the past and continuing into the present:

> I *have been* with this company for seven years. (and still am)
> He *has held* that job for three years. (and still does)

NOTE: In speaking, avoid the dialectal expression, "I *am* in Washington for 16 years," used instead of "I *have been* in Washington for 16 years."

22c Past tense

The past tense describes an action or state of being as having occurred some time in the past.

> I *received* your letter this morning.
> He *left* the office ten minutes ago.
> I *was giving* the typists their instructions when he *entered*.

Like the present tense, the past tense has an emphatic form, formed by the auxiliary *did*.

> Past tense: I *gave* him the letter, even though he says he can't find it.
> Emphatic: I *did give* him the letter, even though he says he can't find it.

Past tense vs. past participle

The past tense form is used *only* for the past tense. Use the past participle, not the past tense, with auxiliaries to form other tenses. (The past tense and past participle forms of regular verbs are the same; it is the irregular verbs that cause trouble here.)

> Not: I *have went* to the movies this afternoon.
> But: I *went* to the movies this afternoon. (past tense)
> or: I *have gone* to the movies.

Past tense vs. present perfect tense

Remember that the present perfect tense describes an action which may have started some time in the past but which continues up to, and perhaps through, the present.

> I *worked* there for 15 years. (past tense)
> I *have worked* there for 15 years. (present perfect tense)
>> (The first sentence, by the use of the past tense, implies that I no longer work there. The second sentence says that I still work there.)
>
> I *lost* my notes of the meeting. (past tense)
>> (I lost them some time in the past; I may or may not have found them.)
>
> I *have lost* my notes of the meeting. (present perfect tense)
>> (The use of the present perfect extends the action into the present; therefore, it is safe to assume that the notes are still missing.)

22d Past perfect tense

The past perfect tense indicates that the action or condition it describes was completed (perfected) earlier than some other action

Tense of Verbs and Verbals

that also occurred in the past. We use this tense when we need to show that two actions happened at different times in the past.

> He *had finished* his breakfast before I *came* downstairs.
>   (past perfect)   (past)
>
> I *had* mailed the letter when he *called*.
>   (past perfect)   (past)

Past tense vs. past perfect tense

Distinguish carefully between these two tenses. Remember that the past tense can describe an event that happened at any time in the past but that the past perfect tense must describe an event that happened *before* another event in the past. The sentences following may help clarify this usage.

> When I *came* back from lunch, she *finished* the letter.
>   (Both verbs are in the past tense; therefore, both actions happened at approximately the same time in the past.)
> When I *came* back from lunch, she *had finished* the letter.
>   (Again, both actions occurred in the past, but the use of the past perfect *had finished* tells us that this action was completed before the other action.)
> We *discovered* that a detective *was following* us.
>   (Both actions happened at the same time in the past.)
> We *discovered* that a detective *had been following* us.
>   (He had been following us some time before we discovered it.)

22e   Future tense

The future tense is used to indicate that an action will take place some time in the future or that a state or condition will exist some time in the future.

> I *shall not be* at the meeting Friday.
> He *will be waiting* for me after work.

Distinction between SHALL—WILL *and* SHOULD—WOULD

In formal writing there is a distinction between these words. There, the simple future tense is formed by the use of *shall* (or *should*) in the first person and *will* (or *would*) in the second and third person.

Reversing this usage expresses the will or determination of the speaker that something is to be done.

  (1) The office of origin *will* furnish this information.
      (A simple statement of fact.)
  (2) The office of origin *shall* furnish this information.
      (This is mandatory; the office *must* furnish the information.)
  (3) The Director *will* be responsible for complying with these regulations.
  (4) The Director *shall* be held responsible for complying with these regulations.

Simple future (expressing probable future action):

I shall	we shall	I should	we should
you will	you will	you would	you would
he will	they will	he would	they would

Emphatic future (expressing the determination or the will of the speaker):

I will	we will	I would	we would
you shall	you shall	you should	you should
he shall	they shall	he should	they should

This distinction is disappearing rapidly in both speech and writing. But a knowledge of this distinction is essential to anyone who writes or reads legal or procedural documents.

22f Future perfect tense

The future perfect tense names an action or condition that will be completed by some specified time in the future.

  I *shall have been* with this company for 10 years on next Tuesday.
  He *will have finished* that project by April 10.

23 Sequence of Tense

Knowing how *to form* the various tenses is not enough; we must also know how *to use* tense logically in our sentences. To do this, we must understand *sequence* of tense.

What is sequence of tense? It is the logical time relation (expressed by tense) between the verbs in a sentence or passage. It is the way we tell our reader in what order events occurred.

Tense of Verbs and Verbals

23a Tense of verbs in principal clauses

The verbs in principal clauses should be in the same tense if they refer to the same time.

Be consistent in your point of view. When you describe a series of actions that occurred at the same time, keep the verbs in the same tense. But if you interrupt the series with an action that happened earlier or later, be sure to change tense to show the time relation of this new action.

> My new supervisor STRODE into the office. He SAT down at his desk and BEGAN to read the letters which the stenographer *had finished* typing just a few minutes before. As he read, she CROSSED her fingers, hoping he would find no errors.
> (The verbs in capitals are in the past tense, denoting that their actions happened at the same time. The italicized verb *had finished* is in the past perfect tense, indicating that this action took place before the others.)

23b Tense of verbs in subordinate clauses

The verb in the principal clause is taken as a starting point. The tenses of all verbs in subordinate clauses are determined by whether the action they describe takes place before, after, or at the same time as the action described by the verb in the principal clause.

(1) If the verb in the principal clause is in the present or future tense, the verbs in the subordinate clauses *are not restricted to* those two tenses but may be in any tense.

> I HOPE he *is* in his office.
> I HOPE he *was* in his office when you called.
> I HOPE he *will be* in his office when we arrive.

(2) If the verb in the principal clause is in the past or past perfect tense, the verbs in the subordinate clauses must be in some tense that denotes past time.

> I THOUGHT that they *were visiting* you this week.
> I THOUGHT that they *had been visiting* you all summer.
> I THOUGHT that they *had visited* you the previous year.

Exception: The present tense is preferred for the verb in a subordinate clause stating a universal truth, even if the verb in the principal clause is in some other tense.

> He TELLS me that Washington *is* the nation's capital.
> He TOLD me that Washington *is* the nation's capital.
> He DIDN'T BELIEVE that the world *is* round.

(3) In clauses of result or purpose (introduced by such conjunctions as *in order that, so that*)—

(a) if the verb in the principal clause is in the past or past perfect tense, use one of the past auxiliaries (*might, could, would*) in the subordinate clause.

He GAVE (or HAD GIVEN) me a pass, so that I *could* enter the building on Saturdays.

(b) if the verb in the principal clause is in the present or the future tense, use a present auxiliary (*can, may*) in the subordinate clause.

He WILL GIVE me a pass, so that I *can* enter the building on Saturdays.

(4) Often in Revenue writing (particularly in correspondence), it is necessary that we refer to what someone else has said—indirect discourse.

If the verb in the introductory clause is past or past perfect, a present tense verb in the original wording becomes past tense.

Original: I *am enclosing* a copy of . . . .
Paraphrase: The taxpayer SAID that he *was enclosing* a copy . . . .

If the verb in the introductory clause is past or past perfect, a present perfect verb in the original wording becomes past perfect.

Original: I *have sent* a copy of . . . .
Paraphrase: He SAID that he *had sent* a copy of . . . .

If the historical present is used in the introductory clause, the verb in the original wording is unchanged in tense.

Original: I *am sending* a copy of . . . .
Paraphrase: He SAYS he *is sending* a copy of . . . .

If the verb in the introductory clause is past or past perfect, *shall* or *will* in the original wording becomes *would*.

Original: I *shall send* a copy of . . . .
Paraphrase: He SAID that he *would send* a copy of . . . .

24 Tenses of Verbals

In the previous sections we have been concerned with the tense of "finite" verbs—those verbs that perform the functions usually associated with verbs. But finite verbs are not the only verb forms involved in our use of tense. Verbals, too, need to be considered in any discussion of tense and tense sequence.

Even though the three kinds of verbals—gerunds, participles, and infinitives—do not function as verbs, they do retain some of the characteristics of verbs. One of these characteristics is "tense." Participles have three tenses; gerunds and infinitives, two.

24a Gerunds

The gerund has two tense forms: present and perfect.

>Present: *talking, writing*
>Perfect: *having talked, having written*
>
>*WRITING letters* is hard work.
>>(*Writing* is the gerund; *letters* is its object. The gerund phrase is the subject of the sentence.)
>
>It is a treat to watch *his SWIMMING*.
>>(*His* is the subject of the gerund *swimming*.)
>
>>(The subject of a gerund should be in the possessive case. Notice this usage in the sentence above and in the two examples below.)
>
>The *student's WRITING* won him first prize.
>>(The gerund *writing* and its subject *student's* form a gerund phrase which serves as the subject of the sentence.)
>
>We will appreciate *your FURNISHING this information*.
>>(The gerund *furnishing*, its possessive subject *your*, and its object *information* form a gerund phrase which is the object of *appreciate*.)
>
>*Careful, courteous DRIVING* is the trademark of a mature driver.
>>(The gerund and its two modifiers form a gerund phrase which is the subject of the sentence.)
>
>He was honored for *his HAVING DONE* such an outstanding job.
>>(The perfect gerund *having done* and its subject *his* forms a gerund phrase which is the object of the preposition *for*.)
>
>*Our not HAVING ARRIVED on time* meant that we missed the first half of the program.
>>(The gerund phrase is the subject of the sentence.)

24b Participles

The participle has three tense forms: present, past, and perfect.

>Present participle: *talking, writing*
>Past participle: *talked, written*
>Perfect participle: *having talked, having written*

The girl *talking* on the telephone is my secretary.
(The participle *talking* modifies *girl*.)

The article, *beautifully written*, appeared in last week's "Post."
(The participle *written*, plus its modifier *beautifully*, modifies *article*.)

The letter, *having been typed* and *signed*, was ready for mailing.
(The participles *having been typed* and *signed* modify *letter*.)

24c Infinitives

The infinitive has two tense forms: the present and the perfect.

Present: *to talk, to write*
Perfect: *to have talked, to have written*
  To recognize and *define* the problem is our first step.
  He is supposed *to have written* those letters.

24d Verbals in sentence fragments

Sentence fragments (or fragmentary sentences) are parts of sentences erroneously punctuated as complete sentences. A common type of fragmentary sentence is that containing one or more verbals but no finite verb in the main clause. Learn to distinguish between verbals and finite verbs, so that you can avoid writing this type of fragmentary sentence. Remember, mere length does not make a sentence—we need a verb.

Fragment: Sentences of from 1 to 5 years in prison imposed upon six offenders arrested in connection with seizure of a large illicit distillery set up in a tobacco barn in southern Maryland.
Corrected: Sentences of from 1 to 5 years in prison WERE IMPOSED . . . .

Fragment: Your memorandum dated March 4, 1959, requesting information about the availability of certain training materials and about the plans for distribution of these materials.
Corrected: Your memorandum dated March 4, 1959, REQUESTED . . . .

25 *Tense Sequence With Verbals*

Verbals cannot by themselves indicate the exact time of an action. They can express time only in relation to the time of the main verb in the sentence. Verbals show that an action happened at the same time as the action of the main verb or that it happened at an earlier time.

25a Participles

Only two forms of the participle—the present and the perfect—are of interest to us here, since the past participle is usually used as part of a verb phrase.

Tense of Verbs and Verbals

The present participle refers to action happening at the same time as the action of the main verb.

> ENTERING the office he *confirms* his appointment.
> (The main verb is in the present tense; therefore the present participle *entering* carries the idea of present time.)
> ENTERING the office he *confirmed* his appointment.
> (With the change in the tense of the main verb to the past, we also change the time of the participle.)

NOTE: It rests with the writer whether he tells his reader that the passage of time between the action of the main verb and the action of the participle is important or relatively unimportant.

The perfect participle refers to action occurring *before* the action of the main verb.

> HAVING FINISHED the repairs, the plumber *is preparing* to leave.
> HAVING FINISHED the repairs, the plumber *was preparing* to leave.

Study the following pairs of sentences for the use of the present and perfect participles. Remember, the present participle names action occurring at the same time as the action of the main verb; the perfect participle names action occurring before that of the main verb.

> BEING late for work, I ran up the stairs.
> HAVING BEEN late for work, I decided to stay and finish the report after hours.
> INTENDING to return immediately, I left the door open when I went out.
> HAVING INTENDED to return immediately, I was disappointed at having to be away so long.
> SELLING their house, they prepared to move to Florida.
> HAVING SOLD their house, they were free to leave.

256 Infinitives

The present infinitive names an action occurring at the same time as the action of the main verb.

The sentences below all contain present infinitives. Notice that we must depend upon the tense of the main verb to tell us the time of the action of both the main verb and the infinitive.

> I *am trying* TO FINISH this report today.
> (Both actions are happening in the present.)

I *was trying* TO FINISH the report before he asked for it.
    (Both actions happened at the same time in the past.)
I *shall try* TO FINISH the report by the end of the day.
    (Both actions will happen at the same time in the future.)

I *am writing* TO REQUEST three copies of your latest publication
    (Both actions happen in the present.)
I *wrote* TO REQUEST three copies of their catalog.
    (Both happened at the same time in the past.)
I *shall write* tomorrow TO REQUEST a copy of their brochure.
    (Both actions will happen at the same future time.)

The present infinitive also expresses future time, sometimes with the help of a time modifier.

    I *hope* TO ATTEND the meeting next Tuesday.
        (I *hope* NOW *to attend* IN THE FUTURE.)

    I *plan* TO WRITE him about the luncheon.
        (I *plan* NOW *to write* IN THE FUTURE)

    He *expected* TO BE here by today.
        (He *expected* IN THE PAST *to be here* AT SOME FUTURE TIME)

    He *had hoped* TO WIN the trophy.
        (He *had hoped* IN THE PAST *to win* AT SOME FUTURE TIME)

The perfect infinitive expresses action occurring *before* that of the main verb.

    I *am* glad TO HAVE BEEN of assistance.
        (I *am* glad NOW *to have been* of assistance IN THE PAST)

    I *am* honored TO HAVE KNOWN such a person.
        (I *am* honored NOW *to have known* him IN THE PAST)

The sentences below contrast the use of the present and perfect infinitives.

    He *appears* TO BE an Army officer.
        (Present—he *appears* NOW *to be* an officer NOW)

    He *appears* TO HAVE BEEN an Army officer.
        (Perfect—he *appears* NOW *to have been* an officer IN THE PAST)

    I *was* glad TO BE of service.
        (Present—I *was glad* THEN *to be* of service AT THAT TIME)

    I *am* glad TO HAVE BEEN of service.
        (Perfect—I *am glad* NOW *to have been* of service IN THE PAST)

After a verb in the past or past perfect tense, the present infinitive will usually best express your meaning. Be especially cautious of

Tense of Verbs and Verbals

sentences in which both the main verb and the infinitive are preceded by *has, have,* or *had.* These auxiliaries are rarely, if ever, needed in both constructions.

> Not: I *should have liked* TO HAVE SEEN her when she was here.
> But: I *should have liked* TO SEE her when she was here.
>
> Not: I *had hoped* TO HAVE SHIPPED the order by now.
> But: I *had hoped* TO SHIP the order by now.
>
> Not: We *had expected* TO HAVE FINISHED the writing by May.
> But: We *had expected* TO FINISH the writing by May.

25c Gerunds

The present tense of the gerund refers to an action happening at the present time:

> *Taking* a review course will not solve your problems.

The perfect tense of the gerund refers to an action that was completed *before* the time of the main verb.

> He attributes his success to *having studied* whenever possible.

25d Time table

To make the meaning clear for the reader, choose the verb forms that best express the time elements involved. Use the following time table as a quick reminder:

IS	to express a fact or a condition existing now; to express a universal or permanent truth; to express past conditions vividly.
WAS	to express a past or completed fact or condition.
	The reporter said that thousands of men *are* unemployed. (Condition still exists)
	The reporter said that thousands of men *were* unemployed. (Condition may have been remedied)
WILL BE	to express a future fact or condition.
IS	with a modifier to express future time or in a subordinate clause introduced by *when, if, after, before, until,* etc.
	The Director *will be* in the meeting tomorrow.

The Director *is* to be in the Regional Office soon.

Next Friday *is* the end of the filing period. (Will be)
Next Saturday *will be* the end of the pay period. (Is)

The conference *will be* held next Monday (Is)
The conference *is* to be held next Monday (Will be)

HAS ⎫
HAVE ⎭ — to express an action which still exists, or the results of which still exist.
HAD — to express a past or completed action.

The taxpayer says that he *has filed* his return.
The taxpayer said that he *had filed* his return.

He *has worked* in the Service since 1950. (Still is)
He transferred here from the District where he *had worked* for 10 years.

HAS BEEN — to express an action which still exists, or the result of which still exists.

WAS — to express a past or completed action.

The employee *has been working* on a task force.
The employee *was* a member of the task force.

TO BE ⎫
TO DO ⎬ — to express the same time as the main verbs, or future time.
TO HAVE ⎭

TO HAVE BEEN ⎫
TO HAVE DONE ⎬ — to express time before the main verb.
TO HAVE HAD ⎭

The survey *was thought to be* essential. (Indicates same time)
Lincoln *is thought* by our historians *to have been* a man of great vision. (*To have been* indicates time before the main verb.)
It *would have been* unfair *to do* that.
or
It *would be* unfair *to do* that.

SHOULD HAVE LIKED ⎫
WOULD HAVE LIKED ⎭ — to be followed by the present instead of the past of verbs with "to".

Tense of Verbs and Verbals

I *should have liked to see* the report.
I *should have liked to meet* you and (to) *discuss* the matter.

BEING⎫
DOING⎭ ———————————— to express the same time as the main verbs, or future time.

HAVING BEEN⎫
HAVING DONE⎭ ———————— to express time before the main verbs.

There *was* some question of his *doing* the job.
There *was* some question of his *having done* the job.

WOULD BE⎫
SHOULD BE⎬ ———————— to express the same time as the main verbs, or time after the main verbs.
COULD BE⎭

WOULD HAVE BEEN⎫
SHOULD HAVE BEEN⎬ ———— to express time before the main verbs.
COULD HAVE BEEN⎭

It *was* thought that the delinquent tax *could* easily *have been obtained*. (*Or:* could be)
They *decided* that it *would have been* worthwhile to go.

SHALL HAVE BEEN⎫
WILL HAVE BEEN⎭ ———————— to express action performed before some future time and action performed before the present time.

We *shall have* the new instructions before then. (future)
The report *will have been* finished by now. (before present)

TEXT 5

Mood and Voice

26	Mood	30e	To express a condition which may or may not be true
27	The indicative mood	30f	After *as if* or *as though*
28	The imperative mood	31	Abuse of the subjunctive
29	The subjunctive mood	32	Shifts in mood
29a	Forms of the subjunctive	33	Voice
30	Uses of the subjunctive	34	Uses of the active and passive voice
30a	To express a wish		
30b	To express a parliamentary motion	35	The once-forbidden personal pronouns and the passive voice
30c	To express a command, a request, or a suggestion		
30d	To express a condition contrary to fact	36	Shifts in voice

TEXT 5

Mood and Voice

We have seen in earlier texts that, by its properties, a verb can tell the reader more than just the *name* of an action or a condition. By its *tense*, you remember, it tells the reader the *time* of an action and, by *sequence of tense*, the time-order of several actions.

In this text we will discuss two more properties of the verb which the writer can use to make his meaning clear to the reader. These properties are MOOD and VOICE.

26 Mood

Mood (sometimes written "mode") means *manner*. Mood tells the reader the manner, or way, in which the writer regards the statement he is making—that is, whether he sees it as a simple statement, as a command, as a wish, as a statement contrary to fact, or as a statement having a high degree of improbability.

The writer may use any one of three moods—

>   the *indicative*—to make a statement or to ask a question
>   the *imperative*—to give a command, make a request, or make a suggestion
>   the *subjunctive*—to express a wish, a possibility, a statement of doubt

27 The Indicative Mood

The *indicative mood*—used to make a statement or ask a question—is used in almost all our writing and speaking.

>   The conference with the taxpayer and his counsel *was scheduled* fo- May 15.
>   What *is* the correct form to be used?
>   From the evidence submitted, it *seems* that the taxpayer withheld information during the conference.

So natural is the use of this mood that, except for one minor point, we need not discuss it further. That point has to do with its use. You will notice that we have said that this mood is used in "making a *statement*"; if you have referred to books of grammar recently, you may have found it defined as "making a statement *of fact.*" We have purposely omitted this final phrase.

Report writers—in fact, all who write any kind of expository writing—know that limiting the use of the indicative to making statements *of fact* is inexact and perhaps misleading. For they know that the indicative is used just as often to make statements *of inference* and *of assumption.* And some of them believe that the tendency of many writers and readers to assume that any declarative statement is *necessarily* a statement of fact may stem from early training in school—when declarative statements were so defined. This erroneous belief leads the beginning report writer to be inexact in distinguishing between statements that are factual and those that are assumptions—a distinction that must be clear in all our reports. Since this basic course is intended for report writers, as well as for all other Revenue writers, even this passing reference to the distinction is important.

28   The Imperative Mood

The *imperative mood* expresses a command, a request, or a suggestion. The subject of an imperative sentence is ordinarily the pronoun *you* (not expressed, simply understood).

>   *Lock* the safe before you leave the office.
>   *Let* us help you start this program in your organization.
>   Please *sign* the affidavit before returning it to us.
>   (Note that the word *please* may be inserted with no effect on the use of the imperative, but often with a desirable effect on the reader.)

Probably the greatest mistake we make in using the imperative mood is in *not using it enough.* An order or a request stated in the imperative is usually not only more emphatic but much more quickly and easily understood.

>   Indicative: It would be appreciated if you would forward this information promptly.
>   Imperative: Please forward (send) this information promptly.

Current guides for *writing procedures or instructional material* urge greater use of the imperative mood (or, as some of them say, "greater use of command language").

The use of the imperative instead of the indicative wipes out two problems that plague the procedure writer: (1) deciding *when* to use *shall, should, will,* and *may* in such constructions as, "The employee *shall* (or *may*) submit a report"; and (2) avoiding a shift from one to the other of these forms within the same procedure. Using the imperative, the writer avoids these problems by simply instructing the employee to "submit a report."

The use of the imperative helps the reader, too; for it results in procedures that are shorter, crisper, and easier to understand than those written in the indicative. Please compare the following:

Indicative mood predominates:

> The address should be typed in block form, even with the left margin; single-space typing and open punctuation should be used. When letterhead bearing a printed typing dot is used, the address should be started one space below and in line with this typing dot.

Imperative mood substituted:

> Type the address in block form, even with the left margin; use single space and open punctuation. When using letterhead bearing a printed typing dot, start the address one space below and in line with the dot.

Indicative mood predominates:

> Vouchers should be prepared by typewriter with carbon duplicates whenever practicable. Otherwise, ink of a permanent nature should be used.

Imperative mood substituted:

> Whenever practicable, prepare vouchers by typewriter with carbon duplicates. Otherwise, use permanent ink.

29 The Subjunctive Mood

The *subjunctive mood* is used most often to express a condition contrary to fact, a wish, a supposition, or an indirect command.

Grammarians seem to agree (and many writers fondly hope) that the subjunctive is going out of use. Writers accustomed to the subjunctive, however, tend to agree with grammarians that this trend is unfortunate. For, simply by changing the verb to the subjunctive mood, they can express shades of meaning that otherwise would require the insertion of several explanatory phrases.

Be that as it may, the subjunctive is still being used in a number of instances; and the Revenue writer needs to know enough about its use and abuse so that he can use good judgment in determining when to use it.

29a Forms of the subjunctive

The only recognizable forms of the subjunctive (and consequently the only ones to be discussed in this text) are—

(1) the form of the third person singular present (which in the indicative has an -*s* and in the subjunctive has none):

> Indicative: The revenue agent PREPARES his report as soon as he completes the case.
> Subjunctive: We suggested that the revenue agent PREPARE his report immediately.
>
> Indicative: The plane usually ARRIVES on schedule.
> Subjunctive: Should the plane ARRIVE on schedule, we will be able to make our connection.

(2) forms of the verb *be*, which show the following differences between the indicative and the subjunctive:

> Indicative: *I* AM, *you* ARE, *he* IS; *we, you, they* ARE
> Subjunctive: If *I* BE   and Should *we* BE
>   If *you* BE   Should *you* BE
>   If *he* BE   Should *they* BE
>   (Both *if* and *should* frequently introduce the subjunctive)
>
> Indicative: *I* WAS, *you* WERE, *he* WAS; *we* WERE, *you* WERE, *they* WERE
> Subjunctive: If *I* WERE (difference)   If *we* WERE (no change)
>   If *you* WERE (no change)   If *you* WERE (no change)
>   If *he* WERE (difference)   If *they* WERE (no change)

Though *were* is the past form in the indicative, it is used as PRESENT or FUTURE in the subjunctive. Either *had* or *had been* is used to express PAST time in the subjunctive.

> Present subjunctive: If the memorandum *were* available (NOW), we could finish the report.
> Past subjunctive: If the memorandum *had been* available (IN THE PAST), we could have finished the report.
>   or: *Had* the memorandum been available, we could have finished the report.
>
> Present: If he *were* able to do it, I am sure he would.
> Past: *Had* he been able to do it, I am sure he would.

Mood and Voice

30   Uses of the Subjunctive

Most uses of the subjunctive have become so natural to the writer that they cause him little trouble. However, there are some that require him to weigh the *degree of probability* of his statement before he uses the subjunctive instead of the indicative.

In the following sections, we shall list first those about which there is little question and then, in section 30e, those that cause confusion or concern.

30a   To express a wish not likely to be fulfilled or impossible of being realized

> I wish it *were* possible for us to approve his transfer at this time. (It is *not* possible.)
> I wish he *were* here to hear your praise of his work. (He is *not* here.)
> Would that I *were* able to take this trip in your place. (I am *not* able to go.)
> I wish I *were* able to help you.

30b   To express a parliamentary motion

> I move that the meeting *be* adjourned.
> *Resolved*, that a committee *be* appointed to study this matter.

30c   In a subordinate clause after a verb that expresses a command, a request, or a suggestion

> He asked *that* the report *be* submitted in duplicate.
> It is recommended *that* this office *be* responsible for preparing the statements.
> We suggest *that* he *be* relieved of the assignment.
> We ask *that* he *consider* the possibility of an adjustment.
> It is highly desirable *that* they *be* given the authority to sign these documents.

30d   To express a condition easily recognized as being contrary to fact

> If I *were* in St. Louis, I should be glad to attend.
> If this *were* a simple case, we would easily agree on a solution.
> If I *were* you, I should not mind the assignment.

30e   To express a condition or supposition which the writer believes to be contrary to fact or highly improbable, as contrasted with a condition or supposition which the writer considers to be within the realm of possibility

This is the trouble area. Here, the writer has the obligation to tell the reader which way he sees the situation: highly improbable or within the realm of possibility. He does this by his choice of the subjunctive or the indicative.

Subjunctive: If his statement *be* true, this is a case of fraud.
(The writer indicates that he thinks it is highly improbable that the statement is true.)

Indicative: If his statement *is* true, this may be a case of fraud.
(The writer indicates that it is quite possible that the statement may be true.)

Subjunctive: If he *were* at the meeting, he would speak to the point. (or, *were* he at the meeting, he would . . .)
(The writer tells his reader that the man is not at the meeting.)

Indicative: If he *was* at the meeting, he would have been able to speak to the point.
(Perhaps the man *was* at the meeting; the writer doesn't know.)

Subjunctive: *Had* the first payment been made in April, the second would be due in September.
(The writer tells his reader that the payment was *not* made in April.)

Indicative: If the first payment *was* made in April, the second will be be due in September.
(Perhaps it was made; perhaps not—the writer doesn't know.)

Subjunctive: If he *were* able to forecast the degree of interest in the program, he could be more specific in his budget requests.
(The writer considers it highly improbable—unlikely— that the man can forecast the degree of interest.)

Indicative: If he *is* able to forecast the degree of interest in the program, he can be more specific in his budget requests.
(Here, the writer thinks it is *possible* that the man can forecast the degree of interest.)

30f After *as if* or *as though*

In formal writing and speech, *as if* and *as though* are followed by the subjunctive, since they introduce as supposition something not factual. In informal writing and speaking, the indicative is sometimes used.

He talked *as if* he *were* an expert on taxation. (He's not.)
This report looks *as though* it *were* the work of a college freshman.

31 Abuse of the Subjunctive

Some writers, in an overzealous attempt to write correctly, use the subjunctive in all *if*-clauses.

Mood and Voice

If-clauses are, of course, *conditional* clauses; that's what the writer tells his reader by his choice of the subordinate conjunction *if*. But not all *if*-clauses express thoughts that are suppositions or that are contrary to fact.

    Simply conditional: If it *is* assigned to me, I shall do it.
                                 (Perhaps it *will be* assigned to me.)
    Contrary to fact: If it *were* assigned to me, I would do it.
                                 (It has already been assigned to someone else; or it is highly improbable that it will ever be assigned to me.)

    Simply conditional: If the taxpayer *was* married on that date, he is entitled to . . . (Perhaps he was.)
    Contrary to fact: If the taxpayer *were* married . . . (He is not.)

32 Shifts in Mood

Be consistent in your point of view. Once you have decided on the mood that expresses the way you regard the message, use that mood throughout the sentence or the paragraph. A shift in mood is confusing to the reader, because it indicates that the writer himself has changed his way of looking at the conditions.

    Not: It is requested that a report of the proceedings *be* prepared and copies *should be* distributed to all members.
          (*Be* is subjunctive; *should be*, indicative.)
    But: It is requested that a report of the proceedings *be* prepared and that copies *be* distributed to all members.

    Not: Date *stamp* the quiz when it is received in the office, and then the quiz *should be sent* to X Division.
          (Shift from imperative to indicative mood.)
    But: Date *stamp* the quiz when it is received and then *send* it to X Division.

    Not: The reply *should be* administratively verified and signed on the line provided therefor, and *should be* certified by a certifying officer. This officer *should* ordinarily *be* the one against whom the exception was taken. If he is no longer available, STATE his current address in the reply.
          (All verbs except STATE are in the indicative; STATE is in the imperative.)
    But: . . . if he is no longer available, the reply SHOULD STATE (or SHOULD SHOW) his current address.

    Not: *Law and Argument:* In this section, the conferee *will evaluate* the arguments presented by the taxpayer in relation to the recommendations of the examining officer and *make* a concise statement of the position to be taken. Citation of cases *should be limited* to leading cases which are directly in point.

Conclusion and Recommendations: Leave no doubt as to how the issue is to be treated by the examining officer. *State clearly* and explicitly the recommendations to be followed by the examining officer. If the issue is a factual one to be sustained in part, *mention* the exact amount of the adjustment determined.

(In the first paragraph of these instructions, the verbs are in the indicative mood; in the second, they are in the imperative. The whole passage will make smoother reading if the same point of view is maintained throughout.)

But: *Law and Argument:* In this section, *evaluate* the arguments presented by the taxpayer in relation to the recommendations of the examining officer and *make* a concise statement of the position to be taken. *Limit* citation of cases to leading cases that are directly in point.

Conclusion and Recommendations: Leave no doubt as to how the issue is to be treated by the examining officer. *State* clearly and explicitly the recommendations to be followed by the examining officer. If the issue is a factual one to be sustained in part, *mention* the exact amount of the adjustment determined.

33 Voice

Voice indicates whether the subject of the verb is performing or receiving the action described by the verb. There are two voices: active and passive.

If the subject is performing the action, the verb is in the active voice.

> The *Director* APPROVED our report.
> The *report* SUMMARIZES the committee recommendations.
> The *agent* ASKED the taxpayer to bring his receipts.

If the subject is being acted upon, the verb is in the passive voice. (The passive form always consists of some form of *be* plus the past participle.)

> Our *report* WAS APPROVED by the Director.
> The committee *recommendations* ARE SUMMARIZED in the report.
> The *taxpayer* WAS ASKED by the agent to bring his receipts.

34 Uses of the Active and Passive Voices

We need to use both the active and passive voice. In the past the tendency in Government writing has been to use the passive voice as much as possible, probably in the belief that the resulting

Mood and Voice

sentences sound "more official." Lately, in an effort to put more life into writing, some grammarians have been stressing the use of the active voice, almost to the extent of advising us to avoid the passive voice at all costs. But one extreme is as bad as the other. We need both the active and the passive voice for emphasis and for exact expression.

If you want to emphasize *who* performed an action, let your subject be the person or thing that performed the action and put your verb in the active voice. If it is relatively unimportant *who* performed the action and you want to stress instead *what action* was performed or *who was affected* by the action performed, let your subject be the person or thing "acted upon" (the receiver of the action) and put the verb in the passive voice.

> All supervisors attended the meeting.
>> (*Supervisors* is being emphasized.)
>
> The meeting was attended by all supervisors.
>> (Here the *meeting* is being emphasized.)
>
> The Blank Instrument Co. employs Mr. Johnson.
>> (This form emphasizes the company.)
>
> Mr. Johnson is employed by the Blank Instrument Co.
>> (This form emphasizes Mr. Johnson, not the company.)
>
> The Division Director himself checked the figures in the statistical report.
>> (Here we want to emphasize *who* checked the figures.)
>
> The figures in the statistical report were thoroughly checked by a proofreader.
>> (In this sentence the important idea is that the figures were checked; by whom is relatively unimportant.)
>
> The Commissioner and his staff know that this method will work only in carefully controlled situations.
>> (The writer is emphasizing the doer of the action—the Commissioner and his staff.)
>
> It is generally known that this method will work only in carefully controlled situations.
>> (In this sentence the doer of the action—whoever knows—is unimportant; the receiver of the action—what is known—is the important idea!)

NOTE: We can't say that one voice is "correct" in certain instances and "incorrect" in others. The decision of which voice to use rests with the writer; he is the only one who can say which voice better suits his purpose.

The active voice is, however, simpler and more direct; therefore, if either the active or the passive will serve your purpose, use the active. Notice the increased sharpness of the second version of the paragraph below.

Passive voice predominates:

> Mr. Johnson is employed as a bus driver by the "X" Transport Lines. During the audit of Mr. Johnson's 1957 income tax return, he *was asked* by the agent to substantiate certain deductions. He *was* also *asked* to obtain a record from his employer showing the number of trips he made during the year. On the basis of this information, the agent arrived at a certain amount for each trip and settlement *was proposed* on that basis.

Active voice predominates:

> Mr. Johnson is employed as a bus driver by the "X" Transport Lines. During the audit of Mr. Johnson's 1957 income tax return, the agent *asked* him to substantiate certain deductions and to obtain a record from his employer showing the number of trips he made during the year. On the basis of this information, the agent arrived at a certain amount for each trip and *proposed* settlement on that basis.

35 *The Once-Forbidden Personal Pronouns and the Passive Voice*

Government writers often make a verb passive for no other reason than to avoid using the personal pronouns *I*, *we*, and *you*. And, for a long time, we were not permitted to use these pronouns. To some extent, this explains our overuse of the passive voice and the resultant heavy, phrase-laden sentences.

Even now, we are careful to use the third-person construction (*it*—and, less often, *this office* or *the Service*) in certain kinds of writing in which we want to maintain an impersonal, objective, disinterested (not uninterested) point of view.

But, by using the personal pronouns *you* and *we* when they can appropriately be used, we can write sentences that are more direct, more concise, and more clear to the reader.

> A brochure is enclosed which sets forth the dates and locations of the schools.
>> (Passive voice; no personal pronoun. This is an example of the "untouched-by-human-hands" type of sentence.)
>
> We are enclosing a brochure which gives the dates and locations of the schools.
>
> OR
>
> The enclosed brochure gives the dates and locations of the schools.

36 Shifts in Voice

Like the shift in mood, which we have discussed, a shift in voice is confusing to the reader. Even when it does not confuse him, it may distract him momentarily.

Shifts in voice—often accompanied by shifts in subject—usually occur in compound or complex sentences. Although it is not essential that all clauses in a sentence be the same in structure, any unnecessary shifts result in a disorganized sentence. Therefore, unless you have a good reason for changing, use the same subject and voice in the second clause that you used in the first.

> Not: I have more confidence in WHAT THE TAXPAYER TOLD ME than in WHAT I WAS TOLD BY HIS COUNSEL.
> (First verb is active; the second, passive.)
> But: I have more confidence in WHAT I WAS TOLD BY THE TAXPAYER than in WHAT I WAS TOLD BY HIS COUNSEL.
> (Both verbs are passive.)
>
> Not: As I SEARCHED through the files for the memorandum, the missing REPORT WAS FOUND.
> (The first subject is *I*—its verb is active; the second subject is *report*—its verb is passive.)
> But: As I SEARCHED through the files for the memorandum, I FOUND the missing report.
> (Subject is *I* in both clauses; both verbs are active.)
>
> Not: As soon as WE RECEIVE his signed contract, ARRANGEMENTS CAN BE MADE to pay him.
> (*We* is the first subject—its verb is active; *arrangements* is the second subject—its verb is passive.)
> But: As soon as his CONTRACT IS RECEIVED, ARRANGEMENTS CAN BE MADE to pay him.
> (Both verbs are in the passive voice, but we still have different subjects.)
> or: As soon as WE RECEIVE his signed contract, WE CAN MAKE arrangements to pay him.
> (Now both verbs are in the active voice and the subjects are the same.)
>
> Not: A SUMMARY of the minutes of the meeting WILL BE PREPARED and WE WILL DISTRIBUTE copies to all members.
> (The subject of the first clause is *summary*—the verb is passive. The subject of the second clause is *we*—the verb is active.)
> But: A SUMMARY of the minutes of the meeting WILL BE PREPARED and COPIES WILL BE DISTRIBUTED to all members.
> (The subjects of the two clauses are still different but the fact that the verbs are both passive makes this an improved sentence.)
> or: WE WILL PREPARE a summary of the minutes of the meeting and (WE WILL) DISTRIBUTE copies to all members.
> (*We* is the subject of both clauses; both verbs are in the active voice.)

TEXT 6

Modifiers

37	Introduction	43a	Adjectives and adverbs that cannot be compared
37a	Importance of modifiers		
37b	Purpose of the text	43b	Comparison with *other* or *else*
37c	Classification of modifiers	43c	Incomplete comparison
38	Types of adjectives	44	Verbals and verbal phrases as modifiers
38a	Articles		
		44a	Infinitive
39	Types of adverbs	44b	Infinitive phrase
		44c	Participle
40	Identifying adjectives and adverbs	44d	Participial phrase
		44e	Gerund phrase
40a	The *ly* ending	44f	Dangling verbal phrases
40b	Words that are both adjectives and adverbs	44g	Nominative absolute—the sentence modifier
40c	Adverbs with two forms	45	Prepositional phrase as a modifier
40d	Distinguishing between a predicate adjective and an adverb		
		45a	Dangling prepositional phrase
		46	Dependent clauses as modifiers
41	Compound modifiers (with and without hyphens)		
		46a	Dependent clauses as adjectives
41a	Modifiers preceding a noun		
41b	Modifiers following a noun	46b	Dependent clauses as adverbs
41c	Suspending hyphens	46c	Elliptical clauses
41d	Two-word proper adjectives	46d	Relative pronouns introducing clauses
41e	Separate modifiers preceding a noun		
		47	Placement of modifiers
41f	Adverb ending in *ly* with adjective	47a	Modifier between subject and verb
		47b	Single adjectives
42	Comparison of adjectives and adverbs	47c	Multiple adjectives
		47d	Single adverbs
42a	Degrees of comparison	47e	Phrases and clauses
42b	Using *-er* and *-est* vs. *more* and *most*	47f	Relative clauses
		47g	Squinting constructions
42c	Irregular comparisons	47h	Adverb clauses
43	Problems with comparison	47i	Long modifying phrases

95

TEXT 6

Modifiers

37   Introduction

37a   Importance of modifiers

"Modifiers—the mark of the mature writer" might well be a better title for this text. For a writer's ability to write clear, effective sentences depends largely on his ability to choose his modifiers judiciously and use them effectively.

Why are modifiers important? For one thing, they form a part of almost every sentence we write. Important though the subject and the verb are (and this was stressed in preceding texts), few sentences consist solely of these words. The sentence "Honesty pays" best illustrates the sentence that has only a subject and a verb, but how unusual such a sentence is.

Even a simple sentence like, *"The revenue* agent submitted *a timely* report" contains four modifiers—*the* and *a* as articles, *revenue* modifying *agent*, and *timely* modifying *report*. And the more complex the thought becomes, the more relationships are shown between the ideas it contains—the more modifiers the writer must use. Modifiers are important, then, because they are a part of virtually every sentence we write.

Modifiers are important, too, because of the function they perform. They *describe, restrict, limit,* and *make more exact* the meaning of other words. Consider how essential it is, in Revenue writing, that we decide just when certain terms that we use must be restricted, limited, or made more exact. To use an obvious illustration, it would be inconceivable that we should speak of just "income"—we must instead *restrict* the meaning of the word, make it more exact; so we speak of it in such terms as "gross" income, "net" income, "adjusted net" income. Because of the technical nature of our writing, we rely heavily on modifiers to make our meaning clear—and to make it exact.

The writer, then, must use judgment in deciding *when* to use modifiers and in choosing the "precise" modifier to get his meaning across. In addition, if he is to write effectively he must be discriminating in his use of modifiers. He must not use too many, for this will result in "wordy" letters; he must train himself to shorten clause modifiers to phrases and phrases to single words whenever that is possible. And, finally, he must use modifiers with discretion, lest they change the "tone" of his writing. In letters, it is often the modifier that may unwittingly offend the reader; in reports, it is often the modifier that tends to destroy the objective, impartial tone of the exposition. Take this sentence for example:

> The taxpayer's counsel stated that he did not agree with the agent's findings.
>
> The taxpayer's counsel stated *flatly* that he did not agree with the agent's findings.

In the first example we have a simple statement of fact, objective and disinterested. In the second example, by adding one modifier (*flatly*) we have changed the tone of the sentence and injected a personal and biased note.

376 Purpose of the text

What, then, must the writer know about modifiers if he is to choose them wisely and use them effectively?

As a minimum, he must know:

(1) that in choosing his modifiers—

    (a) he may use a single word, a phrase, or a clause
    (b) he may modify a subject, a verb, a complement, or another modifier
    (c) he must use adjective modifiers (whether words, phrases or clauses) to modify subjects, objects, and predicate nominatives
    (d) he must use adverbial modifiers to modify verbs, adjectives, and other adverbs

(2) that in using his modifiers—

    (a) he must place them as close as possible to the word(s) being modified
    (b) he must not misuse modifiers lest he confuse the reader
    (c) he must not overuse modifiers lest he ruin the conciseness of his writing

Modifiers

This text will explain and illustrate these and other related points and will point out some of the more serious problems writers face in applying the principles governing modifiers. Later texts will guide the writer in applying these principles in his own writing.

37c Classification of modifiers

Modifiers fall generally into two categories: *adjectives* and phrases or clauses used as adjectives; *adverbs* and phrases or clauses used as adverbs. Sometimes the form of the modifier clearly shows whether it is an adjective or an adverb; sometimes the form is the same for both.

Adjectives describe, limit, or make more exact the meaning of a noun or pronoun (any substantive).

Adverbs describe, limit, or make more exact the meaning of a verb, an adjective, or another adverb.

38 Types of Adjectives

There are six main categories of adjectives:

Limiting:	*many* people, *much* work
Numerical:	*four* letters, *nine* regions
Descriptive:	*accurate* description, *long-term* gain
Proper:	*American* flag, *British* embassy
Pronominal:	*my* assignment, *this* book
Article:	*a* letter, *an* hour, *the* return

38a Articles

The articles are *a*, *an*, and *the*. Use *a* before words beginning with a consonant sound, *an* before those beginning with a vowel sound.

    a desk, *a* book
    an agent, *an* error, *an* LWOP case (el-W-O-P)

The article used before each of two connected nouns or adjectives signals that the words refer to different people or things.

    We elected *a* secretary and *a* treasurer (two persons).
    She uses *a* tan and green typewriter (one machine, two colors).

Do not use *a* or *an* after *sort of, kind of, manner of, style of,* or *type of.*

    Not: What *kind of a* book do you want?
    But: What *kind of* book do you want?

39 Types of Adverbs

Adverbs may be classified according to the questions they answer; in general, there are five types:

    Adverbs of manner: run *swiftly*, write *legibly*, compute *accurately*
    Adverbs of place and direction: *above, before, below, here, out*
    Adverbs of time and succession: *immediately, today, ago, lately*
    Adverbs of degree and measure: *almost, enough, far, little, much*
    Adverbs of cause, reason, or purpose: *because, hence, therefore*

40 Identifying Adjectives and Adverbs

Sometimes the writer has difficulty distinguishing between adjectives and adverbs. Here are a few helps.

40a The *ly* ending

Some adverbs, chiefly the adverbs of manner, are formed by adding *-ly* to the adjective or participle form. However, not all adverbs end in *ly;* and some adjectives end in *ly*. The writer cannot, then, look upon the *ly ending* as a means of distinguishing between adjectives and adverbs.

Adjectives that end in *ly:*

    cleanly, deadly, friendly, likely, lively, lonely, lovely, kindly, orderly, timely

    a *friendly* discussion, an *orderly* arrangement, a *timely* return

Adverbs that do not end in *ly:*

    soon, often, around, down, very, now, yet

    write *soon*, call *often*, *very* high production

40b Words that are both adjectives and adverbs

The following words may be either adjectives or adverbs, depending on their use:

Modifiers

above, bad, better, cheap, close, deep, early, fast, first, hard, late, long, loud, much, only, quick, slow, very, well

Mary types *better* than Joan does. (adverb)
The chief had a cold, but he is *better* now. (adjective)

We climbed a *very* high hill. (adverb)
That is the *very* return I was looking for. (adjective)

If you must use the detour, drive *slow* (or slowly). (adverb)
A *slow* driver is often a hazard on the highway. (adjective)

40c Adverbs with two forms

Some adverbs have two forms—one ending in *ly*, the other not. The longer form is nearly always correct and is preferable in formal writing. The short form is properly used in brief, forceful sentences (in commands—such as the road sign "Drive Slow") and may be used in informal writing. The *ly* form should, however, always be used to modify an adjective.

Following are examples of adverbs having two forms:

slow, slowly	clear, clearly	quick, quickly
cheap, cheaply	sharp, sharply	loud, loudly
soft, softly	deep, deeply	direct, directly

Sometimes the meaning desired will determine which form should be used. Notice that either *direct* or *directly* may be used when the meaning is "in a straight line," but *directly* is the only choice when *soon* is meant.

NOTE: In informal speech, we sometimes drop the *ly* ending from some often-used adverbs. This practice is incorrect and, even though we occasionally let it slip by in our speech, we must not allow it in our writing.

Correct usage:

I am *really* glad you could come. (Not, *real* glad)
I'm feeling *considerably* better. (Not, *considerable*)
He *surely* is lucky. (Not, *sure*)

40d Distinguishing between a predicate adjective and an adverb

A predicate adjective is, as its name implies, an adjective appearing in the predicate and modifying the subject.

The following categories of verbs (called *linking verbs*) are usually followed by a predicate adjective rather than by an adverb. A predicate adjective can occur only after these verbs:

(1) Forms of the verb *to be*

    That man IS *old*.   (old man)
    The report WAS *accurate*.   (accurate report)

(2) Other no-action verbs, such as *become, appear, seem*

    The town APPEARS *deserted*.   (deserted town)
    The air SEEMS *humid*.   (humid air)

(3) Verbs pertaining to the senses

    The reports SOUND *exaggerated*.   (exaggerated reports)
    The peach TASTES *sweet*.   (sweet peach)
    The work LOOKS *hard*.   (hard work)

NOTE: Be sure to distinguish between the predicate adjective and the adverb when the sense verbs are used. Usually these verbs are followed by adjectives, but they may be modified by adverbs.

    She LOOKS *bad*. (She doesn't appear to be healthy.)
    She LOOKS *badly*. (An awkward construction, which could mean that, having lost something, she is doing a poor job of looking for it.)

    The steak LOOKS *tender*. (Has the appearance of *tender* steak)
    The woman LOOKED *tenderly* at the child. (Tells "how" she *looked* at the child.)

    The child LOOKS *wistful*. (Has a wistful look)
    The child LOOKED *wistfully* at the candy. (Tells how the child *looked* at the candy.)

To determine whether the modifier following a sense verb modifies the subject or the verb, substitute *is* or *are* for the sense verb. If, after this substitution, the sentence is logical, you can be sure your choice (whether of a predicate adjective or of an adverb) is correct.

    The steak IS *tender*. (Logical)
    The woman IS *tenderly* at the child. (Illogical)

41 Compound Modifiers (With and Without Hyphens)

41a Modifiers preceding a noun

Two or more words serving as a single adjective are called a com-

Modifiers 103

pound adjective. When these modifiers *precede* a noun, they are joined by a hyphen.

> Have you an *up-to-date* REPORT on that subject?
> Please submit the *above-mentioned* FORM in duplicate.
> That is a *well-written* DOCUMENT.
> Ours is a *well-equipped* OFFICE.

41b Modifiers following a noun

When the modifying words *follow* a noun, do not use a hyphen unless the words are listed as hyphenated compounds in the dictionary.

> This REPORT is *up to date*.
> The FORM *mentioned above* must be submitted in duplicate.
> That DOCUMENT is *well written*.
> Our OFFICE is *well equipped*.
> This MOTOR is *self-starting*.

NOTE: Since usage is constantly changing, it is best to consult a recent dictionary when in doubt about hyphenated words. Notice that, in the last example above, *self-starting* is hyphenated, even though it follows the noun. The dictionary gives all "self" words except *selfsame, selfish, selfhood,* and *selfless* as hyphenated compounds. (The Government Printing Office Style Manual lists a great many compound words; it, too, is a good reference book for the Government employee.)

41c Suspending hyphens

In a series of hyphenated adjective-noun words having a common ending, suspending hyphens are used to carry the force of the modifier over to a later noun.

> Is he looking for a two- or three-bedroom apartment?
> It is a 4- or 5-page report.

41d Two-word proper adjectives

Compound adjectives consisting of two-word proper adjectives are *not* hyphenated.

> He is vacationing at a *New Jersey* beach.
> It was a *Comptroller General* decision.

41e Separate modifiers preceding a noun

Do not hyphenate two or more adjectives that precede the noun *if they do not act jointly* to modify the noun. Note, however, the correct punctuation of such constructions.

> He wore a *white* FLANNEL SUIT. (a flannel suit that was white)
> Give me a *current* STATISTICAL REPORT. (a statistical report that is current)
>
> It was a *long, hard* JOB. (a long job *and* a hard one)
> It was an *involved, difficult* CASE. (an involved case *and* a difficult one)

NOTE: One suggestion to help you determine whether to put a comma between the two adjectives: If you can insert the word *and* between the two adjectives without destroying the meaning of the sentence, use a comma; otherwise, do not.

41f Adverb ending in *ly* with adjective

Do not use a hyphen between an adverb ending in *ly* and an adjective or participle.

> This is a *carefully written* REPORT.
> That is a *frequently quoted* PASSAGE.

42   Comparison of Adjectives and Adverbs

42a Degrees of comparison

Adjectives and adverbs change form to show a greater or lesser degree of the characteristic named by the simple word. There are three degrees of comparison.

Positive degree.—The positive degree names the *quality* expressed by the adjective or adverb. It does not imply a comparison with, or a relation to, a similar quality in any other thing.

> *high* morale, a *dependable* worker, work *fast*, prepared *carefully*

Comparative degree.—The comparative degree indicates that the quality described by the modifier exists to a greater or lesser degree in one thing than in another. It is formed by adding *er* to the positive degree or by inserting *more* or *less* before the positive form.

> Our organization has *higher* morale now than ever before.
> He is a *more dependable* worker than she.
> She can work *faster* than I.
> This report was prepared *more carefully* than the one he submitted last month.

Modifiers

Superlative degree.—The superlative degree denotes the greatest or least amount of the quality named. It is formed by adding *est* to the positive degree of the adjective or adverb or by inserting *most* or *least* before the positive form.

> That organization has the *highest* morale of any Government agency.
> He is the *most dependable* worker in the office.
> This is the *most carefully* prepared report I have found.

The comparative degree is used to refer to only two things; the superlative to more than two.

> This book is the *longer* of the two.
> This book is the *longest* of the three.

42b Using *-er* and *-est* vs. *more* and *most*

There is no difference in meaning between *-er* and *more* or between *-est* and *most*. Either method may be used with some modifiers. However, most adjectives of three syllables or more and almost all adverbs are compared by the use of *more* and *most* (or *less* and *least*) rather than by the endings *-er* and *-est*. In choosing which method should be used with the modifiers that may take either method, you may base your choice on emphasis. By adding *-er* or *-est* to the root word you emphasize the *quality*, while by using *more* or *most* you stress the *degree* of comparison.

> Should I have been *kinder* or *harsher* in handling that call?
> That report is the *longest* of the three.
> Should I have been *more firm* or *less firm* in handling that caller?
> Of all the forms, this one is the *most simple* and that one is the *least simple* to fill out.

42c Irregular comparisons

Some modifiers are compared by changes in the words themselves. A few of these irregular comparisons are given below; consult your dictionary whenever you are in doubt about the comparison of any adjective or adverb.

Positive	*Comparative*	*Superlative*
good	better	best
well	better	best
bad (evil, ill)	worse	worst
badly (ill)	worse	worst
far	farther, further	farthest, furthest
late	later, latter	latest, last
little	less, lesser	least
many, much	more	most

43   *Problems With Comparison*

43a   Adjectives and adverbs that cannot be compared

Some adjectives and adverbs express qualities that do not admit freely of comparison. They represent the highest degree of a quality and, as a result, cannot be improved. Some of these words are listed below.

complete	infinitely	square
correct	perfect	squarely
dead	perfectly	supreme
deadly	perpendicularly	totally
exact	preferable	unique
horizontally	round	uniquely
immortally	secondly	universally

However, there may be times when the comparison of these words is justified. If we use these modifiers in a relative or approximate sense, they may be compared. But proceed with care. It is usually better, for example, to say *more nearly round* or *more nearly perfect* than *rounder* or *more perfect*.

43b   Comparison with *other* or *else*

When we use the comparative in such an expression as *This thing is better than any other*, we imply that *this thing* is separate from the group or class to which it is being compared. In these expressions we must use a word such as *other* or *else* to separate the thing being compared from the rest of the group of which it is a part.

> Not: Our house is cooler than any house on the block.
>   (The mistake here is not separating the item being compared (*house*) from the group to which it is being compared.)
> But: Our house is cooler than any *other* house on the block.
>   (Our house is one of the houses on the block.)
>
> Not: He has a better record than any agent in our group.
> But: He has a better record than any *other* agent in the group.
>   (He himself is one of the agents in the group.)

43c   Incomplete comparison

When you make a comparison between two items, be sure that both terms of the comparison are named. Violation of this rule places the burden on the reader, who may or may not clearly understand which of two items you are comparing. Be sure your reader knows exactly what you mean when you say—

Modifiers

>There have been more successful prosecutions of tax fraud cases in the "X" district this year.

Do you mean *more than in any other district?* or *more than in any previous year?*

Whenever a comparison is not completed, the meaning of the sentence is obscured. This is one form of the incomplete comparison. Here are a few more.

(1) Incomplete comparison—with possessive:

Obscure: Joe's letter states the problem better than John.
(We cannot tell whether it is *John* or *John's letter* that is stating the problem.)
Improved: Joe's letter states the problem better than *John's.*

Ambiguous: John's proposed form is less complicated than Printing.
Improved: John's proposed form is less complicated than Printing's.
(Or: than the one proposed by Printing.)

(2) Incomplete comparison—with conjunction:

Obscure: This text is as good, if not better than that one.
(Because of the omission of the second *as* after *good*, this sentence reads—"as good *than.*")
Improved: This text is as good *as*, if not better than, that one.
or: This text is as good as that one, if not better.

Obscure: This book is shorter, but just as comprehensive as that one.
Improved: This book is shorter *than*, but just as comprehensive as, that one.
or: This book is shorter than that one, but just as comprehensive.

(3) Incomplete comparison—with verb:

Ambiguous: I enjoy this kind of work more than John.
(This could be interpreted—I enjoy this kind of work more than I enjoy *John.*)
Improved: I enjoy this kind of work more than John *does.*

Obscure: I have known him longer than John.
Could mean: I have known him longer than John *has.*
or: I have known him longer than *I have known* John.

44 Verbals and Verbal Phrases as Modifiers

Verbals, words derived from verbs, are sometimes used as modifiers, either singly or in phrases.

44a Infinitive

The infinitive may serve either as an adjective or as an adverb. And, as a modifier, it may be used either with or without the introductory *to*.

As an adjective:

>We heard HIM *speak*.   (heard him.(to) speak)
>The LETTER *to be rewritten* is on my desk.

As an adverb:

>I am READY *to write* the letter now.
>I am UNABLE *to speak* on that subject.
>We will TRY *to finish* before noon.
>We WROTE this letter *to explain* our policy.

NOTE: Much has been written on whether it is good usage to split an infinitive—that is, whether to insert a modifying word between the *to* and the rest of the infinitive (*to carefully consider* instead of *to consider carefully*). The problem most often arises when a modified infinitive follows another verb construction.

Take, for example, the problem the writer faces in inserting the adverb *completely* in this sentence, "He wished to forget the controversy with his staff."

Placed before the infinitive—"He wished *completely* TO FORGET the controversy with his staff"—*completely* becomes a squinting modifier; it could modify either the infinitive or the verb *wished*.

Placed after the infinitive—"He wished TO FORGET *completely* the controversy with his staff"—*completely* interferes with the rhythm of the sentence by coming between the verb and its object.

Placed at the end of the sentence—"He wished TO FORGET the controversy with his staff *completely*"—*completely* loses most of its force because it is so far removed from the infinitive it is modifying.

Now, let's split the infinitive—"He wished TO *completely* FORGET the controversy with his staff." Despite the split infinitive, this construction seems the smoothest and most desirable of the four.

As you can see from this illustration, it is unwise to make the flat statement that an infinitive must *never* be split. Most grammar-

Modifiers

ians recommend that writers avoid splitting an infinitive whenever possible (even if recasting the sentence is necessary), but they endorse the split infinitive if avoiding it would result in an awkward or ambiguous sentence.

44b Infinitive phrase

An infinitive phrase (an infinitive plus the words modifying it or completing it) may also be used as a modifier.

> *To get the most out of this course,* YOU must study regularly.
> The REPORT, *to get favorable attention,* must reach us by May 15.
> *To complete the report on time,* the AGENT should start gathering data now.

44c Participle

The participle, in all three forms (present, past, and perfect) is an adjective.

> Present participle: ends in *ing,* as *talking, building, writing*
>
> Past participle: verb form usually ending in *ed,* sometimes in *t,* and sometimes showing a vowel change, as *talked, built, written*
>
> Perfect participle: verb form consisting of *having* or *having been* plus the past participle, as *having talked, having built, having written, having been written*

> *Rising,* the DIRECTOR greeted his caller.
> (*Rising* is a present participle modifying *director*)
>
> The LETTER, *typed* and *signed,* was mailed today.
> (*Typed* and *signed* are past participles modifying *letter*)
>
> The LETTER, *having been corrected,* was ready for signature.
> (*Having been corrected* is a perfect participle modifying *letter*)

44d Participial phrase

A participial phrase (a participle combined with its object or modifying words) functions as an adjective.

> *Leaving her desk,* the TYPIST opened the file drawer.
> *Covering her typewriter,* SHE prepared to leave the office.
>
> The DRAFT, *typed hurriedly,* was on his desk.
> The LETTER, *mailed in error,* could not be recovered.
>
> The SUPERVISOR, *having called the meeting for 2 o'clock,* was waiting in his office.
> The MEETING, *having been called for 2 o'clock,* had to be postponed.

44e Gerund phrase

The gerund phrase (composed of a gerund plus its subject, complement, or modifier), like the gerund itself, serves as a noun. But when this phrase becomes the object of a preposition, the resulting prepositional-gerund phrase may serve as an *adjective* or as an *adverb*. It is this use of the gerund phrase with which we are concerned in this text.

> *After meeting with representatives of the employee group,* HE announced his decision.
> (Serves as adjective; phrase modifies *he*.)
>
> *In making our decision,* WE carefully considered both sides of the question.
> He ENDED his report *by summarizing his conclusions.*
> (Serves as adverb; phrase modifies *ended*.)

44f Dangling verbal phrases

The term *dangling* is quite descriptive of what happens when an infinitive, participial, or prepositional-gerund phrase cannot refer, both logically and grammatically, to a noun or pronoun serving as the subject of the main clause of a sentence.

Since such phrases are said to *attach* to the subject of the main clause, it is easy to see that they can only *dangle* until the writer takes corrective action. This he can do in either of two ways: (1) by changing the subject of the main clause to one which the phrase may refer to, or (2) by changing the phrase itself into a dependent clause, so that it has a subject of its own.

> (1) Dangling: *To get the most out of this course,* careful STUDY is necessary.
> (The phrase cannot logically modify *study;* so it dangles.)
> Corrected: *To get the most out of this course,* YOU must study it carefully.
> or: If you are to get the most out of this course, you must study it carefully.
>
> (2) Dangling: *To apply for this job,* a FORM 57 must be completed.
> (Dangles; a *form* can't apply.)
> Corrected: *To apply for this job,* the APPLICANT must complete a Form 57.
> or: When the applicant applies for the job, a Form 57 must be completed.
>
> (3) Dangling: *Rushing to meet the deadline for the project,* many ERRORS were made.
> (Dangles; it wasn't the *errors* that were rushing to meet the deadline.)

Modifiers 111

  Corrected: *Rushing to meet the deadline for the project*, THEY made many errors.
  or: Because they rushed to meet the deadline for the project, many errors were made.

(4) Dangling: *By summarizing the information from the questionnaires*, a clear PICTURE of the situation was presented.
  Corrected: *By summarizing the information from the questionnaires*, WE were able to present a clear picture of the situation.
  or: After we had summarized the information from the questionnaires, a clear picture of the situation was presented.

NOTE: An infinitive or a participial phrase that modifies the whole sentence, designating general action rather than action by a specific agent, may be correctly used without relation to the subject of the main clause.

  Generally speaking, these plants grow better in sunlight.
  To summarize, the plan should be ready to put into effect next fall.

44g   Nominative absolute—the sentence modifier

The *nominative absolute*, or simply *absolute*, modifies the whole sentence rather than a specific element in it. Unlike the participial phrase which it resembles, *the absolute has its own subject*. It therefore is grammatically independent of the rest of the sentence and does not dangle when it does not refer to the subject of the main clause.

  All THINGS *considered*, you have done a fine job.
   (*Things* is the subject of the absolute phrase.)
  The GAME *being over*, we went home.
  Clear WEATHER *having been forecast*, we completed our plans for the office picnic.
  The SUPERVISOR *having left the office*, his secretary took the call.

45   **Prepositional Phrase as a Modifier**

The prepositional phrase—composed of the preposition, its object, and any modifiers of the object—may serve as an adjective or as an adverb.

As an adjective:

  The letter was addressed to the OFFICE *of the Director*.
   (modifies *office*)

>   I hope we don't have another CONFERENCE *like the one we had yesterday.* (Phrase modifies *conference. Like* is the preposition; *one* is its object; and the clause *(that) we had yesterday* modifies *one.*)

As an adverb:

>   They HAVE GONE *to the conference.*
>   (The phrase modifies the verb *have gone.*)
>   GIVE it *to the person who answers the door.*
>   (The phrase modifies the verb *give.* Within the phrase, *to* is the preposition; *person* is its object; the clause *who answers the door* modifies the object.)

45a Dangling prepositional phrase

A prepositional phrase *dangles* when it does not, both logically and grammatically, refer to the subject of the main clause.

>   Dangling: *With much effort,* the REPORT was completed on time.
>   Corrected: *With much effort,* WE completed the report on time.

46 *Dependent Clauses as Modifiers*

Dependent clauses may serve as adjectives or as adverbs. The words that introduce them play a dual role—connecting (or linking) the clause with the rest of the sentence and showing the relationship between the dependent clause and the rest of the sentence. (Text 7 on Connectives discusses this topic more fully.)

46a Dependent clauses as adjectives

Dependent clauses that serve as adjectives may be introduced by either relative pronouns (*that, which, who, whom, whatever, whichever, whoever, whomever*) or relative adverbs (*where, when, while*).

By relative pronouns—

>   The MEMORANDUM *that is on your desk* has been revised.
>   The MAN *who called for an appointment* is here.
>   Your LETTER of May 15, *which called our attention to the error,* was answered yesterday.

By relative adverbs—

>   This is the BUILDING *where our office is located.*
>   We caught him at a TIME *when he was not busy.*

An adjective clause may be restrictive or nonrestrictive. Restrictive clauses cannot be omitted without changing the meaning of the sentence. They restrict or limit the word preceding them, and by answering the question, "Which one?" they also serve an identifying function. Because they are an essential part of the sentence, they are not set off by commas.

Nonrestrictive clauses, on the other hand, are not essential to the meaning of the sentence. They may add interesting or helpful information, but they are not necessary as restrictive clauses are. To show that they contain ideas of secondary importance, nonrestrictive clauses are set off by commas.

>The girl *who is sitting at the front desk* is his secretary.
>>(Restrictive clause; essential to meaning of sentence, answers question, "Which one?")
>
>Miss Martin, *who is sitting at the front desk*, is his secretary.
>>(Nonrestrictive clause. Adds another thought, but is not essential to the meaning of the sentence.)

46b Dependent clauses as adverbs

Dependent clauses that serve as adverbs are introduced by subordinating conjunctions. A few of these conjunctions are: *as, because, since, although, if, provided, after*. (See Text 7, Connectives, for a longer list.)

>*While he was reviewing the letter,* he NOTICED several errors in sentence construction.
>*Before he signed the letter,* he INSERTED a qualifying statement.

46c Elliptical clauses

Parts of a dependent clause are sometimes omitted because the writer feels that his reader can easily supply the missing elements. These incomplete clauses are known as *elliptical clauses*. An elliptical clause must be able to modify, both logically and grammatically, the subject of the main clause. If it does not, it dangles.

To correct a dangling elliptical clause we may either (1) change the subject of the main clause to one which the elliptical clause can logically modify or (2) supply the missing elements in the elliptical clause.

>Dangling: *Unless compiled by early June,* we cannot include the figures in this year's annual report.

Corrected: *Unless compiled by early June,* the figures cannot be included in this year's annual report.
or: Unless *the figures are* compiled by early June, we cannot include them in this year's annual report.

Dangling: *While making his periodic tour of the offices,* a few changes in procedure were recommended.
Corrected: *While making his periodic tour of the offices,* he recommended a few changes in procedure.
or: While *he was* making his periodic tour of the offices, a few changes in procedure were recommended.

46d Relative pronouns introducing clauses

Be careful to select the correct relative pronoun to introduce the adjective clause. *Who* refers to *persons; which* refers to *things; that* usually refers to *things,* but is sometimes used to refer to *persons.* (See Note.)

The AGENT *who submitted this report* has had extensive experience.
The monthly REPORT, *which is due tomorrow,* will contain that information.
The statistical REPORT *that you have been submitting weekly* will be required once a month from now on.

Which may introduce either restrictive or nonrestrictive clauses. *That* introduces restrictive clauses only.

The CASE *that* (or *which*) *Agent Jones is working on* is a particularly complicated one.
(Restrictive clause; necessary to identify the case.)

The Adams Manufacturing Company CASE, *which Agent Jones is working on,* is a particularly complicated one.
(Nonrestrictive clause; the case is already identified by name.)

The REPORT *that* (or *which*) *is on my desk* is ready to be typed.
(Restrictive clause)

The monthly statistical REPORT, *which is on my desk,* is ready to be typed.
(Nonrestrictive clause; not essential to meaning.)

NOTE: We may use *that* in place of *who* to refer to persons if we mean *a class or type of person,* rather than an individual.

Any secretary *that works in the general office of the company* is eligible to attend this program.
(Refers to a class or type of employee.)

The secretary *who sits at that desk* is Miss Jones.
(Refers to a specific individual.)

Whose may be used as the possessive of any of these relative pronouns—*who, which, that.*

> The staff member *whose job was abolished* has been reassigned.
> This is the book *whose approach has been the subject of so much discussion.* (This use of *whose* to refer to inanimate objects is acceptable in informal speaking and writing; the phrase "of which" is preferred in formal writing.)

47 Placement of Modifiers

This heading should be printed in red and underscored—anything to call it to the writer's attention. For, high on the list of sentence errors, is the *misplaced modifier*.

Modifiers should be placed as close as possible to the words they modify. This is true, whether the modifier is a single word, a phrase, or a clause. In English, the only way the reader can tell which word is being modified is by the location of the modifier. It's simply a matter of geography.

Many ambiguous (and unintentionally humorous) sentences result from the misplacement of modifiers.

47a Modifier between subject and verb

Wherever possible, avoid placing the modifier between subject and verb and between verb and object.

> Not: The revenue agent, *to explain the difference between gross income and net income,* used several illustrations.
> But: *To explain the difference between gross income and net income,* the revenue agent used several illustrations.
> or: The revenue agent used several illustrations *to explain the difference between gross income and net income.*

47b Single adjectives

A single adjective is usually placed immediately *before* the word it modifies.

> The taxpayer and his wife filed a *joint* return.
> Send the return to your *local* office.

> Not: I would like a *cold* GLASS of water.
> But: I would like a glass of *cold* WATER.

47c Multiple adjectives

To make sure his sentences read more smoothly, the writer may also place immediately after the word—

  (1) A modifier consisting of two or more adjectives.
   (The report—*long, tedious,* and *involved*—was finally completed.)
  (2) A modifier consisting of one or more adverbs plus an adjective.
   (The report—*carefully written* and *well documented*—was submitted to the committee.)

47d Single adverbs

Some adverbs—*only, almost, nearly, also, quite, merely, actually*—are frequent trouble makers. Be sure they are placed as close as possible to the words they modify.

  Example: The problem can *only* be defined by this committee.
  Could mean: *Only* this committee can define the problem.
  or: This committee can *only define* the problem, not solve it.

47e Phrases and clauses

Phrases and clauses, like single-word modifiers, should be placed as close as possible to the words they modify, so there will be no danger of their attaching themselves to the wrong sentence element.

  Not: We need someone to audit REPORTS *with statistical experience.*
  But: We need SOMEONE *with statistical experience* to audit reports.
  Not: Mr. Dough has resigned from the presidency of the Club after HAVING SERVED four years *to the regret of all the members.*
  But: *To the regret of all the members,* Mr. Dough HAS RESIGNED from the presidency of the Club after having served 4 years.

47f Relative clauses

Relative clauses should also be placed immediately after the word they modify, since they attach themselves to the sentence element nearest them.

  Not: The man has an APPOINTMENT *that is waiting in my office.*
  But: The MAN *that is waiting in my office* has an appointment.
  Not: This refers to your memorandum regarding the number of cases closed by agents in the "X" group which are over a year old.
  But: This refers to your memorandum regarding the number of cases over a year old which have been closed by agents in the "X" group.

47g Squinting constructions

Avoid *squinting constructions*—that is, modifiers that are so placed that the reader cannot tell whether they are modifying the words immediately preceding them or those immediately following them.

> Obscure: The lawyer AGREED *after the papers were signed* TO TAKE the case.
> Could mean: The lawyer agreed TO TAKE the case *after the papers were signed.*
> or: *After the papers were signed,* the lawyer AGREED to take the case.

> Obscure: He AGREED *that morning* TO SIGN the offer in compromise.
> Could mean: He agreed TO SIGN the offer in compromise *that morning.*
> or: *That morning,* he AGREED to sign the offer in compromise.

47h Adverb clauses

An adverb clause may be placed either at the beginning of a sentence or, in its natural order, after the main clause. There are two reasons why we might choose to place the adverb clause first: (1) to put greater emphasis on the main clause; (2) to avoid piling up modifying clauses after the main clause.

(An introductory adverb clause—sometimes called an "inverted clause," since it is out of its natural order—should usually be followed by a comma.)

> Natural order: This report must contain information from all the offices in the region *if it is to reflect a true picture of our activities.*

> Inverted order: *If the report is to reflect a true picture of our activities,* it must contain information from all the offices in the region. (*more emphatic.*)

> Piled-up clauses: You cannot claim an exemption for your husband, *since he claimed a personal exemption of $600 when he filed his return,* as neither husband nor wife may use any part of the deduction to which the other is entitled.

> Clearer: *Neither husband nor wife may use any part of the deduction to which the other is entitled; therefore, since your husband claimed a personal exemption of $600 when he filed his return,* you cannot claim an exemption for him.

47i Long modifying phrases

A long or complex modifying phrase at the end of the sentence has an anticlimactic effect. We strengthen our writing when we place such phrases before the main clause.

Weak: We have asked each region to tell us the number of copies it will need *in order to insure adequate distribution of this report.*
Stronger: *In order to insure adequate distribution of this* report, we have asked each region to tell us the number of copies it will need.

Weak: We will send two examination copies of the report to each regional office *immediately after its completion.*
Stronger: *Immediately after the report is completed,* we will send two examination copies to each regional office.

TEXT 7

Connectives

    Introduction
48   Prepositions
48a   Simple prepositions
48b   Compound prepositions
48c   Phrasal prepositions

49   Choice of preposition
49a   Idioms and idiomatic usage
49b   Choice based on shades of meaning
49c   *At, In*
49d   *Between, Among*
49e   *Below, Beneath, Down, Under, Underneath*

50   Using the single instead of the phrasal preposition

51   Placement of preposition

52   Superfluous prepositions

53   Faulty omission of prepositions
53a   Parallel constructions
53b   Split or suspended constructions

54   Prepositional phrase
54a   Function of the prepositional phrase
54b   Overuse of the prepositional phrase

55   Conjunctions, relative pronouns, and relative adverbs

56   Connecting elements of equal rank (coordinate elements)
56a   Use parallelism to show coordination
56b   Use coordinate conjunctions to show coordination (parallelism)
56c   Use correlative conjunctions to show coordination (parallelism)
56d   Use conjunctive adverbs to show coordination
56e   Use punctuation to show coordination

57   Connecting elements of unequal rank (connecting subordinate elements with principal elements)
57a   How to show subordination
57b   Use subordinating conjunctions to show subordination
57c   Use relative pronouns to show subordination
57d   Use relative adverbs to show subordination

58 · Alphabetical List of Troublesome Conjunctions

TEXT 7

Connectives

Introduction

In the very early days of our language, so grammarians tell us, there were no connectives. Short, primerlike sentences were simply placed end to end, with no connectives to show relationships between them.

Man gradually found it necessary to communicate thoughts that were more complex. Thus modifiers and connectives came into being—not necessarily because the writer *wanted* to use them, but because he could not get complex and abstract thoughts across to his reader without using them. And this is exactly where we find ourselves today—both as writers and as readers, we depend on connectives to clarify meaning.

Today our language is rich in connectives. We can be selective in choosing the one that will express our meaning exactly. By our *choice* of connectives, we can tell our reader the precise relationship between two ideas. By our *use* of connectives, we can guide the reader from the beginning of our writing through to the end—signaling along the way when we are going to add a thought, change to a different point of view, or shift to a different subject.

Connectives are to writing what directional signals are to driving. Just as a flashing signal alerts the driver of the car behind that we are going to turn right, so a well-chosen connective signals the reader that we are going to change our approach. Confusion (or worse) results when the driver either fails to signal or signals incorrectly. Confusion also results when the writer fails to signal his reader or signals him incorrectly. One more similarity—as drivers, we sometimes become indignant with the driver in front when he fails to signal, even though we ourselves may not be signaling the driver behind us. As readers, we often rely heavily on the connectives which the writer has used, even though we may not, as writers, be equally concerned about signaling to our readers.

Connectives, then, are important signals which both writers and readers should be familiar with. They should be used skillfully as an effective means of transferring thought from one mind to another.

Four kinds of words can serve as connectives—prepositions, conjunctions, relative pronouns, and relative adverbs. Each not only connects two sentence elements but also shows the relationship between them.

This text describes these connectives and explains briefly how they are used. The final text in the course, Text 10, counsels the writer about how he can use them *effectively*.

48 Prepositions

A preposition *connects* the word, phrase, or clause that follows it (its object) with some other element in the sentence *and shows the relationship* between them.

There are three kinds of prepositions:

48a Simple prepositions

at, but, by, down, for, from, in, like, of, off, on, out, over, per, through, till, to, up, via, with . . .

48b Compound prepositions

about, above, across, after, against, along, among, around, before, behind, below, beneath, beside, besides, between, beyond, despite, except, inside, into, outside, toward(s), under, until, upon, within, without . . .

48c Phrasal prepositions (two or more words that function as a single preposition)

according to	*contrary to*
because of	*inasmuch as*

Connectives

49 Choice of Preposition

Choosing the preposition is usually either no problem at all for the writer or a problem that seems to defy a reasonable solution.

When the choice is simple, it is because prepositions have become such a basic part of our vocabularies that we choose them almost without being aware of making a choice. They seem to slip into our sentences of their own volition. In many constructions, one preposition just *seems right*; another, *wrong*.

When the choice is difficult, it is because we lack this "sensing" of the essential rightness or wrongness of the preposition. Being unable to select the appropriate preposition, we look for a rule of grammar to help us make a choice (or to help us defend or explain the choice we have made). Then we find that there *is* no governing rule of grammar; *idiomatic usage* is the only key.

49a Idioms and idiomatic usage

In English, as in other languages, there has developed over the years a set of language patterns which has become what we call grammar. Within this structure a body of formal rules may be found side by side with a body of informal exceptions to those rules. These "exceptions" reflect traditions of speech and represent popular and accepted usage.

Idiom is often quite different from grammar and often conflicts with it. When we say that something is *idiomatic usage*, we mean that usage has established it as correct and acceptable, whether or not it conflicts with grammar.

It is idiom that requires us to say—

able *to* work	but	capable *of* working
the way *to* cut	but	the way *of* cutting (method)
aim *at* getting	but	try *to* get

Grammar doesn't help us to make this choice. For, as far as grammar is concerned, in each of the three illustrations, *to, of, for,* and *at* are equally acceptable. But idiom says, "It doesn't *make sense* to say *aim to getting*; only *aim at getting* can get the idea across."

Fortunately, if English is our native language, most of these idiomatic expressions are so ingrained that we use them instinctively and cringe when we hear them misused. However, when we cannot make this instinctive choice, we must make it our business to find out what the idiomatic usage is.

Prepositional idioms outnumber most other idioms. For example, one reference book—the Standard Handbook of Prepositions, Conjunctions, Relative Pronouns and Relative Adverbs (Funk & Wagnalls, New York)—lists *more than 2,000 prepositional idioms.*

A few, but only a few, of these idioms are listed in the Writer's Guide to Current Usage. For the hundreds of others, the writer may consult an unabridged dictionary, a dictionary of synonyms, a handbook of grammar, or a specialized handbook like the one referred to in the preceding paragraph.

49b Choice based on shades of meaning

The choice between prepositions is often based on the slight difference in meaning between them or on the preference which grammarians have expressed.

The next few sections explain a few that fall in this category; Part B of the Writer's Guide lists a few others.

49c *At, In*

These two prepositions often may be used interchangeably. However, when they are used in phrases giving the place or locality of an action, writers should be aware of these distinctions:

(1) IN is used when reference to the interior of a building is stressed; AT, when the site itself is stressed.

> We held our conference IN the City Auditorium.
> We arranged to meet AT the City Auditorium.

(2) IN is usually used before the names of countries and sections; AT, before the names of business firms, office buildings, and so on.

> IN France; IN the North; IN the Southwest
> AT the post office; AT Blank and Company
> AT Yale. (He was educated AT Yale.)

(3) IN is used before the name of a city if the writer wants to leave an impression of permanence; AT, if he wants to indicate a temporary stay.

> Following a brief stopover AT Chicago, we spent 2 weeks IN Minneapolis.
> He works AT Dallas, but he lives IN Fort Worth.

(4) In local addresses, IN is used before the name of the city; AT, before the street number of the residence or office.

> He lives AT 745 Main Street IN Silver City.

49d Between, Among

Most of us know and apply the familiar rule: Use *among* when referring to more than two persons, things, or groups considered collectively; use *between* when referring to only two.

> The estate was divided *among* the five heirs.
> The property was divided *between* John and me.

We may not know, however, that *between* can and should be used in certain constructions in which more than two things are referred to. These are, of course, constructions that are somewhat unusual.

Before we explain this further, consider these alternatives: Which would you say—

> (1) A treaty *among* three nations   (or—*between* three nations)
> (2) The contest is *among* the four candidates   (or—is *between* the four)
> (3) We must choose *among* the three plans   (or *between* the three plans)

Perhaps you think that neither *between* nor *among* expresses the relationship clearly. If so, you agree with the grammarians. But the fact is that there is no preposition in our language that can express the relation of a thing to several other things, not only with respect to its relation to the group as a whole but also with respect to its relation to each of the members.

Among expresses the relation collectively and somewhat vaguely; some say it "lumps" the objects too much. *Between*—though it does not do a perfect job—seems to express a little more clearly the thought that the relation of the thing is not just to the group as a whole but to the individual members as well.

Grammarians therefore agree that, in such constructions as those illustrated, *between* is a better and more logical choice than *among*.

This may sound confusing (and it is); but since the writer must work with confusing constructions as well as with simple ones, he needs some such guideline as this.

49e Below, Beneath, Down, Under, Underneath

Sometimes the slight distinction in the use of prepositions concerns us, not because the use of one instead of another will *confuse* the reader but because it may *offend* him.

All five of the prepositions in this section may, in many cases, be used interchangeably. Even when they cannot, the choice is an easy one for us because the distinctions are so natural; for example, we say "his knees trembled *beneath* him" but not "his knees trembled *below* him." Grammatically, either is correct; idiom, however, makes the latter sound ridiculous.

But consider these distinctions:

> The student says: "He is in the class *below* me."
> Not: "He is in the class *beneath* me."
> (Here, *beneath* seems to imply inferiority or contempt.)

We say, quite properly, that someone is *"under* our care" or *"under* our supervision"; but to say that someone is *"beneath* our care" or *"beneath* our notice" would be to speak contemptuously of him.

Here, too, our instinct usually guides us in using the word that will not offend; but courtesy, in both oral and written communication, requires us to be on the alert for any unintentional violation of this idiomatic usage.

50 **Using the Single Instead of the Phrasal Preposition**

This choice (discussed more fully in Text 9) is more difficult for most Government writers, because the use of the phrasal preposition has become almost traditional.

One of the chief criticisms of Government writing is that it is heavy with phrasal prepositions that make it wordy, somewhat

Connectives

pompous, and hard to understand. And it is true that, as Government writers, we seem to have fallen into the habit of rejecting the one-word preposition in favor of the phrasal.

Here are only a few of the phrasal prepositions which writing consultants recommend that we replace as often as possible with single prepositions that would make our writing less imposing and more concise:

inasmuch as	since
for the purpose of	to
prior to	before
subsequent to	after
in regard to	about

Inasmuch as the taxpayer has not signed the affidavit . . . (*Since*)

Unless we receive this information *prior to* . . . (*before*)

Subsequent to our conference with you . . . (*After, since*)

We were asked to submit information *with regard to* available institute sites. (*about*)

51 Placement of Preposition

The strong conviction that a sentence should not end with a preposition was, for a long time, shared by many people; but there is almost universal agreement now that writers need no longer be bound by this restriction.

There are at least three explanations for the growth of this conviction: 1) the rule of rhetoric that a sentence should end with a strong word—a noun, pronoun, verb, etc.; 2) the nature of the word *preposition*—because of its prefix *pre* (meaning *before*), many believed that a preposition necessarily must *come before* another word; and 3) the illiterate use of an unnecessary preposition at the end of the sentence—"Where were you *at?*"

Most of today's writers believe that a studied effort to avoid ending a sentence with a preposition often results in a sentence that is unnatural, awkward, and sometimes confusing.

Consider these illustrations, which most writers agree are much more natural than they would be if they were reconstructed to avoid the terminal preposition:

What did you do that *for?*
Here is the report he sent *in.*
We had many problems to talk *about.*
Tell me what it is you object *to.*

52 Superfluous Prepositions

In talking, more than in writing, we tend to use double prepositions when only one is needed. But we should take care lest this informal colloquial use creep into our writing.

> Not: We will divide *up* the work.
> But: We will divide the work.

> Not: He is standing near *to* the door.
> But: He is standing near the door.

> Not: When are you going to start *in* to write that letter?
> But: When are you going to start to write that letter?

53 Faulty Omission of Prepositions

53a Especially in formal writing, repeat the preposition before the second of two connected elements.

> Not: He seemed interested in us and our problems.
> But: He seemed interested in us and *in* our problems.

> Not: He was able to complete the project by planning carefully and working diligently.
> But: He was able to complete the project by planning carefully and *by* working diligently.

(See the discussion of parallel constructions in this text and in Text 10.)

53b In the so-called *split* (or *suspended*) *construction*, in which two words are completed by different prepositions, be especially careful to use both prepositions.

> Not: He has an interest and an aptitude *for* his work.
> But: He has an interest *in* and an aptitude *for* his work.
> (Commas may be used in this construction: He has an interest in, and an aptitude for, his work.)

> Not: He was puzzled and concerned *about* her behavior.
> But: He was puzzled *by* and concerned *about* her behavior.

NOTE: Many good writers think that split constructions are awkward; they recommend such revisions as these—

> He has an interest in his work and an aptitude for it.
> He was puzzled by her behavior and concerned about it.

54 Prepositional Phrase

The prepositional phrase is the preposition plus its object plus any modifiers of the object. The object of the preposition may be a word, a phrase, or a clause; and the modifiers of the object may likewise be words, phrases, or clauses. (In the text on Case we discussed the fact that a word used as the object of the preposition must be in the objective case.)

54a Function of the prepositional phrase

The prepositional phrase functions most often as an adjective or an adverb; occasionally it may also serve as a noun. In the text on Modifiers we discussed the modifying function of the prepositional phrase.

54b Overuse of the prepositional phrase

Too many prepositional phrases make a sentence unwieldy and hard to understand; moreover, they give the writer a real problem—the problem of putting each phrase as close as possible to the word it modifies.

The writer who uses verbs in the active voice will find this problem greatly simplified. Compare these two sentences:

> Passive voice: This matter should be looked into *by your office* and a report furnished us *on the case at the earliest possible date.*
>
> Active voice: Please look into this matter and let us have a report as soon as possible.

See Text 10 for a further discussion of this point.

55 *Conjunctions, Relative Pronouns, and Relative Adverbs*

These three types of connectives perform two distinctly different functions: some of them connect coordinate sentence elements (elements of equal grammatical rank); others both introduce a subordinate element and connect it with the rest of the sentence.

Three types of conjunctions connect coordinate elements:

> Coordinate conjunctions—*and, but, or, for, so, yet, nor*
> Correlative conjunctions (used in pairs)—*neither . . . nor, either . . . or, both . . . and, if . . . then, since . . . therefore, whether . . . or, not only . . . but also*
> Conjunctive adverbs—*therefore, otherwise, hence, nevertheless, however, besides, accordingly*

The function of the subordinating clause governs the type of connective to be used in introducing it:

> Adverb clauses are introduced by SUBORDINATING CONJUNCTIONS—*as, since, because, if, provided, after, before, where*
> Noun clauses are introduced by RELATIVE PRONOUNS—*that, whether, whichever, whatever, whoever*
> Adjective clauses are introduced by either RELATIVE ADVERBS (*where, when, while*) or RELATIVE PRONOUNS (*who, whom, which, that*)

The rest of the sections in this text will help the writer to—

> determine whether constructions are or are not *grammatically* coordinate
> identify constructions that are subordinate
> recognize connectives that can be used to tell his reader whether the constructions are considered to be coordinate or subordinate
> avoid the misuse of connectives.

56 Connecting Elements of Equal Rank (Coordinate Elements)

56a Use parallelism to show coordination

Sentence elements are said to be *coordinate* (or *parallel*) when they are of equal rank (of equal importance) both grammatically and logically.

Determining equal *grammatical* importance is relatively simple: words = words; phrases = phrases; subordinate clauses = subordinate clauses; principal clauses = principal clauses.

Determining equal *logical* importance is more difficult. This requires that the writer weigh the importance of the thoughts he is expressing. Only he can determine this value; and he signals his reader by choosing the type of connective that makes his decision clear.

>Elements not grammatically equal (not parallel):
>>His main virtues are *that he is sincere* and his *generosity*.
>>(a clause linked to a word)

>Improved:
>>His main virtues are *that he is sincere* and *that he is generous*.
>>(two noun clauses, now parallel; noun clause = noun clause)

>>His main virtues are his *sincerity* and his *generosity*.
>>(two words)

>Elements not equal in importance:
>>*Please advise us if our assumption is incorrect* and *a further adjustment of your tax liability will be made.*

>Improved:
>>*If our assumption is incorrect,* please advise us and we will make a further adjustment of your tax liability.
>>(Italicized element is both logically and grammatically subordinate, as the *if*-clause tells the reader.)

566 Use coordinate conjunctions to show coordination (parallelism)

The coordinate conjunctions—*and, but, or, nor, for, yet*—are the connectives most frequently used to show that two ideas are equal (are parallel). Notice in the following illustrations that the two ideas connected are parallel.

>The *Director* AND the *Assistant Director* will attend.
>(connecting a word with a word)

>He is a man *of great capability* BUT *of little experience.*
>(connecting a phrase with a phrase)

>He said *that he had filed a claim for refund* BUT *that he had not heard anything further from this office.*
>(connecting a subordinate clause with a subordinate clause)

>*I was eager to attend the seminar,* FOR *I knew that the exchange of ideas would be helpful.*
>(connecting an independent clause with an independent clause)

NOTE: See section 58, Alphabetical List of Troublesome Conjunctions, for a discussion of common problems in the use of these coordinate conjunctions—such problems as the use of too many *and's*, the confusion of *and* with *but*, and the popular fallacy that a conjunction cannot be used to begin a sentence.

56c Use correlative conjunctions to show coordination (parallelism)

The correlative conjunctions—*either . . . or, neither . . . nor, not only . . . but also, both . . . and, if . . . then, since . . . therefore*—work in pairs to show that words and ideas are parallel (equal in importance).

>   EITHER the *Director* OR the *Assistant Director* must attend.
>   (connecting a word with a word)

>   The report is designed NOT ONLY *to present a list of the problems facing us* BUT ALSO *to recommend possible solutions to these problems.*
>   (connecting a phrase with a phrase)

The significant point which the writer must bear in mind when he uses pairs of correlatives is that each member of the pair must be followed by the same part of speech (same grammatical construction). That is, if NOT ONLY is followed by a verb, then BUT ALSO must be followed by a verb; if EITHER is followed by a phrase, OR must likewise be followed by a phrase.

>   Not: EITHER *cases of this type* are much fewer in number OR *are not attended* by the same administrative difficulties.
>   (*Either* is followed by a noun, *cases;* or is followed by a verb phrase.)
>   But: Cases of this type EITHER *are much fewer* in number OR *are not attended* by the same administrative difficulties.

>   Not: His reply NOT ONLY *was prompt* BUT ALSO *complete.*
>   But: His reply was NOT ONLY *prompt* BUT ALSO *complete.*

>   Not: One of the reporters who arrived shortly after the raids had started complimented the agents NOT ONLY *on the systematic method in which the raids were conducted* BUT ALSO *with respect to their conduct while on the premises.*

>   But: One of the reporters who arrived shortly after the raids had started complimented the agents NOT ONLY *on the systematic method* in which the raids were conducted BUT ALSO *on their conduct* while on the premises.

When this plan is not followed, the result is "faulty parallelism." To turn faulty parallelism into effective parallelism, sometimes we need add only a word or two.

Connectives

Not: The project was a disappointment NOT ONLY *to me* BUT ALSO *my assistant.*
(*Not only* is followed by the prepositional phrase *to me;* but also is followed by a noun.)
But: The project was a disappointment NOT ONLY *to me* BUT ALSO *to my assistant.*
(Note that each of the correlative conjunctions is followed by a prepositional phrase.)
Not: His assignment was BOTH *to conduct* the course AND *the evaluation* of it.
But: His assignment was BOTH *to conduct* the course AND *to evaluate* it.

56d Use conjunctive adverbs to show coordination

The conjunctive adverbs—*therefore, however, consequently, accordingly, furthermore, besides, moreover, nevertheless, still*—serve the double purpose of connecting independent clauses and of showing relationship between the clauses. Although the clause introduced by a conjunctive adverb is *grammatically independent*, it is *logically dependent* on the preceding clause for its complete meaning.

The conjunctive adverb has more modifying force than the coordinate conjunction, but less connecting force. Therefore, the clauses joined by a conjunctive adverb are not so closely related as are those joined by a coordinate conjunction. Clauses joined by a conjunctive adverb must be separated by a semicolon or a period.

The regulations have not yet been published; *nevertheless,* we must proceed with the preparation of our course.
The special study committee has approved our program. *Moreover,* it has commended us on our proposed method.
The meeting was held at 3 o clock; *however,* I was not able to attend.

NOTE: Certain phrases—such as *on the contrary, on the other hand, in the first place, in fact, in addition, for this reason, for example, at the same time, in the interim*—have the same modifying and connective force as conjunctive adverbs.

The survey committee may propose a solution to our problem; *on the other hand,* it may only define the problem.
We discussed the items on the agenda. *In addition,* several members proposed new topics.

56e Use punctuation to show coordination

The semicolon may be substituted for the connective between coordinate elements.

I have almost finished these letters; there are only three more on my desk.
The reception of this course will be interesting to watch; it is the first of its kind to be offered.

57 Connecting Elements of Unequal Rank (Connecting Subordinate Elements With Principal Elements)

57a How to show subordination

In the previous section we discussed how to put ideas of equal importance into structures that show they are equal. But many of our sentences contain ideas that are not equal in importance and that should be expressed in a way that emphasizes their inequality. Weigh the ideas in your sentence to determine which are basic to the purpose of the sentence and to the goal of the whole writing, and which are less important. Then make this distinction clear to your reader by putting the less important ideas into subordinate constructions.

57b Use subordinating conjunctions to show subordination

Subordinating conjunctions—*as, because, since, as though, than, although, provided, if, unless, how, after, before, so that, in order that, when, while, until*—introduce adverb clauses and connect them to independent clauses. The subordinating conjunction shows a relationship between the clauses it connects.

> I must miss that meeting, EVEN THOUGH I would like to attend.
> WHILE he was reviewing the letter, he noticed several references to the manual.
> IF the project is to be finished on time, we must have those figures by Friday.
> He will check in at the office AFTER he returns from the meeting.

Section 58 discusses some problems the writer has in using subordinating conjunctions.

57c Use relative pronouns to show subordination

Some relative pronouns—*who, whom, which, that*—introduce adjective clauses. Others—primarily, *that* and the compound relative pronouns *whichever, whatever, whoever, whomever*—introduce noun clauses. Both types of relative pronouns connect the clause they introduce to the rest of the sentence.

> The man WHO *called for an appointment* has arrived.
> An electric typewriter THAT *is operating properly* is a great help to the typist.
> The officer *to* WHOM *I wrote* has since left the company.
> Give the package to WHOEVER *answers the door.*
> He will tell us WHATEVER *we need to know* about the new system.

Connectives

See Section 58, Alphabetical List of Troublesome Conjunctions, for a further discussion of relative pronouns.

57d Use relative adverbs to show subordination

The relative adverbs—*where, when, while*—introduce adjective clauses and connect them to the rest of the sentence.

> This is the building WHERE *the office is located.*
> This is the time of year WHEN *we are particularly busy.*

58 Alphabetical List of Troublesome Conjunctions

58a AND VS. ALSO

Also, a weak connective, should not be used in place of *and* in sentences such as:

> He writes letters, memorandums, *and* (not *also*) some procedures.

58b AND ETC.

The abbreviation *etc.* stands for the Latin *et cetera,* meaning *and so forth.* Obviously, then, an additional *and* is not only unnecessary but incorrect.

> Not: He requisitioned paper, pencils, pens, *and etc.*
> But: He requisitioned paper, pencils, pens, *etc.*

58c AND WHICH, AND WHO, BUT WHICH

Avoid using *and which, and who, but which, but that,* etc., when there is no preceding *who, which,* or *that* in the sentence to complete the parallel construction.

> Not: We are looking for a program more economical to operate *and which* will be easy to administer.
> But: We are looking for a program *which* will be more economical to operate *and which* will be easy to administer.

58d Too many AND's

Avoid stringing together a group of sentence elements connected by *and*'s.

> Not: The evaluation of the training program was planned and conducted and reported to the appropriate officials.
> But: The evaluation of the training program was planned and conducted; then it was reported to the appropriate officials.

58e   AND VS. BUT

Use *and* to show addition; use *but* to show contrast.

> Not: The Director and his assistant have been called to a meeting, *and* our supervisor will be in the office all afternoon.
> But: The Director and his assistant have been called to a meeting, *but* our supervisor will be in the office all afternoon.

Avoid using *but* to show contrast when the negative idea is already present in the sentence through the use of some other word.

> Not: In vain we tried to convince him, *but* we were unable to do it.
>   (The phrase *in vain* already expresses the negative idea.)
> But: *In vain* we tried to convince him.
> or: We tried to convince him, *but* we were unable to.

58f   AND or BUT to begin a sentence

We may begin a sentence, or even a paragraph, with *and*, *but*, or any other coordinating conjunction. A coordinate conjunction or a conjunctive adverb at the beginning of a sentence is often a handy signpost for the reader, telling him in which direction this new sentence will carry him.

58g   AS, SINCE, BECAUSE

These conjunctions can be used interchangeably to introduce clauses of cause or reason.

> *Because* the book was due at the library, I returned it.
> *Since* the book was due at the library, I returned it.
> *As* the book was due at the library, I returned it.

However, *since* and *as* have another function—*since* introduces clauses of sequence of time, and *as* introduces clauses of duration of time. Because of the double function of these two words, we must be careful to use them only in sentences in which they cannot be misunderstood.

> Not: *Since* this report was prepared to analyze the effects of . . .
>   (Could mean: *Since the time that* this report was prepared . . .)
> But: *Because* this report was prepared to analyze the effects of . . .

> Not: *As* I was typing the monthly report, he gave the assignment to Beth.
>   (Could mean: *During the time that* I was typing the monthly report . . .)
> But: *Because* I was typing the monthly report . . .

Connectives

NOTE: When an *as* or *since* clause comes last in the sentence, the meaning of the conjunction can be made clear by the punctuation of the clause. If *as* or *since* is used as a time indicator, the clause it introduces is not set off from the sentence. But if the conjunction introduces a clause of cause or reason, the clause is set off.

> There have been several changes in policy *since* the committee released its findings.
> (No punctuation; *since* means *since the time that*)

> There have been several changes in policy, *since* the committee released its findings.
> (. . . *because* the committee released its findings)

58h AS VS. THAT or WHETHER

Avoid using *as* in place of *that* or *whether* to introduce clauses following such verbs as *say, think, know.*

> Not: I don't know *as* I believe you.

> But: I don't know *that* I believe you.
> or: I don't know *whether* I believe you.

58i IF VS. WHETHER

If is used to introduce clauses of condition or supposition.

> We will go *if* the meeting is postponed.
> *If* you cannot answer the letter immediately, please send an acknowledgment.

Whether introduces clauses indicating an alternative. The alternative may be expressed in the sentence or understood.

> It will not make any difference *whether* John agrees or disagrees with the proposal.
> Please let me know *whether* you received the check.

Some grammarians endorse the use of either *if* or *whether* in such constructions as

> Please let me know *if* (or *whether*) you received the check.
> I wonder *if* (or *whether*) he will attend.
> I don't know *if* (or *whether*) he is qualified for that position.

Most writers, however, prefer *whether* when there is any danger that the reader may fail to understand the meaning.

58j WHETHER VS. WHETHER OR NOT

It is not essential that *or not* be used with *whether* to complete the alternative choice. These words may be added if they are needed for emphasis.

> Either: Please let me know *whether or not* you received our letter.
> or: Please let me know *whether* you received our letter.

58k THAT introducing parallel clauses

When either *that* or *which* introduces one of a series of parallel clauses, the same conjunction must introduce the other clauses in the series. Do not shift conjunctions or omit the conjunction in later clauses.

> Poor: (conjunction omitted):
>> He said *that* he would call me before noon and his secretary would deliver the papers by two o'clock.
>
> Improved (conjunction supplied):
>> He said *that* he would call me before noon and *that* his secretary would deliver the papers by two o'clock.
>
> Shift in conjunction:
>> The report *that* was written by Agent Smith and *which* was the subject of so much discussion at the last meeting has been accepted.
>
> Improved:
>> The report *that* was written by Agent Smith and *that* was the subject of so much discussion at the last meeting has been accepted.

58l Proper omission of THAT

That may be omitted in noun clauses (especially those following such verbs as *say, think, feel, believe, hope*), and in adjective clauses, if the meaning of the sentence is clear.

> Noun clauses:
>> He said (*that*) he would call me before noon.
>> I hope (*that*) we can finish this project today.
>
> Adjective clauses:
>> The report (*that*) I asked for is out on loan.
>> The instructions (*that*) he gave were perfectly clear.

58m Faulty repetition of THAT

Do not use *that* twice to introduce the same noun clause. This error most often occurs in a long sentence in which a long inter-

Connectives 139

rupting expression occurs between the *that* and the rest of its clause.

> Not: I am sure you can appreciate *that*, in order to protect the interests of all taxpayers as well as the interests of the Government, *that* we must establish whether the original remittances were correctly applied.
>
> But: I am sure you can appreciate *that*, in order to protect the interests of all taxpayers as well as the interests of the Government, we must establish whether the original remittances were correctly applied.

58n WHEN

Avoid using *when* to introduce a definition unless the definition pertains to time.

> Not: Their first important step in the improvement of the conditions was *when* they thoroughly surveyed the situation. (The step was not "when.")
>
> But: Their first important step in the improvement of the conditions was *the thorough survey* of the situation.
>
> Correct usage:
> Three o'clock is *when* the meeting will be held.

58o WHERE

Avoid using *where* to introduce a definition unless the definition pertains to place or location.

> Not: A sentence is *where* you have a subject and a verb. (A sentence is not "where.")
>
> But: A sentence is a group of words containing a subject and a verb.
>
> Correct usage:
> The large conference room is *where* the meeting is being held.

Avoid substituting *where* for *that*.

> Not: I saw in the bulletin *where* the new law has been put into effect.
> But: I saw in the bulletin *that* the new law has been put into effect.

58p WHILE VS. WHEN

While indicates duration of time; *when* indicates a fixed or stated period of time.

> *When* I return to the office, I will call him.
>   (At that fixed time)
>
> *While* I am at the office, I will look for that information.
>   (During the time that I am at the office . . .)

58q WHILE VS. THOUGH, ALTHOUGH, AND, BUT

While pertains to time and should not be substituted loosely for *though, although, whereas, and, but.*

    Not: *While* I did not remember the applicant's name, I thought I could recognize her face.
    But: *Although* I did not remember the applicant's name, I thought I could recognize her face.

    Not: I assembled the material for the manual *while* he wrote the outline.
        (Could mean: *during the time that he* . . .)
    But: I assembled the material for the manual, *but* he wrote the outline.

TEXT 8

Punctuation and Good Sentences

59	Introduction	63c	Introductory elements with connective force
59a	The purpose of the text		
59b	The importance of punctuation	64	Punctuating parenthetical elements
59c	The approach of the text	64a	Interrupting transitional expressions
60	Punctuation—functional and conventional	64b	Interrupting expressions identifying speaker or source
		64c	Addresses, dates, titles
61	Separating main clauses	64d	Nominative absolute
61a	To show close relationship between clauses	64e	Words in direct address
61b	To emphasize individual clauses—using a period to separate	65	Separating coordinate items in series
		65a	Series with coordinate conjunction
61c	To emphasize individual clauses—using a semicolon to separate	65b	Series with no connective
		65c	Series with connective joining last two members
61d	To express special relationships	65d	Consecutive adjectives (two or more)
62	Enclosing modifiers and appositives	66	The punctuation marks
62a	Adjective modifiers	66a	Period
62b	Adverbial modifiers	66b	Question mark
62c	Appositives	66c	Exclamation point
		66d	Comma
63	Punctuating introductory elements	66e	Semicolon
		66f	Colon
63a	Adverbial clauses and verbal phrases	66g	Dash
		66h	Parentheses
63b	Prepositional phrases	66i	Quotation marks

TEXT 8

Punctuation and Good Sentences

59 Introduction

59a The purpose of the text

Should There Be a Comma Here?

This may well be the question we most often ask as we work for correct writing. Punctuation probably gives us more trouble than any other area of writing—yet, correctly used, it can also give us more help in clearly expressing our ideas. We have no more useful tool than punctuation for showing our readers the relationship of the parts of our sentences, and thus of our thoughts.

Should There Be a Comma Here?

This text will attempt to answer this and other questions about punctuation, not so much with a simple "yes" or "no" as with a discussion of the nature of punctuation and its function as a part of our writing.

59b The importance of punctuation

Punctuation is a part of writing. An important part. It is not something separate and distinct—to be stuck on, like a flower in a buttonhole, after an idea is already fully clothed in words. True, some punctuation marks may be added after the writing is finished, as part of our final editing; but mostly they should flow from our pen along with our words, each to its appointed place in the sentence. For punctuation is indeed as much a part of our sentences as the words in them.

It is true that there is a trend these days toward using less punctuation. This trend doesn't prove that punctuation is becoming less important; instead, it shows that sentences are becoming shorter and simpler, that there are not so many twists and turns in our modern sentences—turns that need to be marked for the bewildered reader. If you want to use less punctuation (if you want to "write modern"), go ahead. Just be sure yours are not the long, involved sentences that need lots of punctuation to keep the reader on the right road. Remember, the sentences that need little punctuation are the straightforward, simple ones.

Since punctuation is a part of writing, the only one who can effectively punctuate a piece of writing is the person who writes it. Only he knows the relationships he wants his punctuation to express. Neither the executive who leaves all punctuation to his secretary nor the stenographer who scatters commas through her shorthand notes understands the true role that punctuation plays in writing.

59c The approach of the text

This text approaches the understanding of punctuation by two routes: First, by discussing what to punctuate; and second, by listing the punctuation marks. Sections 61 through 65 discuss what sentence elements we need to punctuate and how we may effectively punctuate them. Section 66 lists the punctuation marks and their uses.

60 Punctuation—Functional and Conventional

Functional punctuation is essential to clear writing. Here, as in *conventional* punctuation—the set of rules controlled by custom—we find certain standards that are followed by considerate writers. But functional punctuation, because it is based on logic and because it directly adds to the meaning of the words it punctuates, does allow for variation within these standards. The freedom given us in this area, however, carries with it a measure of responsibility. Our readers expect and deserve consistency in punctuation.

Most of the punctuation in our sentences can be grouped by function into:

(1) Punctuation that *separates* one idea from another so that the reader may see them distinctly:

Punctuation and Good Sentences 145

The report was accurate, but it was not well organized.

(2) Punctuation that *encloses* incidental or parenthetic expressions:

Our letter of July 6, *a copy of which is attached*, should answer your question.

(3) Punctuation that *emphasizes* certain sentence elements by setting them apart from the rest of the sentence. (These elements are often out of natural order, for increased emphasis.)

This course, *newly revised*, is now available.
(In natural order—*This newly revised course*—the element is emphasized less.)

The comma is the mark that most often performs these functions. And the comma, because of its wide use, is the mark most often misused. We may be able to avoid some errors in punctuation by applying this formula for the use of the comma (it is valid, too, for other marks): *Use one comma to separate; use two commas to enclose.*

61 Separating Main Clauses

Main clauses (also called principal or independent clauses) are those that may stand alone as sentences. When combined with other main clauses, they form compound sentences.

Within certain limitations, the choice of what punctuation to use to separate main clauses is up to us—the writers. We know best how closely related—or how widely separated—are the ideas expressed by the clauses we have written. And it is up to us to choose the punctuation that will come closest to conveying our meaning to the reader.

How do we decide what punctuation to use? By weighing these factors: Is there a conjunction between the clauses? If so, what kind of conjunction is it? How closely related are the clauses?

How important is the thought expressed by each clause? How much emphasis do we wish to give to each clause?

The punctuation marks that may be used to separate clauses are: the period, the colon, the dash, the semicolon, and the comma. The comma may be used, however, ONLY when the clauses have been linked by a connective. (A violation of this use of the comma is called the *comma splice* or the *run-on sentence*.)

61a To show close relationship between clauses

To show the closest possible relationship between clauses, and to give the least amount of emphasis to the individual clauses, use the coordinate conjunctions *and, or,* or *for* with the comma.

> The case has been closed, and the report on it was filed yesterday.

If the clauses are short enough and the relationship is clear enough, we do not need any punctuation mark.

> The case is closed and the report has been filed.

NOTE: Even when the relationship is close, we usually use a comma before the coordinate conjunction *for* to avoid confusing it with the preposition *for*.

> He has not yet filed his report, for the investigation has not been completed.

and before the coordinate conjunctions *but, yet,* and *nor* to heighten the idea of contrast expressed by these conjunctions.

> The case was closed last week, but the report on it has not yet been filed.

61b To emphasize individual clauses—using a period to separate

To give the most emphasis to the individual clauses—when the thought relationship of the clauses is not especially close—separate them by a period, making each a simple sentence.

> The meeting was over. The committee members had returned to their hotels. Some had even left town.

NOTE: Clauses may be separated by a period, even when the clauses need a conjunction to express the exact relationship between them. Using a period between the clauses, even when a conjunction is present, emphasizes the individual clauses by calling the reader's full attention to each one.

> The report was submitted to the Director last week, with the expectation that it would be approved immediately. But as yet no action has been taken.

When the conjunction is a conjunctive adverb, it does not have to appear first in the clause.

> The report was submitted to the Director last week, with the expectation that it would be approved immediately. As yet, however, no action has been taken.

61c To emphasize individual clauses—using a semicolon to separate

If the relationship between two clauses is clear without a conjunction—and if the relationship is a close one—we may separate the clauses by a semicolon.

> The committee evidently arrived at several solutions to this problem; their report was submitted to the Director yesterday.

NOTE: The semicolon is also used to separate clauses linked by a conjunctive adverb, whether the adverb appears between or in the body of the second clause.

> The report was submitted to the Director last week, with the expectation that it would be approved immediately; however, as yet no action has been taken.

61d To express special relationships

Introductory Main Clauses

We may use either the colon or the dash between an introductory clause and a second clause which completes or explains what the first clause says.

> It is just as he predicted—as hard as we worked, we were not able to complete the report on time.
> We can present the information in either of two ways: we can ask for an appointment to report in person, or we can prepare a written report.

The Semicolon With the Coordinate Conjunction

We may use a semicolon between two clauses linked by a coordinate conjunction:

(1) when the clauses contain commas:

> We will, of course, attempt to finish the project by the deadline; but, as you know, we have had several serious delays.

(2) when we wish to emphasize one clause in a sentence that contains three main clauses:

> The money has been allotted, and the staff has been chosen; and now the real work begins.

The Comma With No Conjunction

We may use a comma:

(1) to separate the two parts of an echo question:

> You didn't believe me, did you?
> That was your brother, wasn't it?

(2) to separate short parallel clauses:

> The thunder roared, the lightning flashed, the rains came.
> Some people liked it, more didn't.
> It's a bird, it's a plane, it's Superman.

Punctuation and Good Sentences

SUMMARY

Here, in diagram form, and in the order in which they are discussed above, are the ways in which we may separate main clauses.

61a To show close relationship between clauses:

```
**********  and **********.
**********, and **********.
**********, for **********.
**********, but **********.
**********, nor **********.
```

61b To emphasize individual clauses—using a period to separate:

```
**********.  **********.
**********.  But **********.
**********.  However, **********.
**********.  ***, however, ****.
```

61c To emphasize individual clauses—using a semicolon to separate:

```
**********; **********.
**********; however, **********.
**********; ***, however, ****.
```

61d To express special relationships:

Introductory Main Clauses

```
**********—**********.
**********. **********.
```

The Semicolon With the Coordinate Conjunction

```
***, ***, ****; and ***, *******.
**********, and **********; and **********.
```

The Comma With No Conjunction

```
**********, *****? (echo question)
**********, **********, **********.
```

62 Enclosing Modifiers and Appositives

We may choose any one of three sets of punctuation marks to enclose a modifier, an appositive, or any other expression that interrupts the flow of the sentence.

THE COMMA is the mark most frequently used for this purpose. It is the lightest of the three possible marks, indicating only a slight separation in thought between the element enclosed and the rest of the sentence.

> That textbook, *which was published less than a year ago*, is already out of print.

THE DASH emphasizes the element being enclosed. It may also be used, even when no special emphasis is needed, to enclose an element containing internal commas.

> Miss Holtzman—*who has never taken a day of sick leave in 32 years*—is at home today with a cold.
> (Element enclosed by dashes for emphasis)
>
> Miss Holtzman—*you remember, the woman who welcomed you when you first came to work here*—is retiring next week.
> (Element contains internal punctuation)

PARENTHESES indicate that the element being enclosed is only loosely connected with the thought of the sentence. Parentheses usually enclose material meant for reference or explanation.

> In spite of his resistance (*which still continues strong*), the plan was adopted.
> His latest book (*published by Harper*) will be available later this month.

Below are three variations of the same sentence. Notice the degrees of emphasis we may give the enclosed element by our choice of punctuation.

> The gray frame building, *built during World War I*, which has housed our offices for the past two years is scheduled to be torn down next year.
> The gray frame building—*built during World War I*—which has housed our offices for the past two years is scheduled to be torn down next year.
> The gray frame building (*built during World War I*) which has housed our offices for the past two years is scheduled to be torn down next year.

Restrictive and Nonrestrictive Modifiers

Modifiers and appositives are classed as *restrictive* or as *nonrestrictive*.

A restrictive modifier or appositive cannot be omitted without changing the meaning of the sentence. It restricts or limits the word preceding it, and by answering the question, "Which one?" also serves an identifying function. Because restrictive modifiers are essential parts of the sentence, they are not set off by commas.

A nonrestrictive modifier or appositive, on the other hand, is not essential to the meaning of the sentence. It may add interesting or helpful information, but it is not necessary as a restrictive modifier is. To show that they contain ideas of secondary importance, nonrestrictive modifiers are set off by commas.

62a Adjective modifiers

Restrictive adjective clauses, verbal phrases, and prepositional phrases are not set off from the rest of the sentence by commas. Nonrestrictive modifiers are.

> Restr: The employee *who wrote that letter* is on leave today.
> Nonr: Mr. Jameson, *who wrote that letter*, is on leave today.
>
> Restr: The new agent *from Milwaukee* is doing a good job.
> Nonr: Mr. Jameson, *from Milwaukee*, is new to this office.
>
> Restr: The report *to be presented at tomorrow's meeting* is being duplicated.
> Nonr: The survey committee's report, *to be presented at tomorrow's meeting*, is being duplicated.
>
> Restr: An office in a building *built in 1918* may not meet the needs of today's executive.
> Nonr: That red brick structure, *built in 1918*, is scheduled for demolition.
>
> Restr: The changes *proposed in your letter dated January 17* are being carefully studied.
> Nonr: The changes in the sorting machine operation, *proposed in your letter dated January 17*, are being carefully studied.

Logic will sometimes tell the reader whether a modifier is restrictive or nonrestrictive, the punctuation serving only to point up what is already obvious. But sometimes a sentence may have two possible meanings, depending upon whether the modifier is considered restrictive or nonrestrictive. In these cases the reader is entirely dependent on the writer's correct punctuation of the modifier.

> Restr: His estate was willed to his daughters *who had not married* and to his son.
>> (This sentence says that only his *unmarried* daughters were included in the will; any *married* daughters received no part of the estate.)
>
> Nonr: His estate was willed to his daughters, *who had not married*, and to his son.

(This sentence says that all his daughters—who, incidentally, were not married—were included in the will.)

Restr: We discussed the problem with a lawyer *who was able to explain it.*
Nonr: We discussed the problem with Counselor P. Mason, *who was able to explain it.*

626 Adverbial modifiers

Adverbial modifiers are not always clearly restrictive or nonrestrictive. Often only the writer can determine whether an adverbial modifier is essential to the meaning of the sentence. Then, too, the punctuation of adverbial modifiers is not solely dependent upon whether the modifier is restrictive or nonrestrictive. Factors such as the position and length of the modifier and the amount of emphasis it should have also play a part.

As a general rule we should not set off a restrictive adverbial modifier that occurs at the end of the sentence.

> I have not heard from him *since last Thursday.*
> He will not miss the meeting *if we send him a wire.*
> What is the procedure *under these circumstances?*
> He was in his early thirties *when he worked here.*

NOTE: Both restrictive and nonrestrictive adverbial modifiers are usually set off if they come at the beginning of the sentence.

We may or may not set off a nonrestrictive adverbial modifier that comes at the end of the sentence. We should ordinarily set it off if it is long or if it needs special emphasis.

> This project must be finished on time, *even if it means overtime for the whole staff.*
> The bill is expected to pass, *although there is strong opposition to it in some quarters.*
> This is all the information we have, *so far as I know.*

We have three ways of punctuating an adverbial clause or phrase which immediately follows a conjunction:

(1) no punctuation:

> He is planning to attend, but *if the time is changed* he will have to cancel.

(2) punctuation after the modifier only:

> We may have a slight budgetary surplus; and *if no more urgent use for the money arises before the end of the month,* we may order the new projector.

(3) punctuation before and after the modifier:

> We are working hard now; but, *if the bill is passed,* we will have twice as much work to do.

62c Appositives

Restrictive appositives—those necessary for identification—are not separated from the word they stand in apposition to. Nonrestrictive appositives are set off.

> Restr: My brother *James* will arrive Friday.
> (James is one of several brothers.)
> Nonr: My brother, *James,* will arrive Friday.
> (My only brother, whose name is James.)
>
> Restr: Hemingway's novel *"For Whom the Bell Tolls"* was presented on television.
> (Setting off the title by commas would indicate that this is Hemingway's only novel.)
> Nonr: One of Hemingway's novels, *"For Whom the Bell Tolls,"* was presented on television.

Often an introductory expression—such as *namely, for instance, that is to say, in other words, for example, such as*—is used to emphasize an appositive. Below are some of the ways we may punctuate these expressions.

> One of the officers, *namely Henders,* was on duty.
> A nonrestrictive, *or nonessential,* appositive is set off.
> We have been assigned three new reports: *namely, the statistical summary, the narrative summary, and the budgetary summary.*
> This has presented us with a new problem: *specifically, the lack of staff time.*
> Our office is instituting several new techniques—*the revised filing procedures, for example.*
> The extremes in architecture (*that is, the very modern and the very old fashioned*) do not appeal to me.

63 Punctuating Introductory Elements

63a Adverbial clauses and verbal phrases

An introductory adverbial clause or verbal phrase is usually set off from the rest of the sentence, even when it is restrictive.

> *When you go to the supply room,* bring me some pencils.
> *If you call me before noon,* I can meet you for lunch.
> *Generally speaking,* we approve these requests.
> *In drafting the report,* we developed several new approaches to the problem.
> *To reach my office,* take the elevator to the third floor.

If the clause or phrase is quite short and if there is no danger that it might be misread, the comma may be omitted.

63b   Prepositional phrases

We do not usually separate introductory prepositional phrases from the sentence unless they deserve special emphasis.

> *On August 27* the new rule will go into effect.
> *In Washington* the weather is usually pleasant in May.
> *In spite of his objections* we plan to release the report.

But

> *In the operation of that particular machine,* Jones has the highest production record.
> *In the first place,* he has more experience at that job.

63c   Introductory elements with connective force

If the element is obviously parenthetical, separate it from the rest of the sentence.

> *In the light of this report,* we must review our earlier decisions.
> *On the other hand,* his may have been a hasty decision.
> *As a result,* we will have to postpone our planned meeting.
> *On the contrary,* he may have an answer for us by Thursday.
> *However,* we must not plan on anything as risky as that.

But if the expression is short and closely connected with the thought of the sentence, separating it will only destroy the smoothness of the sentence.

> *Last month* our average was higher than it has been all year.
> *Indeed* the progress is most encouraging.
> *Possibly* we may be able to exceed last year's record.
> *Thus* we will establish a new high in production.

64   Punctuating Parenthetical Elements

By *parenthetical* we mean any element that interrupts the flow of the sentence. Some of the elements we discussed in earlier sections may be considered parenthetical. This section will list some others—elements that are not needed for grammatical completeness but that are related to the thought of the sentence. Parenthetical elements are set off from the rest of the sentence—in most instances by commas. If the parenthetical element occurs in the middle of the sentence, be sure that it is preceded and followed by a punctuation mark.

64a   Interrupting transitional expressions

> We were able, *fortunately,* to catch the letter before it was mailed.
> He was ordered, *therefore,* to return at once.

Punctuation and Good Sentences 155

This, *however*, was impossible.
We will, *of course*, be happy to help you.
This, *on the other hand*, should be easier.
I was, *as a matter of fact*, planning to call you.

64b Interrupting expressions identifying speaker or source

This project, *we feel*, is our most important one.
The results, *it is now believed*, will be successful.
The course, *as you know*, will begin next Monday.
This report, *I might say*, is the best you have done.
"The meeting," *he said*, "was an outstanding success."

64c Addresses, dates, titles

Please send applications to the Training Division, *Room 5700, Internal Revenue Building, Washington 25, D.C.*
He is a member of the Alexandria, *Virginia*, Chamber of Commerce.
The District Director at Los Angeles, *California*, has sent your letter to me.
I read it in a Baltimore, *Maryland*, newspaper.
The representatives will be from Chicago, *Illinois;* Omaha, *Nebraska;* Salem, *Oregon;* Austin, *Texas.*
Your letter of July 6, *1959*, arrived while I was on leave.
   (If the day is not included, the month and year are usually written with no punctuation: *July 1959.*)
Mr. Robert W. Laws, *chairman of the committee*, will speak at the opening ceremonies.
Please forward your estimates to the Director, *"X" Division, National Office*, by close of business June 2.

64d Nominative absolute

All things being equal, I believe he will win.
There being no further discussion, the meeting was adjourned.
The measure having been passed by a large majority, the chairman went on to the next item.

64e Words in direct address

Tell me, *Doctor*, how serious is it?
With your permission, *Mr. Chairman*, I would like to answer that question.
Would you like me to call you when it is ready, *sir*?

65 *Separating Coordinate Items in Series*

Separate coordinate items in series by punctuation unless they are joined by coordinate conjunctions. The comma is the mark most often used, although we may use the semicolon to separate items containing internal commas and the dash to throw strong emphasis on the individual items.

65a Series with coordinate conjunction

When the items are connected by coordinate conjunctions, they do not usually need any punctuation. But we may punctuate if the series is long or if we want to emphasize the items.

> Either: The instructor and his students and the rest of the faculty heard the discussion.
> or: The instructor, and his students, and all the faculty that were able to attend heard the discussion.

65b Series with no connective

To make the meaning clear, we need to separate the items in a series containing no connectives.

> My ambition now is to get away from the office, to lie on the beach, to listen to the surf.
> He was making a typical departure for a meeting, calling instructions to his staff, hurriedly signing last-minute correspondence, stuffing papers into his brief case.

65c Series with connective joining last two members

A series with a connective joining the last two members may be punctuated in either of two ways:

> Either: He ordered paper, pencils, and erasers.
> Or: He ordered paper, pencils and erasers.
> Either: Every piece of writing has a beginning, a middle, and an end.
> Or: Every piece of writing has a beginning, a middle and an end.

NOTE: Many writers (and certainly most readers) prefer the use of the comma before the connective because this punctuation leaves no doubt in the reader's mind that the last two members of the series are to be considered separately.

65d Consecutive adjectives (two or more)

Separate by commas only those consecutive adjectives which are coordinate. Adjectives are coordinate if (1) they can be linked by *and* and (2) they independently modify the substantive:

Coordinate (each adjective independently modifies the substantive):

> a lengthy, overdue report
> (a lengthy *and* overdue report; an overdue *and* lengthy report)
> a careful, painstaking review
> a busy, ambitious, clever man

Not coordinate (each adjective modifies all that follows it):

> the new statistical chart   (not: new *and* statistical)
> a gray flannel suit   (a flannel suit that is gray)
> a green ballpoint pen

66 The Punctuation Marks

Intended more for reference than for study, this section lists the punctuation marks and their major functions. Many of the items will necessarily repeat, in different sequence, material covered in sections 61 through 65.

66a Use the period:

. . . to mark the end of a sentence that is not a question or an exclamation.

> An agreement was reached on that case last week.

. . . after a request—to distinguish it from a direct question.

> Will you please send us three copies of the January 17 memo.
> Will you let us know whether you can attend the conference.

. . . after words or phrases that stand as sentences. (This is not an endorsement of fragmentary sentences; but if sentence fragments must be used, they are followed by periods.)

> True.
> What time will you be back?   By noon.

. . . after abbreviations and initials.

> The taxpayer, R. D. Pale, M.D., is employed by the Central Medical Association.

. . . to show that material has been omitted from a quotation. Omissions are usually shown by three periods, in addition to any other punctuation needed at that point in the material.

> The report stated, "Preliminary investigations . . . disclose no reason for discontinuing the procedure at this time."
> The report stated, "Preliminary investigations by the committee members disclose no reason for discontinuing the procedure . . . ."

66b Use the question mark:

. . . after a sentence that asks a *direct question*. (Not after a request, even though it is phrased as a question.)

>Have you heard from Mr. Rollins this morning?
>You know the letter I mean, don't you?

>But: He asked where Mr. Rollins was.   (Indirect question.)

. . . to indicate doubt about the correctness of a statement.

>The company was established in 1920(?) and was incorporated in 1921.
>About a year after the company was established (1920?), it was incorporated.

. . . to replace the commas in an interrogatory series in order to emphasize the individual members of the series.

>Do you have the letter? the cards? the file?

66c Use the exclamation point:

. . . after an exclamatory sentence or remark, to show strong feeling. (The exclamation point should be used sparingly—rarely in expository writing.)

>That's the longest report I've seen yet!
>Whew!   What a day!

66d Use the comma:

. . . to separate main clauses joined by a coordinate conjunction.

>The case has been closed, and the agent has reported.
>The case is closed, but the agent has not reported.
>The case is closed, yet no report has been filed.

. . . to separate short, parallel main clauses not joined by a coordinate conjunction.

>The table was cleared, the books were brought out, the evening's work was begun.

. . . to separate the two independent clauses of an echo question.

>You thought I'd be late, didn't you?

Punctuation and Good Sentences

. . . to set off a nonrestrictive adjective modifier.

> Mr. Jameson, *whom you met last week*, will help you.
>
> The "X" Company, *established in 1873*, is the city's oldest business firm.
>
> *Exhausted from a long day of meetings*, he stuffed some papers into his briefcase and left for the airport.
>
> *Elated*, he called his staff in to tell them the news.

. . . to set off a nonrestrictive adverbial modifier at the end of a sentence, especially if it is long or needs special emphasis.

> I will call you at 4 o'clock, *after the messenger brings the mail*.
>
> I have not seen him since Tuesday, *when he spoke at the luncheon*.
>
> We must finish this report by Friday, *even if we have to work on it at night*.

. . . to set off a nonrestrictive appositive.

> My brother, *James*, has been visiting me.
>
> James, *my youngest brother*, has been visiting me.
>
> Office equipment, *such as typewriters and adding machines*, must be oiled regularly.

. . . to set off an introductory adverbial modifier. (If the modifier is short and if no confusion will result, it is not set off.)

> *When you get back to the office*, look up that information and call me.
>
> *If your figures are correct*, we will have enough money left to buy that new equipment.
>
> *Because she was familiar with the files in the division*, she was able to assemble the data on time.

. . . to set off an introductory prepositional phrase that demands special emphasis.

> *In spite of his head cold*, he put in a full day at the office.
>
> *In the light of his objections*, we may reconsider the proposed change.

. . . to set off an introductory transitional expression that is not closely related to the meaning of the sentence.

> *On the other hand*, his statement may be based on nothing more than opinion.
>
> *In the first place*, we do not have the funds to undertake the project right now.

... to set off an interrupting transitional expression.

> We may, *of course*, postpone the meeting indefinitely.
> He will, *therefore*, be forced to submit a written statement.
> We must be sure, *however*, that he understands the serious nature of the charges.

... to set off an interrupting expression identifying speaker or source.

> A little change of pace, *we decided*, was just what we needed.
> The report, *as you may remember*, was not approved immediately.
> That, *I feel*, may be the root of our problem.
> "Your organization," *he said*, "has done an outstanding job."

... to set off addresses, dates, titles.

> He moved to Omaha, *Nebraska*, shortly after he graduated.
> Your letter of July 6, *1959*, explains the problem clearly.
> The reports are due in the office of the Director, *Personnel Division*, by noon Friday.

... to set off a nominative absolute phrase.

> *The meal having been paid for*, he felt he must eat it.
> *The report having been submitted*, he prepared an errata sheet.

... to set off words in direct address.

> *Sir*, your letters are ready for signature.
> Your letters are ready for signature, *Mr. Brown*.
> May I interrupt, *Mr. Chairman*, to ask that the question be repeated.

... to separate coordinate items in a series.

> He asked that paper, pencils, and ashtrays be placed in the conference room.
> He said it had been an exciting, exhausting day.

66e Use the semicolon:

... to separate main clauses not joined by a coordinate conjunction.

> We submitted the project plans to the Director this morning; they were approved by noon.
> The Director publicly commended us for our work; he is particularly pleased about the new accounts system.
> We have completed the report; that is, we have completed the first draft.

Punctuation and Good Sentences 161

. . . to separate main clauses joined by a conjunctive adverb.

> The Director publicly commended us for our report; however, he later asked us to rewrite the conclusion.
> The new system is scheduled to begin next Monday; we will, therefore, need the manuals by Friday.

. . . to separate main clauses joined by a coordinate conjunction when the clauses contain commas (if the semicolon is needed for clarity).

> You will, of course, want to notify him; and, unless he is out of town, he will surely attend. (Comma after *and* is optional.)
> He has given his tentative approval; but, naturally, he will wait until after the trial run to make a final decision.

. . . to emphasize one of three main clauses in a sentence.

> The plans have been made, and the staff has been chosen; now we are ready to begin.

. . . to separate coordinate items in a series when the items contain internal commas.

> Attending were representatives from Omaha, Nebraska; Los Angeles, California; Salem, Oregon; and San Francisco, California.
> Meeting to discuss the new plan were: Wilson, just in from New York; Addison, here only for the day; and James, only recently back from his place in the country.

66f Use the colon:

. . . between main clauses when the second clause completes or explains the first.

> There are two courses open to us: We can demand that the issue be reopened, or we can abide by the decision until the group meets again in the fall.

. . . after an expression that formally introduces a list, an explanation, or a quotation.

> Our new secretary will need to possess three qualities: endurance, patience, and humor.
> Our supply list includes the following items: one ream of bond paper, one box of pencils, and three typewriter ribbons.
> The topic of the report is: An Appraisal of the Jacobs System.
> In his talk the Director said: "This division has, in the past few months, made great strides in reducing the backlog of cases."

66g   Use the dash:

. . . between main clauses when the second clause explains or summarizes the first.

> The decision was obvious—we would have to recall all tests until we could recheck them.
> He has done two things of which he is enormously proud—he has led the division to increased production, and he has helped increase the prestige of the division throughout the organization.

. . . to set off a nonrestrictive modifier or parenthetical element that contains internal commas.

> The Williams Building—built, it is believed, in 1900—was torn down three years ago.

. . . to emphasize a nonrestrictive modifier or parenthetical element that is normally set off by commas. (Used rarely in Revenue writing.)

> He was—fortunately—able to deliver the pictures by the deadline.
> I plan to ask Wade—who is the person who surely ought to know—how this plan was first devised.

. . . to set off a nonrestrictive appositive for special emphasis.

> Only one member—the chairman—can break a tie vote.
> There is just one thing wrong with the filing system—you can't find anything!

66h   Use parentheses:

. . . to enclose a nonrestrictive modifier or parenthetic element that is only loosely connected with the thought of the sentence.

> The book (published in 1949) has been most helpful to me.
> His discussion of those principles (pages 44–49) is one of the best I've seen.
> Mr. X (who probably knows more about offers in compromise than anyone else in the Service) is being transferred to our Atlanta office.

NOTE: If other punctuation is needed at the place in the sentence where the parentheses occur, it follows the closing parenthesis. But if the punctuation pertains to the parenthetic matter it is placed within the parentheses.

> If you plan to attend the meeting (to be held at the Statler Hotel), please notify us by June 1.
> The director has approved our report (Publication No. 333); it will be released later this week.
> His promotion is barred by the Whitten Amendment. (See C.S. Reg. 2.501(j).)
> His promotion is barred by the Whitten Amendment (C.S. Reg. 2.501(j)).

Punctuation and Good Sentences

66i Use quotation marks:

. . . to enclose any direct quotation, whether a single word, a sentence, or several paragraphs. Do not include within the quotation marks any explanatory expressions not a part of the quoted material.

> He described the new procedure as "long needed and much appreciated."
> He assured us that the procedure had been "promulgated."
> "We are faced with a difficult task," he stated; "but I am sure we will accomplish it."

NOTE: In Revenue writing, it is frequently necessary to define terms or identifying expressions. The word(s) being defined should be enclosed in quotation marks, whether or not they are preceded by such words as "the term," "the expression," etc.

> For income tax purposes, the term "adjusted gross income" means . . .
> A "nonresident alien" is a person who . . .

. . . to enclose the entire quotation, not the individual sentences, when the quotation consists of several sentences.

> "I am pleased with the progress we have been making in recent months," the Director remarked. "Production is up, and morale seems to be high. All in all, we have come a long way since we first began this project."

. . . before each paragraph of a series of quoted paragraphs, but after only the final paragraph.

> "_____
> _____ .
> "_____
> _____ .
> "_____
> _____ ."

. . . to enclose the title of a published work that is part of a larger whole, such as an article from a magazine, a chapter from a book, a poem from a collection. The title of the complete work is usually italicized in printed copy and underlined in typed copy.

> For examples of this style, read the chapter on "How to Write Like a Pro" in Rudolf Flesch's *A New Way to Better English*.
> Of interest to every executive is "How to Take the Tension Out of Your Job," an article in the May issue of *Management Methods*.

Use single quotation marks to enclose a quotation within a quotation.

> Addison remarked, "The phrase 'initiate any appropriate action' seems to leave a lot to the imagination."

When a quotation is given in indirect form, no quotation marks are used. An indirect quotation is usually introduced by *that*.

> Direct quotation: He said, "I mailed my tax return yesterday."
> Indirect quotation: He said that he mailed his tax return yesterday.

Quotation Marks With Other Marks of Punctuation

The comma and period are placed inside the quotation marks, whether or not they are a part of the quoted material.

> "I wonder," he said, "if we will ever finish it."

NOTE: There is one exception (and only one, so far as we know) to the placing of the comma and period inside the quotation marks, regardless of whether they are a part of the quoted material. When you are writing about insertions in, or deletions from, certain legal work, such as laws and regulations, put the punctuation mark outside the quotation marks *unless it is a part of the material to be inserted or deleted*.

> Insert the words "growth", "production", and "manufacture".
> To be inserted immediately after the words "cadets, U.S. Coast Guard;".
> Change "February 1, 1951" to "June 30, 1951".

The semicolon and colon are placed outside the quotation marks unless they are a part of the quoted matter.

> "We have come far, but we have farther to go"; that is the note on which he began his speech.
> I have only one thing to say about the "X Report": it will be a long time before we hear the last of it.

The question mark and exclamation mark are placed inside the quotation marks if they are a part of the quotation; outside if they are not.

> He asked, "Do you plan to attend the meeting?"
> Could we describe the project as "essentially completed"?

Use *only one* terminal punctuation mark at end of sentences. *Examples:* (1) Who was it who said, "Know thyself"? (2) He frowned when she asked, "Why?" (3) Which student asked, "Why?"

TEXT 9

Watch Your Words

67	Introduction	72	"Concrete" words
68	The importance of words	73	"Current" words
69	Peculiar characteristics of words	74	Words with multiple meanings
69a	Symbols—and more	75	Economy with words
69b	Do words have meaning?		
69c	The emotional meaning of words	76	Idiomatic uses of words
69d	How many meanings?	77	Words that antagonize
69e	Language is never static	78	Words that are impersonal
70	Technical and legal terms	79	Overuse of adjectives and adverbs
71	Simple words		

TEXT 9

Watch Your Words

67 Introduction

The next two texts are unlike the eight you have already completed. We are now going to study about words—words themselves, word order, word relationships. "But," you may say, "what have we been studying about up to this point, if not about words?" It is true that we considered words in the earlier texts, but not in the way we shall look at them in the texts that follow.

The first eight texts laid the foundation for clear and effective writing by pointing out the *functions of words* and by describing and illustrating the way they can properly perform these functions. A knowledge of these functions is basic to good writing. The last two texts in this course introduce the basic principles of writing for which the first eight laid the foundation.

Text 9 discusses words, the symbols we use to express an idea. We cannot think, much less write, without using words. They are, however, packages which should be labeled "Handle with care," for they may have meanings beyond their definition, and they may possess powerful psychological qualities. Text 9 alerts the writer to his responsibility for choosing and using words that will make his writing both clear and effective.

In Text 10 we go one step beyond words and look at sentences and paragraphs. In these larger units we see the importance of word order and word relationships in producing clear and effective writing.

68 The Importance of Words

Words, like the poor, we have with us always. We think, speak, and write with words—everything we do depends on them. Words pour out of our offices daily in an endless stream—in memorandums, in letters, in reports, in face-to-face conversations, and in telephone conversations. Unfortunately, many of these words are an effort to clarify the meanings of words spoken or written earlier, words that didn't get our message across clearly the first time.

How can words be so meaningful, yet so meaningless? How can words cause so much confusion, meaning one thing to the writer or speaker and another to the reader or listener? What can the writer do to insure that his words will carry the meaning he intends?

The first place to look for an answer to these questions is in what may seem an unlikely spot—in *ourselves*, the users of words. The majority of us use words automatically; we take them for granted. We may not think consciously about them, except to look in the dictionary for the spelling of some word that has never been firmly pinned down in our minds. Possibly we carry our concern about words no further than avoiding some expressions and overusing others because we have learned that correspondence containing these expressions will—or will not—be passed by our supervisors. Recognizing word problems to this limited extent is barely scratching the surface.

We need to stop taking words for granted and to get rid of some baseless assumptions we have about them. We often assume that words will be understood without testing them to be sure that they are the right words for the difficult job of getting our meaning across to the reader. Many of us have a false sense of security when we use words: we believe that by putting the thought into words, we have communicated it to the reader or listener. We assume that any adult can use words—after all, he's been using them all his life—and that there is no need to work at the job of improving word power, which is something we have or we don't, like curly hair or musical talent.

The instances we meet daily of words failing to do their work properly ought to prove the fallacy of these assumptions. When a taxpayer does not understand our letter and writes again for further information, or when employees have to ask for interpretation of instructions, do we ever blame the *wording* of the instructions? When readers misinterpret messages and take the wrong action—or fail to take any action at all—do we suspect that *words* may be responsible for this communication failure? When taxpayers receive letters that make them feel the Service is being

Watch Your Words 169

dictatorial or bureaucratic or when employee morale plummets to hit rock bottom after an internal document has been distributed, do we realize that *words* may be at the root of the trouble?

Words are both frustrating and fascinating. Have you ever noticed the strange ways people from other parts of the country use words? And have you ever tried to grasp and take back a word you wish you hadn't used? It's easier to put squeezed-out toothpaste back into the tube.

Only when we recognize the peculiar characteristics of words and come to respect words for what they can and can't do are we willing to learn enough about them to make them serve us well.

69   Peculiar Characteristics of Words

69a   Symbols—and more

Words are the symbols of our ideas, the means by which we communicate. But words are never mere words. They are chameleon-like creatures, changing color to suit the occasion. Justice Oliver Wendell Holmes once said, "A word is not a crystal, transparent and unchanging. It is the skin of a living thought and may vary greatly in color and context according to the circumstances and time in which it is used."

69b   Do words have meaning?

Words are completely unpredictable. They have no real meaning in themselves; they only *stand for* meaning. This statement may seem slightly heretical to those who have always taken words for granted. Of course words have meaning! If not, why do we have dictionaries, huge volumes explaining the meaning of words? But the real meaning lies within the person who speaks and writes the words and within the person who hears or reads them.

For example, we may say that it is the duty of the Internal Revenue Service "to insure compliance with the tax laws." To many Revenue employees this means "to insure that the Government collects from the taxpaying public *all* money due it under the law *but no more than that due it.*" Within the employee there has been built up a concept of the Service which includes this meaning.

But what does the phrase mean to taxpayers? And does it mean the same to *all* taxpayers? Certainly not. For to everyone (employee and taxpayer alike) the meaning lies not in the *words* themselves but in the knowledge and understanding that the *people* bring to the words. This is true, whether we use an abstract phrase like this example or simply a term like "in connection with his trade or business." Each reader and writer tends to assume that the other uses a word just as he would; and the resulting interpretations may be poles apart.

69c The emotional meaning of words

The meaning a word *suggests* is known as its *connotation*. The recognized dictionary definition, the typical or possible meaning, is its *denotation*. The denotation of the words "Form 1040" might be "a form used to report income received and tax to be paid." The connotation, or what the words suggest, will vary with each person who files a return. The connotation of a word is affected by the circumstances in which the word has been used generally and by the context in which it occurs. In addition, a word may hold a special association for an individual.

Because a reader reacts to the meaning he associates with a word, we can never be sure what emotional impact a word may carry or how it may affect our readers. Words which we may think are synonymous can differ greatly in emotive force. Call a man a "politician" and we imply that he is concerned with artifice and intrigue; call him a "statesman" and we have said that he is broadminded and wise in affairs of state. We can arrange nearly any group of synonymous words on a scale ranging from the most approving term to the most disapproving. If we label a man a public servant, we pay him a compliment. If we say he is a government official, we have used a neutral term that is neither approving nor disapproving. If, however, we call him a bureaucrat, we come close to name calling. Revenue writers must present facts objectively and impartially; therefore, try to select the neutral word that will not bias your writing by its hidden emotional meaning.

69d How many meanings?

Words, we sometimes find from experience, don't always mean what we thought they did; there may be several other meanings for the same word which make it inappropriate (perhaps even ridiculous) in the way we have used it. Very few words have a single, fixed meaning; common words—for example, *run*—may have more than 100 different meanings. Of approximately 750,000 words in the English language, only about 150,000 (or one-fifth) have meanings that have been established and documented—that is, their meaning has been frozen so that the word means today what it did years ago and what it will years from now. This small group of words comprises legal and scientific terms, which are purposely precise. Unless you are using words from this restricted-meaning group, you are faced with the problem of selecting from among the multimeaning words the ones that will best carry your message. Considering these odds against our communicating effectively, we may be mildly surprised, not that our words get our meaning across efficiently, but that they get it across at all.

We cannot say that once we have learned several meanings for a word that word is pegged and labeled and we can chalk up another mark toward a fuller vocabulary. It would be easier—and far less interesting—to study words if they would stand still for any length of time, but this is exactly the thing we can depend on them *not* to do.

69e   Language is never static

Language is a living, growing thing—adding, according to some estimates, from 3,000 to 5,000 new words every year. Every field of activity contributes its share. Not all these new words, of course, will survive; some may flourish for a few years and then drop from sight. Words atrophy and die, and others take their place. Words sprout additional meanings to meet new needs. As an illustration of the way language changes, try to think of some words used in your grandparents' time which are now obsolete or well on their way toward that classification. Compare these with words that have come into your vocabulary during the last 10 years through, for example, advances in science or medicine. How, then, is the Government writer to know whether a word is currently acceptable? We must steer a middle course in selecting words when we write as representatives of the Revenue Service. Alexander Pope had never heard of our problem, but he gave us the right answer with his words,

"Be not the first by which the new is tried,
Nor yet the last to lay the old aside."

How do we select the right words to get our meaning across to the reader? Perhaps the first place to look for help is in your vocabulary. The larger your vocabulary, the better the chances are that you will express yourself effectively. A few generations ago the mark of a learned man was his knowledge of grammar; today the standard of excellence is the quality of his vocabulary. Many popular magazines carry quizzes about words as a regular feature— it is becoming increasingly smart to be curious about words.

This is not to say, however, that a knowledge of words alone is enough. The test is whether you can *use* that knowledge. Can you, for instance, differentiate between shades of meaning in such words as *explain* and *interpret, apology* and *excuse, discover* and *invent?* Increasing your vocabulary will not, as you may infer from some magazine articles, insure your rise from a GS–3 position to a GS–13. Expanding one's vocabulary will, however, help both the GS–3 and the GS–13 to speak and write more clearly and effectively.

From our discussion of words up to this point we can see that the problem of managing words boils down to a question of word choice. We must know how to choose the word that will be *clear* to the reader and will be *effective*, or appropriate, in the kind of writing we are doing. It is almost impossible to group words in neat little bundles and say, *"These* are the words that will make your writing clear" and *"Here* are the words that will make it effective." Clarity and effectiveness go hand in hand, as we find when we try to pin a word in one category and not in the other. For this reason we are making no attempt to separate our discussion of principles of word choice under these two headings. Instead, we shall discuss general guidelines for choosing words that improve writing by making it both clear and effective. Let us begin by considering some words with which Revenue writers are most familiar—technical and legal words.

70   Technical and Legal Terms

We would be less than human if we did not, among ourselves, use the jargon of Revenue. But it is one thing to use this language to fellow employees and quite another to use it to taxpayers unfamiliar with our terms. Perhaps you can remember the feeling you had on entering the Service when you first encountered some of the legal and technical terms—those terms that have become so commonplace to you that now it is hard to think of them as unfamiliar to newcomers to the Service or to the taxpaying public.

Much of the work of the Revenue Service depends on the use of legal and technical terms; we are obliged to phrase our letters in such a way that there are no loopholes for possible misinterpretation. Because we must use this language, our words tend to be formal and legalistic; and our writing has a stiff, unyielding tone.

We have no choice in this matter of legal language: we have to live with it. There is, however, no rule that says we are forbidden to add translations of passages into language taxpayers can understand. Will the average taxpayer understand the word *situs* when we write:

> The sum of $500 on deposit in the First National Bank, Blankville, Anystate, did not have a *situs* in the United States.

Some of the legal terms we use seem formidable to many taxpayers because the terms contain words of foreign origin. The average reader will appreciate our translating these terms into simpler language:

in lieu of	in place of, instead
e.g.	for example
i.e.	that is
viz, videlicet	namely
supra	above
pursuant to	following
aforesaid, the said—	this
promulgate	issue
per annum	yearly
hold in abeyance	wait, suspend action
you are advised	informed
compounds of here, there, where (herein, thereon, etc.)	usually these can be omitted entirely

If you are sure the reader also speaks legal language, there is, of course, no reason why you should not use it. Be sure to distinguish, however, between true legal terms and those inflated words we sometimes think of as quasi-technical terms. If we want to tell a taxpayer that complete records are his best friends, we need not hide the message behind such words as "Maintaining proper records would do much to alleviate the difficulties inherent in determining the allowability of expenses claimed by taxpayers." If there is any suspicion in your mind that any term you use will not be clear to your reader, try to find a simple word to substitute for it. If you cannot find a substitute, at least define the term and illustrate it.

71 Simple Words

One statement upon which we can all agree is that writing representing a government agency should be dignified. The means we use to achieve this goal vary. To some writers dignity means a formal style; to others, an impersonal style characterized by long words and pompous phrases. Writing can be dignified when the language is simple, direct, and strong. In fact, strength and simplicity are basic requirements for dignity. We are not advocating a return to primer words and primer thinking. But to make your writing clearer and easier to read—and thus more effective—prefer the simple word to the inflated governmentese word.

How many of these sesquipedalian words have you used in your writing today? How many in your conversation?

What we write	What we mean
construct, fabricate	make
accomplish, perform	do
initiate, commence, inaugurate	begin
therefore	so
nevertheless	but
terminate, conclude, finalize	end
utilize	use
deem	think
assistance	help
substantial portion	large part
reside, dwell	live
stated	said
anent	about
ascertain	learn, find out
afford an opportunity	allow
procure	get

Sometimes little words are not suited to what you are writing; long words carry your message more effectively. By all means use the long word if it says what you mean and if it will be clear to your reader. One long word may say what it takes 20 little ones to express. (An example of this is the word *serendipity*, which means the faculty for finding something of value while looking for something else.) But when you use a long gobbledygookish word, be sure you know what you are saying. When we use the word "expedite," that Government term that means to hasten, perhaps we are, after all, using the simple direct word. *Expedite* originally meant "to free one caught by the foot," which may be exactly what we are trying to say.

72 "Concrete" Words

The old Chinese saying, "One picture is worth a thousand words," applies very well to writing. If we write, "Government building" or "machines," the reader has only a general idea of what we mean; if we change these words to "Treasury Department" or "typewriters," clear pictures come to our reader's mind.

A great deal of Government writing concerns abstract subjects about which it is hard to be specific. We need abstract words to express ideas, opinions, and generalizations; it is ridiculous to suggest that we try to find concrete words to substitute for such generalities as "eligibility," "responsibility," and "administration."

However, where it is possible to pin a word down more exactly, we should do so. "Personnel," for example, might become "temporary typists" or "office auditors." "It is the opinion of this office" could be "This office thinks (believes)." "Cases" might be "delinquent accounts" or "applicants for positions."

If we are writing to a taxpayer about his refund (a word which has a beneficent effect on almost every taxpayer), he is not interested in "claims" *in general* and "statutory provisions" under which they may be filed. He is looking for two specific words—"your refund."

We can be so general in our written instructions that they are open to misinterpretation. We may fall into the habit of using "weasel words"—vague, general words that can be understood different ways. Put instructions in simple, concrete words. If we want a stenographer to make two extra copies of a special kind of letter, we do not say, "When preparing correspondence for the signature of certain Treasury officials, it may be well for the stenographer to take into consideration the channels through which the correspondence must pass, and to be guided accordingly."

Too great reliance on abstract words and general terms is habit-forming, a habit into which it is easy to fall. Lack of concrete, specific words makes writing harder to read and, consequently, less effective. Clarity, too, suffers when we try to avoid calling a spade a spade. There are times, of course, when policy or self-preservation keeps us from using the blunt word *spade;* but perhaps we can safely say *shovel*, which is more specific than "a short-handled bladed instrument used for the purpose of delving into sod."

73 "Current" Words

Tightrope walkers are not the only people who must know how to maintain a good balance. Anyone who writes must also know the art of balancing, of choosing words that are, besides being clear and precise, not leaning too much toward the side of quaint archaic language or too much toward the language of the space age. The government writer, in particular, must maintain this balance: his words must reflect favorably upon his agency, representing a middle course that is acceptable by today's standards of good usage.

The writer's task is constantly being made more complex because language is not a static thing. Words are daily added to the language; many of them never become accepted members of society, and we must know which these are. If words are not used, they may be dropped or may remain as curios of their time. Compare the words in the "New Words" section of an up-to-date dictionary with those in a similar section 10 years ago. You may marvel at our word poverty of a decade ago. Every field of activity contributes its share of new words; you will read social history as you check the words people were using in any given time. The "New Words" section will help you decide whether a word has been temporarily accepted, but this does not necessarily mean that its use is always acceptable in government writing. Many of these creations are slang or colloquialisms that are colorful but unsuited to represent our agency.

Some words are depreciating in value while others are increasing. For example, in the early days of railroading two words were used to describe stopping points for trains—*station* and *depot*. *Depot* quickly became the more popular word, but today it is almost obsolete, connoting dreary waiting points in small towns. Would *Grand Central Depot* have the same meaning as *Grand Central Station*?

Two words which have bettered their status are *transpire* and *contact*. *Transpire* has the specialized meaning of exhaling or breathing through tissues. This meaning has been pushed to the rear, and *transpire* is now used to mean *happen* or *come to pass*. *Contact*, a noun, has sprouted into a verb meaning *to get in touch with*. Purists deplore these uses, but the fact remains that these words are gaining acceptance.

An interesting example of the acceptance of a word is "notarize." Once there was no single word that carried the meaning "to take a document to a notary public and have it attested to"; but writers, eager to economize on words, coined the verb "notarize." It was not found in the dictionary for some time after its birth; but soon, as often happens, recognized writers began using it. And it became legitimate. Now it is included in the dictionary, and only the purists object to its use.

Some word meanings have changed beyond recognition. That is why writings of earlier times—such as Chaucer, Shakespeare, or even the King James version of the Bible—may sometimes puzzle us. King James once described a cathedral as "amusing, awful, and artificial." At that time "amusing" meant "amazing," "awful" meant "awe-inspiring," and "artificial" meant "artistic."

Government writers following the stilted pattern of what they believe to be their agency's style of writing need to be especially on the alert against using outdated words. We do not call a letter "an esteemed favor" or even "an epistle," as earlier writers did. But we do continue to use such outmoded expressions as *"kindly* refer to the symbols," "in this *connection* it may be *stated,*" and please *"advise."*

Think of words as articles of clothing. How shall you dress your message? Would you send to a taxpayer's office a representative of the Service dressed in the frills of George Washington's time or in the abbreviated sport clothes of today's informal living? In many cases we are dependent upon written words to represent us. Select these words with care: to the reader your letter *is* the Internal Revenue Service.

74   Words With Multiple Meanings

The problem of making words do the work they should is further complicated by the assumption that words mean the same thing to all readers. The fact is that the meaning of words varies with each writer and reader; the person who reads the words you write may not see your meaning in them. He is far more likely to interpret them according to his background, his education, his experience—even according to the part of the country from which he has come. What a given word will do to a given reader cannot be predicted.

Suppose you use a word in a letter—slightly unfamiliar perhaps (you even had to look it up in the dictionary), but you felt it gave your writing an added desirable quality. Out of the many meanings the dictionary gave for this word, there was one, buried halfway down the column, which you seized upon as your authority for using this word. But how can you be sure that your reader, also driven to the dictionary, will select that same meaning? The fact that the definition *includes* the meaning you choose to select for your word does not mean that you have used the right word—the word that will make your meaning clear to the reader. Can you be sure the meaning he attaches to the word is the one you intended?

We can illustrate this point by the following example:

> A statement of account is forwarded when the copies are furnished to a *proper* applicant.

The word *proper*, as the writer used it, means *duly authorized*. The dictionary, however, lists many other definitions, such as *well-behaved* or *fit*. Will the taxpayer reading this sentence understand what we intended this word to mean?

There is no question in the minds of Revenue employees what is meant when it is said that a tax is *abated*, but the taxpayer may not know whether his tax has been *partially reduced* or *entirely forgiven*. The dictionary will not help him, for he can find both meanings there; if there is nothing in our writing to hint which meaning he should choose, he can only fall back on his imagination to grasp the meaning. It is only fair to the reader to make unmistakably clear the meaning we wish a word to communicate.

There are other words which have specialized meanings for us. The law *precludes*, we write; and the uninformed reader may wonder whether we mean *impede, shut up,* or *forbid*. When we hold an action in *abeyance*, we *suspend* it; but abeyance can also mean *suppression*—and perhaps does mean just that to the reader. We say the taxpayer may, at his *election*, compute his tax in one of two ways; and *election* may, to some, have only a connotation of voting booths and political candidates. When we say the statute of limitations has been *tolled*, we are using the word *tolled* in a sense unfamiliar to many readers. These words, although clear to us, may not convey to the reader the meaning we intend.

We cannot be sure that even ordinary words—those unrelated to our work—always say what we think they do. For instance, *to comprehend* means *to understand*, but it also means *to include*.

>He comprehends (understands) the contents of this text.
>This course comprehends (includes) 10 texts.

How many words can you name which have only a single meaning? Because most words have multiple meanings, we must recognize the problem of selecting the one which will most nearly express our meaning. Exactness in words is difficult to achieve; we can be only roughly accurate.

75 Economy With Words

Why should we be economical with words? Why, when there are so many words in the world, should we work to save a few of them? Economy of words makes the meaning of a piece of writing clearer to the reader; he does not have to search through a heap of meaningless, repetitive phrases to find a clue to what the writer is saying. When we say that the Government writer should strive for economy with words, this does not mean that he should be stingy or miserly, writing in a style used in telegraphic messages; dropping such words as *a*, *an*, *the*, and *I*, as we do in telegrams, makes a memorandum or letter harder to read.

Economizing with words is a matter of compression rather than one of omission; it is packing the same (or more) meaning into a smaller unit to save your reader's time and to better your chances of communicating what you have to say.

Do not be so economical with words that your letters or memorandums are skeltons, shivering in the bare bones of their outlines. Use the words you need, but do not be afraid to cut down on the unnecessary words, some of the high-sounding phrases that through habit have become a part of government writing, the padding that covers the real meaning, the long "windups" with which we start a letter, a paragraph, or a sentence.

The cure for much of our wordiness is simple: *Economize.* Cut out groups of words and substitute one or two words.

One small connecting word can do the work of three or four words:

What we write	What we mean
until such time as	until
with regard to	about
with reference to	about
in view of the fact that	because, although
in the amount of	for
on the occasion of	when
for the purpose of	for
prior to	before
subsequent to	after
in the event that	if
at the present time	now
along the lines of	like
during such time as	while

Verbs can turn into full-blown phrases under the hand of even an inexperienced Government writer. Watch your verbs. Make them work. Don't bury them this way:

make inquiry concerning	ask about
he is of the opinion	he believes
it is our understanding that	we understand
give consideration to	consider
in compliance with your request	as you requested
afford an opportunity	let, permit
appreciate it if you would furnish	appreciate your furnishing

Sometimes whole clauses can be reduced to one or two words:

Enclosed is your application, *which has been approved.*
Enclosed is your *approved* application.

Information *which is of a confidential nature.*
Confidential information.

The information was given to Mr. Black, *in view of the fact that he is the chairman of the committee.*
The information was given to Mr. Black, *committee chairman.*

Doublets are phrases which say the same thing twice, as "entirely complete." Initially these phrases may have been attempts to achieve emphasis, balance, or euphony; but their use today stamps us as habit writers. If you stopped to think about it, would you write "important essentials" or "necessary essentials"? If something is essential, it *is* necessary and important. Don't waste your words on these doublets. What others can you add to the list from your own writing?

ask a question	ask
carbon copy of	carbon of *or* copy of
consensus of opinion	consensus
entirely complete	complete
first began to	began
first and foremost	first
still remains	remains
repeat again	repeat
strict accuracy	accuracy

We can save words and sharpen our writing by lopping off some of the stock phrases used at the beginnings of sentences. When we use these "windups," it is as if we backed off to take a running jump at a sentence; but we back off so far that we lose the impetus to jump when we get there.

Your attention is directed to the fact that these reports are due on the 15th of the month. (Begin "These reports . . . .")

It should be noted that the taxpayer failed to sign his return. (Omit italicized part.)

For your guidance and information there are enclosed *herewith* several samples of the forms. (There are enclosed . . . or, Several samples of the forms are . . .)

Examination of records of this office reveals that the case was closed last month. (Or, "Our records show that . . .")

Don't smother your reader with wordiness. Trim away excess words from your writing; cut away the underbrush of "with reference to's" and "in the event that's." This paring down of words is not the string-saving type of economizing; rather, it is recognizing the power of words and the value of your reader's time. Your writing will be clearer and easier to understand; you will also find that it becomes more and more challenging to find the exact phrase that says precisely and concisely what you mean.

76 Idiomatic Uses of Words

An idiom is an expression peculiar to a language. It may be ungrammatical or illogical, but through usage it has become an accepted part of the language. If you have studied a foreign language, you no doubt recall grappling with lists of idioms, ways of saying things that defied all the rules of grammar you had learned. If we use the expression "to catch a cold" or "look up an old friend," we are speaking idiomatic English.

The most common error made in using idioms comes from using the wrong preposition with a noun, adjective, or verb. Notice the difference in meaning each preposition gives to the word *agree:*

>   agree in (an opinion, a characteristic)
>   agree on (a plan)
>   agree to (a proposal)
>   agree with (a person)
>   agreeable to

We may write for pages with all the idioms matched to their correct prepositions. But use one incorrect preposition, and you are sure to hear about it. The use of the incorrect word distracts the reader and interferes with his clear comprehension of what you are saying.

A list of all the idiomatic phrases comparable to this example would be impractical. However, some of the idiomatic uses of words that cause Revenue writers trouble are included in the Writer's Guide to Current Usage attached to this course. For a check on any idiomatic use, the best reference is the unabridged dictionary.

77   *Words That Antagonize*

The oldtime westerner could say to his adversary, "When you say that word, SMILE!" Unfortunately, we cannot express in our written communications the gestures and inflections that make the difference between what we say and what we mean: we are dependent upon the written word to carry the message for us. Perhaps it is not always possible to smile about tax matters; but it *is* possible to choose words in writing about such matters that do not make the wrong impression on or antagonize our readers. Perhaps we have never realized that some of the words so commonly used in Government writing may be fighting words to those who receive them.

No one likes to be told that he has made a mistake. We may be trying only to be very exact when we use some of the following terms, but the reader is likely to miss that fact entirely and see only that he is being blamed:

>you misunderstood
>your undated letter
>you failed to enclose
>your error

(Some of the misunderstanding and failure and error may have been our fault, too; perhaps our instructions were not clear.)

With one word we can cast doubt on our correspondent's or reader's statement or intentions:

>the return you *claim* you filed
>the *alleged* (or *so-called*) proof you present
>we *infer* that you mean

Sometimes in our efforts to write in the impersonal style found in Government correspondence, we use words that have a pompous or patronizing sound. By inserting a phrase like "of course" or a word like "obviously" or "undoubtedly," we can change the whole tone of a sentence, giving the impression of talking down to the reader as if we questioned his ability to understand. If we begin a sentence, "It stands to reason," "we would like to point out," "we call your attention to the fact," or "we are sure you can see," we are by our choice of words laying the groundwork for poor public relations.

Often paraphrases of regulations tend to follow the language of the law, and the result is an arbitrary, unyielding statement. "The return *shall be filed* on or before . . . ." "Since the burden of proof is on the taxpayer, *you are to submit* . . . ." A choice of different words to soften these statements would in no way change the mandatory legal requirement; less blunt words could, however, help the taxpayer-reader to accept the requirement with better grace.

The coldly impersonal style of much Government writing can give readers the impression of correspondence written by robots. Long sentences in the third person and the passive voice only strengthen this impression. The following paragraph illustrates the indifference and bureaucratic tone which antagonizes many readers. Would *you* like to receive a letter containing this paragraph?

As you were previously informed, the "X" Administration is charged with determining the extent to which claimants are eligible for benefits under the Blank Act, as amended. Accordingly, the possibility of administrative action to include in your wage records for benefit purposes any of the amounts received by you from the companies referred to is a question for consideration by that Administration.

We might comment on the words that make sparks fly. "As you were previously informed" needs only the addition of the word, "Stupid," to emblazon our meaning. "Claimants"—not you, not people. "Eligible" and "possibility" make the chances of your winning seem very remote. "Administrative action" might mean anything. "A question for consideration by that Administration" is like the kiss of death.

Words can attract or repel readers. Most readers generally like such words as *home* and *mother,* and dislike those which have an unpleasant connotation, such as *death* and *taxes.* If we can substitute for a negative word one to which people react favorably, we are building good public relations.

Most people like these words:

ability	guarantee	reliable
achieve	helpful	service
advantage	liberal	truth
benefit	industrious	useful
comprehensive	judgment	you
determined	please	
economy	reasonable	

They generally dislike these:

alibi	exaggerate	prejudiced
allege	hardship	ruin
blame	impossible	standstill
complaint	insolvent	unfortunate
deadlock	liable	waste
discredit	oversight	wrong

Tone, like some personal qualities, is hard to define. A piece of writing has good tone or it hasn't. And it is mainly our choice of words that determines tone. We need empathy, or the ability to know how others think and feel, if our writing is to have the right tone; but we also need a knowledge of and an appreciation for words to express this feeling.

78 Words That Are Impersonal

Whether we write letters, memorandums, or reports, they are written *to* people *by* people. This fact may never be suspected, however, because much government writing is wholly impersonal and live human beings are never mentioned. Programs are formulated, taxes are collected, and reports are made; but we never realize from our writing that *people* are doing these things. It is true that many of the subjects covered in our writing are abstract or technical and should be discussed impersonally; at the same time, however, it is possible to humanize our writing a little without detracting from its dignity.

Of course we cannot always say "I believe" or "I think" when we are writing as representatives of the Service. We need not, however, hide behind such phrases as "It is believed," "It may be stated by this office," "It is requested that your amended return be filed at once," "It is provided by law," etc. Instead, make the verbs active; and if it is not a violation of security or policy, say *who* believes, *who* states, etc. "*We* believe." "*This office* may state." "*Please* file the amended return at once." "*The law* provides . . . ."

The first line to be filled in on a tax return is the name of the taxpayer, yet often we write about the taxpayer as if that line did not exist. It is much more specific to say "Mr. Jones"—or even "this taxpayer"—instead of "the subject taxpayer" or "the instant taxpayer." We have been fairly successful in eliminating from our correspondence such opening statements as "Yours of the third instant received and contents noted." Those openings have whiskers, we say. They date the Service—make a bad impression on the public. Yet we continue to say "the subject taxpayer" or "the instant taxpayer," expressions which also connote whiskers. If we are writing *to* the "instant or subject taxpayer," the Service will not suffer if we use the direct address, "you."

A familiar legal term in our work is "the taxpayer and his spouse." In this use, we have no quarrel with the use of the word "spouse." Because it can mean either husband or wife, it is a convenient carry-all sort of word for formal writing. But when we are writing *to* (not about) Mr. Jones, we may use the word *wife*, and if we are writing to Mrs. Jones, we are correct in speaking of her *husband* or *Mr. Jones*. By clinging to the formal legal usage, we are making Government writing stilted and impersonal.

Another word we use to hide behind is "incumbent." The use of this word in internal documents is perfectly proper; we use comparable technical terms when we are writing for readers within the Service. When we are writing for readers outside the Service, however, we should avoid using the term "incumbent." And then there are the countless other *people*, taxpayers, applicants, claimants, personnel. If we are writing *to* (or about) any of these groups, it is better to use specific names, titles, or descriptions instead of lumping these people together in a general category. But, you may say, this makes more words and a longer piece of writing. If by the addition of extra words, we make the meaning clearer, the paragraph easier to read, and our message more palatable to the reader, we have not wasted words.

Readability increases in direct proportion to the number of personal words used; writing that is impersonal is hard to read. We should not, of course, switch our style of writing to match that of Madison Avenue or the breezy familiarity of some sales letters; we should, however, recognize the fact that there are situations where a stiff, formal style is inappropriate. In these cases we should try to write simply and directly, in a person-to-person style, remembering that our readers, too, are people, and that wearing a high silk hat does not necessarily make the wearer dignified.

79   Overuse of Adjectives and Adverbs

Adjectives and adverbs are words which add emphasis to our writing—the words which underline what we are saying. There is a place in writing for such intensives, we all agree; but when we are writing for Uncle Sam we must know when and where to use words that emphasize.

We may in all good faith think that the words we use are helping our cause, but they may be just as diligently working against us. High on the list of such turncoats are the adjectives and adverbs. Overuse of these words can defeat our purposes; one adjective too many or a poorly selected adverb, and our readers begin to suspect our sincerity and honorable intentions.

Watch Your Words

Reports and memorandums must be factual and free from bias. It is very easy for one adjective or one adverb to "slant" the writing to the side we may want our readers to see. For example, you might write, "He asserted his claim stubbornly (or bitterly or fanatically)." Would the reader have the same impression if you changed the adverbs to "tenaciously, vigorously, zealously"? Watch your use of such modifiers in reports; use them sparingly, for you will find them saying things you never meant them to say.

We want our letters to be factual, of course; but we also want them to have a ring of sincerity. Too much reliance on adjectives and adverbs will not give them this quality; in fact, these words can destroy the sincerity you tried to express. Words to be watched are "very" and "quite." "It is *quite* clear" may mean "fairly clear" or "exceptionally clear"; it may also detract from the tone of your writing by implying that you are talking down to your reader.

The words *very, highly,* and *somewhat* (as in "very glad," "highly successful," and "somewhat uncertain") add little as intensives, but they have the potential to exaggerate the importance of facts. When we say we "greatly appreciate" the opportunity to review an application, which has received "careful consideration," we weaken our statement by the use of these intensives. The words *appreciate* and *consideration* can stand alone without the help of crutch words which may make the reader suspect your sincerity.

"At the earliest practicable date" is a word-wasting phrase, as is "to the fullest extent possible." Furthermore, overuse has worn these expressions thin; no amount of screaming by the adjectives can turn them into attention-getting phrases. Piling up descriptive words will not make your sentences more effective; it will only make your readers say with Hamlet, "Methinks the lady doth protest too much." Perhaps the government writer would say, "It is the opinion of the undersigned that too great emphasis in expression in written communications causes certain questions to be raised relative to the veracity of the statements and the intentions of those uttering same." Or how would you say it?

Once we have recognized the power of words and consciously try to increase our knowledge of words, we are started on the way to better writing.

TEXT 10

The Effective Sentence

80	Introduction
81	What makes a sentence effective?
82	An effective sentence is planned and organized
83	An effective sentence is clear
84	Putting grammar to work to make sentences clear
84a	Use connectives as grammatical signposts.
84b	Delegate subordinate thoughts to subordinate clauses
84c	The comma splice
84d	Avoid dangling modifiers
84e	Don't misplace modifiers
84f	Complete your comparisons
84g	Don't change your point of view
84h	Avoid split constructions
84i	Avoid faulty reference of pronouns
85	Using readability factors to make sentences clear
85a	Use language the reader understands
85b	Shun gobbledygook
85c	Use parallel constructions
85d	Use itemization
85e	Don't overuse the passive voice
86	An effective sentence is concise
86a	Economy of expression
86b	Avoid the too-full sentence
87	An effective sentence is expressed in an appropriate style
87a	Formal and informal styles
87b	Use variety in sentence types
87c	Use variety in sentence length
87d	Put important ideas in emphatic positions
88	Sentence identification table
89	The sentence and the paragraph
	A note in conclusion

TEXT 10

The Effective Sentence

80 Introduction

Throughout this course we have been trying to lay a solid foundation for effective writing. In doing so we have refreshed our knowledge of grammar, knowing that grammar provides an essential knowledge of words, word order, and word relationships. In this final text we will discuss what it is that makes writing effective and how the grammatical tools we have been acquiring (or polishing up) can make it easier to write effective sentences.

What do we mean by effective writing? Like some of the other abstract words we studied in Text 9, "effective" probably has as many meanings as there are people using it. We know that making writing effective does not mean adding superlatives, underscoring words, or sprinkling exclamation marks liberally throughout our letters and memorandums; neither can we say that because a sentence is grammatically correct it is also effective. It is strange, but true, that some of the worst sentences in Government correspondence contain no errors in grammar; but they are not effective.

From the several definitions we might list for an effective sentence, can we agree that a sentence (or letter or memorandum) is effective if it accomplishes the purpose for which it was intended in a way that does credit to the writer and to the Service?

Writing does not accomplish its purpose unless it transfers a thought from the mind of the writer to the mind of an unknown reader. The Revenue writer must select the right words from the thousands in our language and use them in such a way that his message will be clear to his reader and properly reflect the attitude of the Service toward the taxpaying public—an attitude of courtesy (even in the face of discourtesy) and of both firmness and fairness. But this is only one phase of the problem. Rarely does a Government writer write to *a* reader; instead, he writes to a *reader audience*—his immediate supervisor, perhaps a reviewer, the top man in the office, other offices to which information copies will be sent, and—ultimately—the person to whom the letter or memorandum is addressed. To accomplish its purpose our writing not only must be *clear* to the "ultimate" reader and an effective means of expressing the writer's thought; it must also be clear to, and meet the standards for effectiveness set by, the "reader audience."

81 What Makes a Sentence Effective?

Unfortunately, there is no pat formula for making sentences effective. If there were, the man who came up with it could make a fortune; for all around us are writers looking for the sure way—and, if possible, the painless way—to make their sentences effective.

But we cannot say, "Take the following ingredients: one part judgment, two parts careful arrangement, a half measure of grammar, a full measure of common sense—and the result will *always* be an effective sentence."

Most writers—and readers—will agree, however, that these four ingredients are necessary for effective sentences. Perhaps they will not call them by just these names; they may say, instead, that to be effective a sentence must be

(1) Planned and organized
(2) Clear to the reader
(3) Concise (but not abrupt)
(4) Expressed in appropriate style

Under each of these headings we are going to discuss guidelines or principles of writing, that will help you write more effective sentences. By applying the rules you have learned in earlier texts, you will write sentences that are *grammatically correct*. And because they are grammatically correct, they will be logically developed; for grammar requires a sentence to have a logical organization with its parts in proper order and in proper relationship one to another. You have learned about the signposts (the words which coordinate and subordinate) which show the relative values of the parts of the sentence, the words which say, "This is the main idea; this thought and that thought are of secondary importance." Other guides—for example, tense or punctuation—point out the relationship between parts of the sentence. In our

The Effective Sentence

study of grammar we have learned about connectives and linking words which tie thoughts together into unified sentences, paragraphs, and larger units of writing.

This text, then, summarizes these principles and shows the writer how to apply them to make his own writing more effective. Don't push these grammatical tools to one side as if you considered them unnecessary and impractical. Few tools will serve you better—if you will let them.

82 An Effective Sentence Is Planned and Organized

Did you ever hear about the man who jumped on his horse and rode off in four directions at once? He must have been closely related to some writers who tear into the job of writing with the same energy and lack of planning. Like the horseman, they won't get anywhere. Their sentences will not move forward in orderly progress toward a predetermined goal; they will be cluttered and unarranged, trailing ideas and grammatical constructions behind them. Before you write, take time to think. Know where you are going before you start.

Sentences are like icebergs. The words we get on paper—the ice that shows above the water—are only a small part of the whole process of sentence construction. The part that is hidden from sight is many times larger. Under every clear sentence is a mass of clear thinking. For no sentence can be clear if it is based on thoughts that are vague, rambling, or disorganized.

A writer's first task, then, is to decide what he wants to say—what his goal is. He looks at this idea and that, rejecting those that are immaterial and selecting those he considers most important. He arranges these ideas in a logical pattern, showing their relationship; he does not let minor ideas shoulder their way into places properly belonging to major thoughts, nor does he let major thoughts stand stiffly side by side without any links to show him they are related. He completes his plan before he starts to write, for he knows that clear sentences do not just grow—they result from planning and organization.

As a matter of intelligent self-interest, the writer does not leave it to the reader to determine the goal of the sentence or to sort out and arrange the ideas so that they make sense. He himself decides upon the goal and arranges ideas grammatically according to their importance so that he can get his ideas across to the reader. If you write for the Internal Revenue Service, these duties are as much a part of your job as if they were spelled out in your job sheet.

83   An Effective Sentence Is Clear

The problem of how to communicate clearly is not one which you alone have discovered. Confucius knew about it a long time ago; perhaps what he said about it could apply to your office today:

> "If language is not correct, then what is said is not what is meant; if what is said is not what is meant, then what ought to be done remains undone."

Sentence clarity begins with sentence correctness; for we have agreed that grammatical correctness comprises correct word choice, correct word order, and clear word relationships. In the sections that follow we shall see how applying knowledge of grammar can help us write sentences that will be clear to the reader.

84   Putting Grammar To Work To Make Sentences Clear

84a   Use connectives as grammatical signposts

In Text 7 we discussed coordinating, subordinating, and correlative conjunctions and conjunctive adverbs. There we were concerned with the grammatical correctness of these connecting words that show relationship between parts of the sentence. In this text we stress these connectives again because of their importance to the writer who wants to make his writing more effective. They are signals to tell the reader what is coming; they also link the parts of the sentence into the logical pattern you have selected. Watch these signals if you want your writing to be clear; don't signal for a left-hand turn and then blame the reader if he doesn't realize that you meant to stop short.

Coordinating conjunctions and conjunctive adverbs join principal clauses. Use the precise connective to show the relationship of the second clause: there are words that mean addition, contrast, choice, or result.

The Effective Sentence

Coordinating Conjunctions

What they say	*Examples*
AND: The next thought is equal in content and in grammar.	I wrote to him, AND he wrote to me.
BUT: Stop! The next idea is opposite in thought.	I wrote to him, BUT he did not write to me.
OR: Here is an alternate thought.	You may write to him, OR I will write to him.
FOR: Next comes evidence in support of the first statement.	It must be late, FOR I am hungry.

Conjunctive Adverbs

BESIDES, FURTHERMORE, MOREOVER—add ideas of equal rank.	The applicant does not meet our requirements; FURTHERMORE, his application was not received in time.
HOWEVER, NEVERTHELESS—signal contrasting ideas.	The applicant meets our requirements; HOWEVER, we did not receive his application in time.
OTHERWISE—choice between two ideas.	This applicant lacks a few months' experience; OTHERWISE, he is qualified for the position.
ACCORDINGLY, THEREFORE—express result.	This applicant meets our requirements; ACCORDINGLY, he has been selected for the position.

Correlative Conjunctions

Correlative conjunctions are used in pairs to connect equal constructions. The most common of these pairs are *either—or*, *neither—nor*, *both—and*, *whether—or*, *not only—but also*. After each member of the pair, the same grammatical construction must be used.

Incorrect: He *not only* found shelter *but also* a friendly welcome.
(The first part of the correlative is followed by *found*, a verb; the second, by *welcome*, a noun.)

Better: He found *not only* shelter *but also* a friendly welcome.
He *not only* found shelter *but also* received a friendly welcome.
(In the first example the correlatives are followed by nouns; in the second, by verbs.)

Incorrect: This ruling will interest *both* agents *and* those who pay taxes.
(One member of the correlative is followed by a noun, the other by a clause.)

Better: This ruling will interest *both* agents *and* taxpayers.
(Nouns follow correlatives.)

Incorrect: *Either* fish *or* you can cut bait.
(Both correlatives are followed by verbs; however, one is in the imperative mood and one in the indicative.)

Better: *Either* fish *or* cut bait.
(The verbs following the correlatives are in the same mood.)

84b Delegate subordinate thoughts to subordinate clauses

Suppose we write, "The agent's report, however, reflected additional tax of $25, and it was consequently assessed, and you received a notice for payment of this amount." The reader assumes that all the thoughts are of equal value—we have told him that by our use of *and* connecting the clauses. It is part of your work to decide what part of the sentence should be emphasized, to put that in the main clause, and to delegate the job of expressing secondary thoughts to subordinate clauses and phrases.

As we saw in Text 7, subordinate ideas may be expressed in adverbial and adjective clauses. Still shorter forms are the phrases (prepositional, gerund, participial, and infinitive). Sometimes subordinate ideas can be reduced to a single word instead of to a clause or phrase. The following illustration shows some of the ways our example may be rewritten to convey a unified impression:

If we use—	the sentence would read
ADVERBIAL CLAUSE	*Because* (*since, when, inasmuch as,* etc.) *the agent reported additional tax due of $25,* this amount was consequently assessed and you received a notice for payment.
ADJECTIVE CLAUSE	You received a notice for payment of $25, *which is the amount of additional tax assessed on the basis of the agent's report.*
PHRASES	*On the basis of the agent's report showing additional tax of $25,* you received a notice for payment of this amount.

84c The comma splice

Among the most common enemies of sentence clarity is the comma splice (or comma fault). The comma splice occurs when two main clauses are joined by a comma without a coordinating conjunction; for example, "Most State and local taxes are deductible, Federal taxes are not."

We can revise this sentence in any of four ways:

(1) By connecting the main clauses with a coordinating conjunction (*and, but, for, or, nor, yet*):

   Most State and local taxes are deductible, *but* Federal are not.

(2) By using a semicolon instead of a comma:

   Most State and local taxes are deductible; Federal taxes are not.

(3) By writing each clause as a separate sentence:

   Most State and local taxes are deductible.   Federal taxes are not.

(4) By subordinating one of the clauses.

   Although most State and local taxes are deductible, Federal taxes are not.

The comma splice is more than misuse of a punctuation mark; it is a failure to show clearly the relationship between the two clauses.

84d Avoid dangling modifiers

A clear sentence is logically sound and grammatically correct; only when grammar and logic work together can clear writing result. Because we are dependent upon the order of words to show their relationship to other parts of the sentence, we must make sure that the word arrangement makes sense logically and grammatically. When we are pursuing an idea and writing furiously as if we feared that first fine careless rapture might escape forever—watch out. A misplaced phrase, a dangling modifier, a faulty reference of a pronoun, and the fine burst of writing has become ridiculous.

Some of the best examples of meaning one thing and saying another come from dangling modifiers—words, phrases, or clauses which cannot logically and grammatically attach to the proper sentence element. No matter where modifiers occur in a sentence, they are attracted grammatically to the nearest substantive as iron filings are attracted to a magnet, and logic be hanged.

Dangling modifiers are usually phrases (participial, gerund, infinitive, or prepositional). They may be corrected by the addition of words or by the change of structure so that the reader may associate the modifier with the logical substantive.

Participial phrase:

>Following the supervisor's instructions, the work was soon finished.

The work was not following the orders; rewrite to show *who* was following the orders, as "Following the supervisor's instructions, *the clerks* soon finished the work."

Gerund phrase:

>After sitting in the outer office for an hour, the interviewer arrived.

It was not the interviewer who had been sitting. Revise to "After *we had been sitting* in the outer office for an hour, the interviewer arrived."

Infinitive phrase:

>*To get* the most out of the course, a definite *time* should be set aside for study.

Logically, *to get* cannot modify *time*. Correct to read, "*To get* the most out of the course, *one* should set aside a definite time for study."

Prepositional phrase:

>I talked to the agent who is sitting at the desk *without a coat.*

It was not the desk which was coatless. Correct by putting the prepositional phrase at the beginning of the sentence, near the word it modifies.

84e Don't misplace modifiers

A modifier is sometimes placed in a sentence so that it can be taken to modify two words, and the reader is left to guess which of two

The Effective Sentence

meanings may be intended. The following sentence illustrates such a "squinting" modifier. "The agent assured me *when the papers came* he would do it." This clause should be moved from its present location to a place where it will say exactly what it it means. Does the sentence mean, "*When the papers came*, the agent assured me he would do it," or "The agent assured me he would do it *when the papers came*"?

84f Complete your comparisons

In the text on Modifiers we studied problems of comparison and saw how to correct mistakes arising from incomplete comparisons. This subject is also discussed in this text because incomplete comparisons make sentences both foggy and illogical.

Many incomplete comparisons leave the reader wondering which of two possible meanings you wanted to convey. If you say, "I like peanut butter sandwiches better than Jimmy," you may mean, "I like peanut butter sandwiches better than I like Jimmy," or "I like peanut butter sandwiches better than Jimmy likes them." While you may never have occasion to use this exact example in Revenue correspondence, you will find that it will pay to check every comparison you start to write. Finish the job so that there will be no doubt what you mean.

If we say a cigarette "contains less tar and nicotine," we have not made a complete statement. We are leaving it to the reader to guess the second term of the comparison. Less tar and nicotine by what standard of comparison? Comparison with another brand of cigarettes or with all other brands? It is your job, as a writer, to spare the reader the indecision that invariably attaches to an incomplete comparison.

A sentence may contain a structurally complete comparison, but the incongruity of the two things compared may make the sentence illogical.

    Example: The streets and houses of my town are nothing exceptional, but are just like any other country town.
        (*Streets and houses* are not logically comparable to *country town*.)
    Better: The streets and houses of my town are nothing exceptional, but are just like *those of* any other country town.

Example: He thought his playing sounded like Paderewski.
(His playing may be compared to the playing of Paderewski, but not to Paderewski himself.)

Better: He thought his playing sounded like *that of* Paderewski.

84g Don't change your point of view

Both clarity and the reader suffer when we switch subjects in mid-sentence without warning. Errors of this type may be no more than annoyances or distractions to the reader; perhaps they merely slow up his thought. On the other hand, they can bring his reading to a complete standstill while he realigns your sentence to get its meaning.

Maintain one point of view unless there is a reason for changing.

Shift in subject:	From her desk *the clerk looked* across the room and near the door *stood the files*.
Better:	From her desk *the clerk looked* across the room and near the door *saw* the files.
Shift in voice:	Several bank deposits *were analyzed* and the agent *found* the answer to his problem.
Better:	The agent *analyzed* several bank deposits and *found* the answer to his problem.
Shift in tense:	The agent *has evaluated* the information and *came* to the conclusion that investigation is not warranted.
Better:	The agent *has evaluated* the information and *has come*, etc.

or

The agent *evaluated* the information and *came*, etc.

84h Avoid split constructions

When we split closely related parts of a sentence, such as a subject and verb, a verb phrase, or parallel parts of a sentence, we cloud the meaning. If we want to emphasize some part of the structural unit, it is, of course, permissible to split the construction. As a general rule, however, avoid splitting sentence elements that belong together.

The following example shows how a sentence can mark time instead of moving forward—all because the subject and verb got separated in the crowding phrases:

The Internal Revenue Service has held that nonresident alien *participants* of the Exchange Visitor Program, under State Department sponsorship, especially those employed in hospitals as interns, resident physicians, and nurses who perform services which are of material benefit to the hospital and receive substantially the same amounts as paid to citizens performing similar services, *are* subject to tax on the income . . . .

84i Avoid faulty reference of pronouns

When we substitute a pronoun for a noun, we must make clear to the reader the word for which the pronoun stands. When a pronoun seems to refer to any one of two or more antecedents, an ambiguous statement results.
There are three methods of eliminating ambiguous reference:

(1) By changing from indirect to direct statement.

> The supervisor told the revenue agent that *his* post of duty was being changed.
> (Whose post of duty? Revise to, "The supervisor told the revenue agent, 'Your post of duty will be changed.'")

(2) By repeating the antecedent.

> Our job was to remove the labels from the old bottles and wash *them*.
>
> Better: Our job was to remove the labels from the old bottles and wash the bottles.

(3) By putting the pronoun closer to the antecedent.

> The President appointed Senator Moore as chairman of the new committee because *he* was interested in the committee's work.
> This might mean that the President was interested in the work. It could also mean that the Senator was interested. Write the sentence to show the exact meaning you wish to convey.
> The President, who was interested in the committee's work, appointed Senator Moore as chairman.
>
> The President appointed as chairman Senator Moore, who is interested in the committee's work.

A pronoun should not refer to a whole preceding statement or idea. A summarizing word should be added or the sentence revised to eliminate the pronoun.

> He missed the bus, *which* kept him from being on time for his appointment.
>
> Grammatically, *which* appears to modify *bus;* logically, it modifies the whole idea in the main clause. We may correct the sentence by inserting a summarizing word or by recasting the sentence.

He missed the bus, *an unfortunate occurrence* which kept him from being on time for his appointment.

Because he missed the bus, he was not on time for his appointment.

85 Use "Readability Factors" To Make Sentences Clear

Suppose you have produced a paragraph made up of sentences that are models of correctness—any grammarian would commend you for them. The minor ideas are properly subordinated; the modifiers are neatly tucked in with no participles dangling; the sentences move vigorously along toward your predetermined goal. And yet—when you ask someone in the office to read it, you find that this gem of correctness just doesn't do the job of getting your idea across. What can be done?

Professional writers who have studied this problem have found that certain factors make writing readable, or understandable, to the lay reader. The Revenue writer (who is also a paid professional writer with the job of making complex tax ideas understandable) can profit by these findings to get his message across. In this section we will discuss some of these factors that are applicable to Revenue writing.

85a Use language the reader understands

You have received a letter from a taxpayer asking a routine question about filing a return. Would you answer that letter in a foreign language? By doing so you might give the impression of great learning, but you would not have answered the letter.

Text 9 discusses some words which, although routine to us, are as incomprehensible to the taxpayer as if we wrote in a foreign language. Taxation is a complex subject filled with difficult legal and technical terms which must be explained or interpreted to taxpayers in a firm, fair, and reasonable way. These legal and technical terms are the jargon of our business. It is easy for us to write in the mother tongue of Revenue; but we must remember that not all our readers speak this language. Clarity, as well as readability, requires us to put our message into everyday language.

If our only sin against clarity were using the jargon of our business, we might be forgiven. But we are also guilty of writing a language that is unintelligible outside Government service: the language of gobbledygook. Call it governmentese, federalese, jargon—these names describe writing that is wordy, pompous, and inflated. The taxpayer receiving a letter written in this language has to hunt for the answer to his question with a dictionary in his hand and faith in his heart that Uncle Sam will treat him fairly.

856 Shun gobbledygook

Gobbledygook is a monster with many heads; many characteristics of ineffective writing lumped loosely under one general descriptive title go to make up this kind of writing.

Gobbledygook never uses one word if it can use two or more. "If" becomes "in the event that." "Because" becomes "in view of the fact that." Even the little word "to" is blown up to "for the purpose of." Instead of saying, "This potential loss will be partially offset," gobbledygook inflates it to "It may be said that this potential loss will be offset in part." Gobbledygook turns "during our examination for July and August" into "during the course of our examination for the months of July and August."

Following the theory that if one word is good, more are better, gobbledygook delights in building big words out of little ones:

substantial portion	means	large part
visitation		visit
utilization		use
accomplished		done
presently		now

Gobbledygook does not recognize concrete, specific words. It uses abstract terms, generalizations, and roundabout ways of identifying its subject.

Gobbledygook has but one voice—the passive. Verbs never act—they are turned into weak nouns or shunted into the passive voice. "Some improvement was effected in the work area as a result of installation of a new lighting system" is the way gobbledygook tells us that installing a new lighting system improved the work area.

Gobbledygook hides the real subject and weakens the verb. In the sentence, "Refusal of employment of women workers is common on the part of employers," the word that should be carrying the burden of the sentence is disguised as a noun and made the grammatical subject of the sentence—*refusal*. The real subject—what we are talking about—is *employers*. What this sentence really means is "Employers often refuse to employ women." If you were required to twist sentences out of shape this way, you would rightly feel that your supervisor was expecting too much. Yet after only a short exposure to Government writing we have no trouble writing, "The court requested that an arrangement should be effected by the taxpayer for the payment of the tax liability prior to sentencing." In straightforward language we would say, "The court requested the taxpayer to pay his tax before being sentenced." For a more complete discussion of this aspect of jargon, the student should refer to Effective Revenue Writing 2.

No doubt your circle of readers within the Government will understand your letter written in gobbledygook. They may even praise it, suggesting a change of phrase here or there to give a more effective sound; but think how unintelligible it may be to the taxpayer receiving it. If it is not clear to him, your attempt at communication has failed.

85c Use parallel constructions

Long sentences are almost a trademark of Government writing. They are the source of one of the most common complaints against writers for Uncle Sam; however, long sentences would not be at all objectionable if they were clear. To help us write sentences which are clear in spite of their length, we have one of the most effective tools in writing—parallelism. By putting logically parallel thoughts in grammatically parallel constructions, whether words, phrases, or clauses, parallelism helps the writer to express his thought effectively; and it helps the reader to grasp the thought.

The basic rule governing parallelism is simple: like ideas must be expressed in like form. Perhaps in a civil service examination you have been asked to pick out the one item in a group which is unlike the other members. In the series, "Flower—leaves—branches—monkey," you know that the discordant item is the monkey. If you read the sentence, "He likes to swim, rowing, and skating," you can easily spot the word that is out of step. Make all items parallel—either *to swim, to row, and to skate*, or *swimming, rowing, and skating*.

> Incorrect: He marched to the front of the room, *shivering* inwardly, but *he hid* his fears with a calm appearance.
> (The participle *shivering* and the clause beginning *he hid* are not parallel.)
>
> Better: He marched to the front of the room, *shivering* inwardly but *hiding* his fears with a calm appearance.
> (The participles *shivering* and *hiding* are parallel.)

Incorrect: We are looking for a candidate *with a knowledge of accounting* and *who is willing to accept assignment in Washington.*
(The phrase "with a knowledge of accounting" does not parallel the clause "who is willing to accept assignment in Washington.")

Better: We are looking for a candidate *who has a knowledge of accounting* and *who is willing to accept assignment in Washington.*
(The clauses introduced by *who* are parallel.)

Once you have begun a parallel construction, follow through with it. If we write, "Through this course in public speaking the student learns to think on his feet, to maintain poise, and better enunciation," we mislead the reader. He expects a third item similar to *to think* and *to maintain;* when he does not find it, he experiences a slight jolt, comparable perhaps to missing the stair step he thought was there.

Signals

Parallel constructions usually call attention to themselves by the similarity of words which introduce them—prepositions, conjunctions, the infinitive sign *to*, and auxiliary verbs. Don't be afraid to repeat these signals. The reader relies on them to point out parallelism; furthermore, repetition is part of the secret of effective parallel structure.

Example: I do not remember being taught anything *about* diagramming sentences and *about* sentence structure.

Secretaries may be expected *to* receive callers, *to* answer telephones, and *to* do miscellaneous clerical work.

85d Use itemization

In the Internal Revenue Service we have many opportunities to use another form of parallelism—itemization. Many of our sentences are unwieldy, perhaps because of their length, content, or legal nature. We tell taxpayers that they must file returns if they meet certain conditions, subject, of course, to certain exceptions to the rule. The resultant overstuffed sentence is routine reading for us; for the taxpayer it is more likely to be hopelessly confusing. If we itemize the list of conditions to be met, we are making our instructions more readable.

Example: However, if your itemized deductions total less than 10 percent of your Adjusted Gross Income, it will usually be to your advantage to—
(1) claim the Standard Deduction;

(2) determine your tax by use of the tax table as explained below;
(3) file your return on Form 1040A as discussed in Chapter 2.

The basic rule for parallelism is illustrated here—express like ideas in like form. In this case, each item in the series begins with an infinitive (*claim, determine, file*). If you begin your itemization with a noun, begin all the other items with nouns. If you use a participial phrase or a brief sentence for a first item, follow through in the same way with the remaining items.

85e Don't overuse the passive voice

Earlier texts in this course have stressed the importance of using strong live verbs in the active voice. We are emphasizing that point again, because, generally speaking, Government writers overwork the passive voice, as we have seen in our comments on gobbledygook. It is true that there are places and uses for the passive voice: if we want to emphasize that the action is performed by an unknown person or thing or that the recipient of the action should be stressed, we are justified in making the verb passive. However, the passive voice makes it harder for the reader to understand what the writer is trying to tell him. Which of these two examples does the better job of getting its meaning across? Which is the more readable?

> The matter *was referred* to the Director at Bigtown for his comment, and under date of September 6 this office *was advised* that as the result of a conference with the official having jurisdiction over the area in which Crossroads Junction *is located*, it *has been concluded* that it would be impractical to maintain regular office hours at Crossroads Junction.

> We *asked* the Director at Bigtown for his comment, and on September 6 *learned* that officials in the Crossroads Junction area *had conferred* with him and *recommended* against maintaining regular office hours at Crossroads Junction.

86 *An Effective Sentence Is Concise*

An effective sentence saves the reader's time and patience by saying directly and concisely what it means. A measure against which we might check our sentences is the question, "Does this sentence contain only essential facts?" If the taxpayer asks whether he must file a return under circumstances peculiar to his case, we sometimes tend to put too many facts in our answer: we try to cover *all* the possibilities that might occur instead of keeping our sights trained on the one question we are answering.

Perhaps concise writing has its beginnings in the planning and organizing stage. If we think the problem through, we can see more clearly how to separate the essentials from the trimming, the basic line of action from possible contingencies. Write to meet the needs of your reader; though it may be a struggle, omit those "if" clauses that show your expert grasp of the subject but that burden the reader unnecessarily.

86a Economy of expression

Writing cannot be effective if its message is buried beneath a mass of useless, repetitive words. In Text 9 we discussed word economy; in this text we have seen that word wasting is one of the characteristics of gobbledygook.

We can make our sentences more concise—and more readable—by cutting out the unnecessary words in introductory statements, in prepositional phrases, and in roundabout grammatical constructions. For example, sentences beginning with *There is* or *It is* add unnecessary words and detract from conciseness.

Compare these sentences:

> *There is* enclosed a copy of Mr. Doe's report.
> A copy of Mr. Doe's report is enclosed.

> *It is* on the fifteenth of the month that this report is due.
> This report is due on the fifteenth of the month.

The introductory words *there* and *it* slow the writing and waste words. If we begin sentence after sentence in this way, the message we hope to communicate loses both vigor and clarity.

Perhaps a word of caution should be added. Prune away the deadwood in your sentences, the beside-the-point information; but do not chop so enthusiastically that you reduce the sentence to a bare stick. Conciseness is not abruptness or curtness; the words that make the difference in the tone of your writing are *not* the unnecessary ones that should be trimmed away. Shorten and sharpen your sentences by planning and organizing them and by omitting words which fatten your writing instead of nourishing it.

866   Avoid the too-full sentence

Many Internal Revenue sentences lack conciseness (and clarity) because they are too full; they try to say too much. Most of these too-full sentences contain more than one thought. Many also include unnecessary words and jargon phrases that lengthen them but add nothing to their meaning.

Two types, in particular, cause most of our trouble:

(1) The sentence filled with legal material, often an indirect quotation from the Code or regulations.

> *For example:*
> It may be stated in general that the income of an estate in process of administration in the courts of a foreign country is taxable as an entity insofar as the income received is from United States sources, irrespective of the fact that the decedent may have been either a nonresident alien or a citizen of the United States and the beneficiaries in the distribution may be either nonresident aliens or citizens or residents of the United States.

(2) The rambling sentence strung together with "and's" and "but's."

> *For example:*
> He subsequently filed an amended return containing a breakdown of these expenses, but the total of such itemized expenses amounted to only $700, and the effective dates of the trips involving this travel, as set forth in the explanation, were very indefinite.

What can be done with the first type of too-full sentence? Several things. We can often make such a sentence clearer and more concise by simply breaking it into shorter, bite-sized pieces. A period and a short space between sentences gives the reader a chance to catch his breath before he starts the next thought. Perhaps the content falls logically into a pattern that suggests itemization—an arrangement that breaks bulk into more readable segments. Legal citations can often be pulled out of the middle of the sentence and put into a separate parenthetical sentence. Exceptions also can be pulled away from the main statement to comprise a separate sentence.

The second type—the rambling sentence—may suffer from nothing more than improper subordination or improper arrangement of ideas. It, too, can often be broken into shorter, bite-sized pieces by substituting a period for a conjunction—or even by using a period and letting the conjunction begin the next sentence.

87 An Effective Sentence Is Expressed in Appropriate Style

The two key words here are *style* and *appropriate*—both hard to define because they are abstract terms that mean different things to different writers. Perhaps a better heading would be "Fit words in fit places," which is the way Jonathan Swift defines style in writing.

As we begin our discussion of appropriate style, we leave solid ground. We leave the security of rules of grammar (and, to some extent, of specific principles of writing) and move to the less precise area of concepts and of judgment. Here we have no precise rules that we can memorize and apply, with the confidence that the result will inevitably be an effective style. We have only *guidelines;* and even they will not help us unless we make full use—at the same time—of all our writing skill, our empathy, and our judgment.

Style, as we have said, is hard to define. It is partly a matter of word choice and partly a matter of word order and word relationships. Style is how we say a thing. But it is more than that. It is a mirror in which *we* are reflected—it reveals something of our judgment, our habits, our capacities, our biases, our understanding of people, as well as our knowledge of what we are writing about.

Style is not something that we may *decide to acquire;* for if we write, we *have* a style. The only decision we need to make is whether we will work at *improving* our style. In making this decision, we must realize that style is not trimming that can be added to writing as a final touch or as a cover for deficiencies; it is built into our writing, revealing our identity as clearly as if we had left our fingerprints on the margin of the page.

And—now—*appropriate* style. What style is *appropriate* for Revenue writing? Here, too, our decision reveals our judgment. Certainly we must put our message in a style that does credit to the Service—a style that is dignified, but not pompous; direct and natural, but not chatty; simple, but not primerlike. Certainly, too, we must fit the style to the type of communication we are writing and to the reader who will receive it. We must know when a formal style is needed and when an informal style would be more effective and more appropriate.

87a   Formal and informal styles

We should recognize the fact that there is no one kind of writing that we can label "Style for Internal Revenue." We can, however, distinguish between the formal and informal style and know when the use of each is appropriate.

A formal style should be used in documents prepared for a wide range of readers—in published material, rulings, top-level correspondence. Following are some of the characteristics of this type of writing:

Word Choice—The words used in formal writing are carefully chosen from a large vocabulary to express the writer's thought with exactness. Many of the words, which may be long, are not of Anglo-Saxon origin, as are those we use in ordinary conversation. Contractions and abbreviations are seldom used. Technical terms are not oversimplified, for discriminating, informed readers will be among those who read this writing.

Sentence Structure—Sentences tend to be long and complex. They are not, however, of the nonstop or too-full variety; they are planned, closely knit, and carefully constructed. Parallelism is used freely, as are connectives and transitional words.

Grammar—The formal style holds to the conservative or purist viewpoint. When there is a choice between two forms or usages, formal English will prefer the conventional. The grammar is meticulously correct, following rules that informal English may gloss over.

Because the formal style occurs more often in written than in oral communications, it can be more polished, more exact, and more elaborate. Although it is dignified, the style is human; in spite of its complex structure, it is unobtrusive and clear.

Much of the ineffective writing in Government comes from striving for but failing to reach the standards of formal English. The result is the ponderous style we call governmentese: it bears the same relationship to formal English as a caricature bears to a portrait. By overemphasizing the very points that make the formal style effective, we bog down in the wordiness of governmentese. The specialized vocabulary of formal English to express an exact meaning becomes in governmentese the overuse of big words with vague meanings. The language becomes stilted; passive verbs and roundabout constructions lengthen the sentences. Grammatically, governmentese may be correct writing; but it is not effective writing.

Complementing the formal style is the informal style, appropriate for replying to questions from taxpayers, for interoffice memorandums, and for issuances within the Service. This style is fundamentally the spoken language of educated people; it is dignified but not stiff; direct and sincere but not chatty or slangy.

Word Choice—The vocabulary of informal English is more nearly that of everyday speech. The words are shorter, more direct, and often less exact than those of formal English. Contractions may be used, as well as vivid idioms.

Sentence Structure—Sentences tend to be shorter and more direct. Loose sentences are the rule instead of the exception, and the construction tends to be less complex.

Grammar—The informal style pays less attention to exact grammatical rules; when there is a choice of usage of words, informal English leans toward the popular choice. Punctuation, too, may be omitted in instances when the formal style would require it.

When it is used effectively, informal English is coherent and fluent, vital and spontaneous. Like the formal style, it too lends itself to caricature in the hands of the careless writer. Its loose sentences may ramble in an unguided fashion; it may be chummy or cliche-ridden; its attempt to be natural can result in artificiality.

Perhaps the difference in these styles can be better explained by example. Suppose you have received a letter written in pencil on rough, lined paper from a taxpayer who wants to know "kin i take off on my income tax for Lovina she is my daughter in law." Your reply should be simple and direct, written to meet the needs of *that* reader. Contrast the style of this reply with that of a policy statement you prepare for the signature of a Treasury official. The difference in the needs of the reader-audience requires a different—a more formal—style. The keyword here—as in most writing—is *appropriate*. Write in a style that is appropriate to your subject and for your reader.

876 Use variety in sentence types

We can make our writing more readable by introducing variety in our sentences. In writing, as in everything else, too much of the same thing is boring. Analyze a paragraph from something you have written recently. Jot down a list of sentence types in the paragraph. What does it look like? Is it, for example, topheavy with simple sentences? Too many short, simple sentences following each other will not make your writing effective; instead, they will do much to produce a style your supervisors may label as "primer stuff." Don't be afraid to use a variety of sentence types—some simple, some compound, some complex. Mix them and match them, as with color combinations.

Express your thoughts in the type of sentence suited to what you are saying. There is no one hard-and-fast way of writing any sentence; there are, however, patterns of arrangement of the words within a sentence which can vary its emphasis, its rhythm, even—at times—its meaning. For example, here are some of the ways of expressing the thought contained in the sentence, "Show me the writing and I will see the man."

Personal: You show your character in your writing.

Conditional: If you will show me a man's writing, I will know what he is like.

Participial phrase as opener: Having read his writing, I know the kind of man he is.

Head-on, direct: Writing reveals the man.

Prepositional phrase: Through writing one shows the kind of person he is.

Parallel construction: When I read your writing, I see not only the words which you wrote but also the man who wrote them.

Clause at beginning: How you express yourself in writing tells much about the kind of person you are.

Specific: Is your writing dull, disorganized, incorrect? Or is it vital, effective, the result of planning? In your writing you reveal your character.

The Effective Sentence

In your first draft, write the sentence as it occurs to you; getting it down on paper is the main consideration at that point. When you are revising and editing your draft, select the sentence structure that will make your paragraphs more effective. Revising is a part of writing. It is in the editing and revising stage that you add what we might call the "plus factors" that go to make up an effective style.

87c Use variety in sentence length

Sentences are more emphatic when they are short and simple. It is, of course, logical to express the important idea in a main clause, bedecked with subordinate clauses; but the importance of the main idea is heightened when it stands in a sentence by itself. This technique is even more effective when the extremely short sentence is surrounded by long sentences.

> Example: He tackled the difficult problems as though his life depended upon his finding an immediate solution. *It did.*
>
> You cite the case of a missionary whose taxable income was less than $600 while he was in the United States on a prolonged furlough to receive medical attention, returning to his residence abroad as soon as his physical condition permitted. *A return of income is unnecessary.*

87d Put important ideas in emphatic positions

Where words are placed in a sentence often determines the amount of stress they receive. The most emphatic positions in a sentence are at the beginning and at the end. It is natural to begin with the subject, the most important thing; and it is also natural to build up to a climax at the end.

> Example: They now find that their early training becomes valuable to them.
>
> Better: Their early training now becomes valuable to them. (Emphasis at beginning.)
>
> Example: We came upon some fresh evidence after we had interviewed 10 people.
>
> Better: After we had interviewed 10 people, we came upon some fresh evidence. (Emphasis at end.)

If you must choose between emphasizing the beginning or the ending of a sentence, emphasize the end. Arrange items in a series in ascending order of importance, building up to a climax. "The agent *sorted* his papers, *found* the statement, and *made* his report." When the items are out of the logical ascending order, the resulting anticlimax is often ludicrous.

Sentences also follow this principle of emphasizing the end and the beginning. The loose sentence emphasizes the beginning, being grammatically complete before the end is reached; the periodic sentence, which withholds its statement until the end, is typical of emphasis at the end.

    Loose: The taxpayer can request a conference if he does not agree with our findings.
    Periodic: If he requests a conference, we will schedule it within 10 days.

Following this page is a chart summarizing this material on sentence variety. It shows graphically how little excuse we have for writing monotonous sentences.

88   *Sentence-Identification Table*

1. Sentences identified by type:

    Declarative—statements of fact or of assumption
    Interrogative—questions
    Imperative—commands or requests

2. Sentences identified by number and kinds of clauses:

Simple:	containing one independent clause
Compound:	containing two or more independent clauses
Complex:	containing one independent clause plus one or more subordinate clauses
Compound-complex:	containing two or more independent clauses plus one or more subordinate clauses

3. Sentences identified by order of their parts:

Direct:	Modifier—SUBJECT—VERB—OBJECT—Modifier
Inverted:	VERB—SUBJECT—OBJECT
Interrupted:	SUBJECT—Modifier—VERB—Modifier—OBJECT

4. Sentences identified by suspense in completion of meaning:

Loose:	Meaning completed before end of sentence
Periodic:	Meaning not completed until end of sentence

5. Sentences identified by degree of fullness (number of ideas):

    Segregating: quite short; unified idea
    Aggregating: quite long; shows cumulative effect of combining of ideas

6. Sentences identified by language-choice:

    Informal: Conversational—in Internal Revenue correspondence, the kind of conversational language appropriate in face-to-face discussion with taxpayers; recommended for letters to lay taxpayers and for informal interoffice memorandums
    Formal: Suitable for documents prepared for a wide range of readers. Includes all published material, rulings, top-level correspondence

89   The Sentence and the Paragraph

A disjoined series of clear, effective sentences, fascinating as they may be for dissection, serves no good purpose by itself. It is only when these same sentences work together in a group, or paragraph, that they are worth the pain it has cost us to produce them. In many respects paragraphs are like sentences; what we have learned about making sentences effective can also apply to paragraphs.

Like a good sentence, a good paragraph shows evidence of planning and organizing. It is built around a topic sentence, which serves as a guidepost to the reader and as a steering device for the writer. This is the sentence that tells the reader, "Now we are going to discuss this angle of the subject." It also serves to keep the writer on the subject, making sure his sentences develop the thesis introduced by the topic sentence. Each paragraph, like each sentence, should be a step forward in a logical plan of development of the piece of writing.

The paragraph must be clear. The reader must not have to wonder what it is about or why it occurs when it does. Just as word order is important in the sentence, arrangement is important in the paragraph. Sentences must be linked together in the paragraph as words are linked in the sentence. The ending and the beginning of the paragraph are, like those of a sentence, the strong positions; the careful writer will take advantage of these points for emphasis.

The paragraph must be readable—preferably not too long. Short or medium-length paragraphs invite the reader's attention. As in sentences, however, the length should vary, to break what might otherwise be a monotonous pattern.

A Note in Conclusion

After you have chosen the right words, arranged them in a sentence in proper order—grammatically and effectively—and fitted the sentence into a unified paragraph, your job is not complete. For the writer the job is never finished; there are always more words, more sentences, more paragraphs—better ways of saying what you have tried to express. The next course, Effective Revenue Writing 2, challenges the writer to probe deeply into these problems. Neither that course (nor this) guarantees to turn out finished writers after ten easy lessons. Only the writer himself, through practice, can improve his own writing; in Effective Revenue Writing 2 the writer who is sincerely interested in improving his skills will learn more about writing principles and about applying them to even the most difficult types of writing.

Writer's Guide to Current Usage . . .

This brief guide contains an alphabetical list of some words and phrases that are often misused or overused. It is for the reviewer, the writer, and the secretary who need something they can refer to quickly to reassure themselves that a word or phrase will increase, not detract from, the effectiveness of Revenue writing.

Part A contains four types of expressions: (1) some that are frequently confused and misused; (2) some that, because of their unpleasant connotation, should be avoided in letters to taxpayers; (3) some that are threadbare from overuse and that writing consultants recommend be supplanted by more vigorous expressions; and (4) some that are controversial because, though once frowned on by careful writers, they are slowly becoming acceptable for use in official writing.

Part B contains the short list of prepositional idioms referred to in Text 7 on Connectives.

The Guide is, of course, not intended to take the place of a handbook of grammar, a dictionary of synonyms, or a dictionary of current American usage. In fact, we hope it will so pique the interest of writers that they will want to get and use such reference books.

PART A

About (at about), around. Avoid the dialectal expression *at around* or *at about* in sentences like "He will arrive *about* 9 o'clock."

Above, the above. Avoid except in legal documents. Considered by many writers to be vague and hackneyed.

    Substitute: May I have *this* information?
    For: May I have *the above* information?

Above-listed, above-mentioned. Stilted and stiff in all except legal writing. (If you must use *above*, then place it after the word *mentioned*.)

    Instead of: The *above-listed* deductions must be substantiated.
    Say: *These* deductions must be substantiated.
    Or: The deductions *listed above* must be substantiated.

Accordance, in accordance with. Also stilted—and wordy. Try substituting *as, in, according to*—or omit entirely.

    Instead of: *In accordance with* your request . . . .
    Say: *As* you requested . . . .

Acknowledge. In informal writing, try substituting "Thank you for your letter of May 16 . . ." for "This will acknowledge your letter of May 16."

Admit. Use with care in letters to taxpayers. Although the dictionary may defend its *accuracy*, it connotes to many readers a *conceding only after pressure has been brought to bear*. In internal documents, the sentence "The taxpayer *admits* having failed to report these sales" is quite acceptable. But in letters to taxpayers, "You *admit* having failed to report" sounds like an accusation and therefore has an adverse effect on public relations.

Advice, advise. Watch the spelling of these words. *Advice* is the noun, meaning opinion or counsel given. *Advise* is the verb, meaning to counsel or give an opinion.

Advise, inform, tell. Many writers overuse *advise*, using it when either *inform* or *tell* would be preferable. This distinction between *advise* and *inform*, however, should be kept in mind: *inform* means to communicate certain facts; *advise* means to suggest or recommend a course of action.

Affect, effect. Often misused, these two are totally unlike. *Affect* is *always a verb*; it means (1) to act on; to impress; or to produce a change in; (2) to pretend; to put on.

>   This change in policy will *affect* production. (produce a change in)
>   The supervisor *affected* a stern manner. (put on)

Effect is used *as a verb* and *as a noun*. As a noun, it means result or consequence.

>   What *effect* will this change have? (result)
>   The *effect* of this will be felt by everyone. (consequence)

As a verb, it means to bring about, to accomplish.

>   His transfer will be *effected* soon. (brought about)
>   We shall try to *effect* the change at once. (accomplish)

Aforementioned. Legalistic and too stiff for routine correspondence.

Aggravate, irritate, annoy. In formal English, *aggravate* means to *increase* or *make worse*—"The humid weather *aggravated* his suffering." (Refer to a dictionary of synonyms for shades of meaning of *aggravate, irritate, annoy, exasperate, vex, provoke*.)

All (of). *Of* is redundant. "They interviewed *all* the candidates."

All right. Must be two words, even though both *already* and *almost* are properly spelled with one *l* and as one word.

Allege. Once used, according to some authorities, to mean "to state under oath." Now used most often to mean "to state something, making clear that it is offered without adequate proof." Properly used in report writing, it should be avoided in most letters to taxpayers, many of whom see it as implying doubt of their truthfulness. "The taxpayer *alleges* that he contributed the full support of . . ." may mean to us simply that he has not yet submitted proof; to him, it may mean that we strongly doubt the truth of his statement.

Amount (in the amount of). Be economical with words. Instead of "Your check *in the amount of* $175.00," use "Your check *for* $175.00." Instead of "your tax refund *in the amount of* $200.00," use "your tax refund *of* $200.00" or "your $200.00 tax refund."

Amount, number. *Amount* is used to refer to things judged by their weight, bulk, or sums; *number* is used to refer to things that can be counted.

> an *amount* of tax BUT a *number* of tax returns
> an *amount* of correspondence BUT a *number* of letters

And/or. Reserve for legal documents. In memorandums and letters, this legalism destroys preciseness and clarity. Instead of, "This action may be taken by the taxpayer *and/or* his counsel," substitute, "Either the taxpayer or his counsel, or both, may take this action," or "This action may be taken by the taxpayer or his counsel, or by both of them."

Anticipate, expect. *Anticipate* means to look forward to. Some writing consultants consider it a somewhat pompous substitute when it is used to mean *expect*.

> Instead of: We *anticipate* that we will be in a position *to* furnish this information soon.
> Say: We *expect* to be able to send you this information soon.
> Or: We *can* send you this information soon.

Apparent, obvious, evident. Whether something is *apparent*, or *obvious*, or *evident* is something the writer should decide by consulting a dictionary of synonyms to determine the shades of meaning between the words.

All should be used with discretion in correspondence, since telling the reader that something is *apparent* or *obvious* may imply that anyone who does not see it as being so is lacking in intelligence.

Appreciate. A perfectly good word, but avoid using it constantly in such wordy constructions as "We would *appreciate it if you would* . . . ."

> Instead of: We would *appreciate it if you would* furnish this office with a copy of the proposed telegram.
> Use: We should *appreciate* your sending us a copy of the proposed telegram.
> Or: Please send us a copy of the proposed telegram.

As, like. Despite the frequent counsel to "write *like* we talk" and the assurance that a certain product "tastes good *like* it should," we suggest that in Revenue writing *as* be used as a connective between clauses, and *like* as a preposition.

> This method is *like* the one we have been using. (preposition)
> Audit this return *as* you audited the others. (conjunction)

As per. Considered to be stilted and overformal in correspondence.

> Instead of: As per your instructions . . . .
> Use: As you instructed . . . .

As such. Sometimes used when it adds nothing whatsoever to the meaning of the sentence.

> The accusation, *as such*, means nothing.
> The data, *as such*, add nothing to our fund of information.
> There is no objection to the sale of the real property, *as such*.

As to. Serves us best at the beginning of a sentence as a means of introducing a new subject. "*As to* your tax liability for 1957, we note that . . . ." But, used in the body of the sentence, it has led many a writer astray by tempting him to roundabout constructions.

As to whether (who) (what) (how). In such expressions as these, *as to* is often unnecessary.

> The Director expressed doubt (*as to*) whether these precautions are sufficient.
> We have just received an inquiry (*as to*) whether his claims have been processed.

Its use leads the writer into a false sense of security in a sentence like this—

> He asked for information *as to whom* the information should be given. (Having the *to* in *as to*, the writer overlooks the fact that there is no preposition that *whom* can properly be the object of.)
> Substitute: He asked for information *about* whom the report should be given to.
> Or: He asked for information *about* who should be given the report.

Attached (hereto). In this expression *hereto* is redundant. If one thing is *attached* to another, it can be no more firmly attached by being attached *hereto*. The fact is that it is either attached, or it isn't; and *hereto* is excess baggage.

Writer's Guide to Current Usage

Bad, badly. For an interesting discussion of the change that is taking place in the acceptable use of these two words, consult either an up-to-date handbook of grammar or a dictionary of synonyms. (*A Dictionary of Contemporary American Usage*, by Bergen Evans and Cornelia Evans, has a long discussion of this and similar usage problems.)

Because (reason is because). *Because* means *for the cause that* or *for the reason that.* Therefore, "The reason is because . . ." is both ungrammatical and illogical.

> Not: The *reason* I took this course is *because* I wanted to improve my writing.
> But: The *reason* I took this course is *that* I wanted to improve my writing.
> Or: I took this course *because* I wanted to improve my writing.

Balance. This word is incorrectly used for *rest* or *remainder* except when you refer to the balance in an account.

> The *rest* of the correspondence . . . NOT . . . the *balance* of the correspondence.

Be good enough to. This phrase annoys many readers because they consider it patronizing (even though the writer may not intend it to be).

> Instead of: Will you *be good enough to* send me a personal copy of the report?
> Substitute: *Please* send me a personal copy of the report.
> Or: I should *appreciate* your sending me a copy . . . .

Can, may. Both may be used to indicate *possibility.*

> The management analyst *can* attend the Management Institutes.
>   (He is physically able to; and it is *possible*, under established criteria, for him to attend.)
> The management analyst *may* attend the Management Institutes.
>   (We do not have definite information about his plans—he *may* and he *may not* attend; it is *possible* that he will attend.)

Only *may* is used to indicate *permission:*

> Management analysts *may* attend the Management Institutes.
>   (They are permitted to attend.)

Can, could. *Can* indicates ability or freedom to do something; *could* implies much the same, but may also indicate doubt or willingness.

> We *can* ship the training materials so that they will reach you next Friday.
>   (We are able to.)
> We *could* arrange to have them delivered earlier if you can justify the payment of airfreight charges.
> *Could* you (are you willing to) be here by 3 o'clock?

Could is used in a subordinate clause when the verb in the main clause is in some tense expressing past time. *Can* is used in the subordinate clause when the verb in the main clause is in the present or the future tense.

> He *gave* me a pass so that I *could* enter the building on Saturdays, Sundays, and holidays.
> He *will give* me a pass so that I *can* enter the building on Saturdays, Sundays, and holidays.

(See *may, might*)

Case. This certainly has a legitimate use, especially in referring to legal cases—in the *case* of *Smith* vs. *Doe*. But—when used like *field, line,* and *factor*—*case* is generally considered to be a sinner, tempting the writer to abandon his effort to find a word that precisely expresses his thought and to settle for a *blanket word* that frequently results in flabby writing.

> Instead of: In *case* you cannot attend the meeting . . . .
> Use: If you cannot attend . . . .
>
> Instead of: In many *cases*, the revenue agent will be wasting his time if he . . . .
> Use: Often, the revenue agent will be wasting . . . .
> Or: In many instances, the revenue agent will be . . . .
>
> Instead of: Our Division is not now so burdened with past-due correspondence as was formerly the *case*.
> Use: . . . as it used to be.

Character, nature. These two contribute much to the verbosity of Government writing; often, they add nothing to meaning.

> Instead of: These claims are of a far-reaching *character*.
> Say: These claims are far reaching.
>
> Instead of: The positions may be classified higher because they require incumbents to perform duties which are more difficult *in nature*.
> Say: These positions . . . duties which are more difficult.
> Or: These positions . . . require incumbents to perform more difficult duties.

Claim, assert, maintain. *Claimed* is often used in Revenue writing to mean *asserted, maintained, stated,* or simply *said*. To some extent, these words can be used interchangeably. But *claimed*, in letters to taxpayers, can have an adverse effect on public relations. (See Text 9 for a discussion of its connotation.)

Capacity, ability. *Capacity* is used to show the *innate power* of a person or a thing *to receive something*. *Ability*, to show the *power* of a person or a thing *to do something.* Ability can be developed; capacity cannot.

> He has the *ability to manage* an organization effectively. (*to do*)
> He has the *capacity* for long hours and hard work. (*to receive*)

Close proximity. Redundant. *Proximity* itself means nearness in place or in time.

Complaint, your complaint. Even though they may be used accurately (or, perhaps, *especially when they are used accurately*) these words antagonize the reader. Whenever possible, substitute *suggestion, comments, observations.*

> We were glad to get your *comments* about the way Mr. Doe handled your tax problems.

Compliance, comply with. These words are quite all right in formal writing, but are heavy and overformal in most correspondence.

> Instead of: *In compliance with your recent request,* we are enclosing herewith a copy of *Your Federal Income Tax.*
> Say: We are glad to send a copy of *Your Federal Income Tax,* which you requested.
> Or: We are enclosing a copy of *Your Federal Income Tax,* as you requested.

Compare to, compare with. These two are quite different. To *compare* one thing *to* another is to call attention to the *ways in which the two are alike.* To *compare* one thing *with* another is to call attention not only to the ways in which they are alike but also to the ways in which they are different.

> He *compared* Washington *to* San Francisco.
> (Pointed out the many ways in which they are alike; tried to describe Washington by showing its similarity to San Francisco.)
> He *compared* Washington *with* San Francisco.
> (Pointed out both similarities and differences—size, climate, activities, and so on.)

Comprise, constitute, compose. Totally unlike, these three are often confused. *Comprise* means to embrace, to include, to contain—the "whole thing" *comprises* a number of smaller items. Conversely, a number of smaller items or elements *constitute* or *compose* the whole body. (Some authorities offer this difference between *comprise* and *include:* Use *comprise* when *all* the component parts of the whole are given; use *include* when only some are given.)

> The course *comprises* 12 chapters.
> The course *includes* three chapters on Taxpayer Interviews.
> Twelve chapters *constitute* the course.

Consensus (of opinion). *Of opinion* is redundant, since *consensus* means *agreement of opinion.*
>The *consensus* of the group is that he should be selected.

Contact. The verb *contact* still stirs up controversy. (The noun *contact* has never caused trouble.) Many writers cringe when they read, "Please *contact* Mr. Jones about this matter," preferring, "Please *call (write, get in touch with)* Mr. Jones . . . ." Others maintain that it is an excellent word, since there is no other that covers approach by telephone, letter, memorandum, or face-to-face conversation. Certainly the verb *contact* has no place in formal Revenue writing; in informal, its use is a matter of personal preference.

Contemplating. This word is considered pompous when *thinking* or *planning* may be substituted. To *contemplate* means *to observe thoughtfully.*
>Instead of: We are *contemplating* installing a new procedure.
>Say: We are *thinking about* installing . . . .
>Or: We are *planning to install* a new procedure.

Costs the sum of. This is wordy and repetitious; substitute *costs.*
>Instead of: This handbook *costs the sum of* $5.
>Say: This handbook *costs* $5.

Covers. This word is often loosely used; *for, on,* or *about* may be substituted.
>Instead of: The enclosed check *covers* your expenses to and from the Regional Office.
>Say: The enclosed check *is for* your expenses to and from the Regional Office.

>Instead of: We are enclosing pamphlets *covering* the Summer Management Institutes.
>Say: We are enclosing pamphlets *describing* the Summer Management Institutes.

Data. The plural form of the Latin word *datum,* but used in both the singular and the plural sense. When used to refer to a BODY of statistics or findings, the singular is frequently preferred:
>Very little *data is* available.
>The *data is* inconclusive. (The *body* of statistics)

When used to refer to a body of information being considered by individual units, the plural is preferred:
>We gathered the *data* painstakingly and classified *them* according to geographical location.

Writer's Guide to Current Usage 225

Though both singular and plural uses are correct, avoid the illogical—and ungrammatical—shift from one point of view to the other:

> Very little DATA ARE available. (illogical)
> Very few DATA ARE available. (grammatically correct, but seems more awkward than "Very little DATA IS available.")

Substitute *information, facts, statistics*, etc., whenever possible.

Deem. Considered by many authorities to be a somewhat overformal and pompous way of saying *think* (except in legal documents).

> Not: If you *deem* it necessary.
> But: If you *think* (*consider*) it necessary.
> Not: As you *deem* advisable.
> But: As you *think* (*consider*) advisable.

Definite(ly). Often an unnecessary modifier that does not give the emphasis the writer intended that it should. "This is *definitely* harmful to our employees" is considered no more emphatic than "This is harmful to our employees."

Develop. Often loosely used when *arise, happen, occur*, or *take place* might be more precise. (Also often misspelled by the addition of an "e"—develope; some advocates of mnemonics suggest this device for remembering the correct spelling—remember to LOP off the "e" in "deveLOP.")

> Not: Circumstances *developed* that made his dismissal necessary.
> But: Circumstances *arose* that made . . . .
> Not: Unless events *develop* that would . . .
> But: Unless events *occur* (*take place*) that would . . . .

Different from, different than. *Different from* is preferred usage in America. In speaking and in informal writing, little attention is given to the distinction between the two; in formal writing and in writing for publication, *different from* should be used.

> Not: His final draft is *different than* his first.
> But: His final draft is *different from* his first.
> (*differed from* his first)

Direct(ly). *Direct* is both an adjective and an adverb. It may be used (and many prefer that it be used) in such constructions as

> Please send the memorandum *direct* to this office.
> (though *directly* is equally correct)

Directly, though correctly used to mean *immediately*, is seldom so used in Revenue writing:

> The Division Chief will arrange *directly* to have the statement signed.

We seem to prefer:

> The Division Chief will *immediately* arrange to have the statement signed.
> *or*
> The Division Chief will arrange to have the statement signed *immediately*.

Disinterested, uninterested. Often confused, these two are quite different in meaning. DISINTERESTED means *unbiased by any personal interest; impartial; objective.* UNINTERESTED means *not interested;* an uninterested person is indifferent, not interested.

> He was a *disinterested* observer.   (unbiased)
> He was *uninterested* in office matters.   (not interested)

Difference, discrepancy, disparity. Because there are shades of meaning between these words, writers should consult a dictionary of synonyms if they want to be *exact* in their choice.

Disclose, expose, reveal, divulge. These words, often used interchangeably, differ somewhat in meaning. *Divulge,* in particular, should be used with care in letters to taxpayers, because of its unpleasant connotation. "If you care to *divulge* . . ." seems to imply to the taxpayer that we think he is deliberately withholding information, whereas he may simply be unaware of the need for giving it. (Look in a dictionary of synonyms for differences in meaning.)

Due to, because of, owing to. These are often used interchangeably. Most grammarians and purists concede that they are fighting a losing battle in trying to persuade writers to use "due to" as an adjective—not as a preposition. As an adjective, it must, of course, have a noun to agree with or refer to—

> Strict use of *due to*
>   as an adjective: The closing of the Type C office was *due to* the small number of taxpayers being served.   (*Due to* correctly modifies the noun *closing*)
>
> Loose use of *due to*
>   as a preposition: The Type C office was closed *due to* the small number of taxpayers being served.

Strict conformity to rule would require the writer of the second sentence to (1) recast the sentence to read as the first sentence did or (2) substitute either *because of* or *owing to*, both of which are accepted prepositions.

Many writing consultants say simply "It is not good practice to start a sentence with *due to;* instead, use *because of.*"

> Not: *Due to* a previous engagement, I cannot confer with him tomorrow.
> But: *Because of* a previous engagement, I cannot confer . . . .

Due to the fact that. This expression is wordy; often either *since* or *because* may be substitited.

> Not: *Due to the fact that* our supply of Instructors' Guides is limited, we cannot send you more than 12.
> But: *Since* our supply of Instructors' Guides is limited . . . .

Duly. Acceptable in legal material, but often wordy and overformal in letters.

> Not: When the affidavit has been *duly* signed . . . .
> But: When the affidavit has been signed . . . .

Each and every. A pair of doublets that weakens writing; companion terms are *first and foremost* and *the sum total of*. Greater force and clarity result when only one of the pair is used.

> Not: *Each and every* clerk is required to report time spent on the project.
> But: *Each* clerk is required . . . OR . . . *every* clerk is required.

Effect. (See *affect*)

Else's, everyone else's, somebody else's. At one time, the correct form was *everyone's else* and *somebody's else*. But usage has now made *else's* the preferred form.

Earliest convenience. A term so vague that the writer and the reader may be far apart on when something is to be done. Substitute *immediately, soon, promptly*, or—even better—name a specific time.

> Not: Please send your list of candidates *at your earliest convenience*.
> But: Please send your list of candidates *promptly*.
> Or: Please send your list of candidates by Friday, August 14, so that we can have a complete list ready for the Commissioner by August 31.

Even date. An old-fashioned term now infrequently seen in Revenue writing:

> Not: Your letter *of even date*.
> But: Your letter of May 16 . . . .

Event (in the event that). A wordy way of saying *if*.

> Not: *In the event that* you are unable to attend, please wire.
> But: *If* you are unable to attend, please wire.

Employ, use. Most authorities say that *employ* is overformal and pompous when it is substituted for *use*. Avoid it, particularly in letters to taxpayers.

> Not: If you *employ* the cash receipts and disbursements basis . . . .
> But: If you *use* the cash receipts and disbursements basis . . . .

Enclosed herewith. *Herewith* is redundant. If something has been *enclosed*, then it certainly is *herewith*. *Transmitted herewith* is acceptable, though.

> The master sheets you requested are *enclosed*.

Enclosed please find. Considered by many writers to be greatly overused and even somewhat absurd. They maintain that one cannot *instruct* another to *find* something, since *find* implies coming upon something *by chance*. And they express confidence that, if the article is enclosed, the reader *will find it* without being so instructed.

> Not: *Enclosed please find* a schedule of the meetings.
> But: *Enclosed is* a schedule of the meetings.
> Or: The *enclosed* schedule of the meetings . . . .

Etc. Should be used sparingly in informal writing. It is incorrectly used when it ends a series introduced by the phrase "such as":

> Not: You may bring with you small articles *such as* books, pens, binders, *etc.* (*Such as* tells the reader that you plan to name only a few)
> But: You may bring with you small articles *such as* books, pens, and binders.

Etc. at the end of a sentence weakens it. Never use the redundant *and etc.*

Farther, further. Though many writers use these words interchangeably, most careful writers still prefer *farther* for indicating physical distance and *further* for indicating degree or quality.

> My new office is *farther* from my home than my old one is.
> I am expecting *further* instruction soon.

Favor. An old-fashioned word for letter.

> Not: Your esteemed *favor* of the 15th inst. is at hand.
> But: Thank you for your letter of May 15 . . . .

Feel free to. Considered old fashioned and patronizing by many writers. And many readers are antagonized by it.

> Not: Please *feel free to* contact this office for any further information about the matter.
> But: If you would like further information about the matter, please let us know. (please write us)

Fewer, smaller, less. *Fewer* refers to number (items that may be counted); *smaller* refers to size; and *less* refers to quantity or degree.

> He has *fewer* cases assigned to him than I have.
> His office is *smaller* than mine.
> We collected *less* money this month than last.

The distinction between *fewer* and *less* is a matter of controversy. Many grammarians and many careful writers insist on the distinction expressed here: *Fewer courses, fewer employees—less training, less assistance.* Others believe that there is a sound basis in the history of language for using the two interchangeably. Since Revenue writing goes to *all* citizens, we suggest that (for the present, at least) the Revenue writer continue to make this distinction between the two words, so as to avoid criticism from the many readers who believe strongly in the distinction.

Field. Like *case*, an overworked word that adds little to clarity and much to verbosity.

>Not: He has had much experience in the *field* of taxation.
>But: He has had much experience in taxation.

For the purpose of. Like *in order to* and *at the present time* is classified as being unnecessarily wordy (even though the constant use of these expressions makes them inconspicuous unless the writer has trained his eye to spot such wordy constructions so that he can write more concisely).

>He called the conference *for the purpose of* discussing the 19__ budget plans. (Substitute *to discuss*)
>
>*In order to meet* the deadline, he asked the group to work overtime. (Substitute *to meet* the deadline)
>
>We are able *at the present time* to send you 25 Writing Handbooks. (Substitute: We can send you *now*. . . .
>Or: At present, we can send you . . .)

For your information. This habit-forming phrase is frequently used when it adds nothing to the meaning of the sentence—what is being said is *obviously* for the reader's information. It is correctly used, however, to alert the receiver (perhaps of an interoffice memorandum) that no action is expected of him—the memorandum is simply an *information* memorandum.

Herein, hereto, herewith. Should be reserved for legal documents and reports. In correspondence with lay taxpayers, they are overformal and often redundant.

I.e., e.g. Reserve these and other similar abbreviations of Latin terms for legal writing, for reports, and for letters to professional taxpayers. The English forms—*that is, for example*—require very little additional typing and make for easier comprehension by the average reader.

Identical (same identical). Rarely seen in writing but often heard, the term *same identical* should be avoided. It is redundant. If two things are *identical*, they are the *same*.

If and when. A doublet, like *unless and until*. Rarely, if ever, does the writer gain anything by using the two terms; one will suffice. Try dropping *and when* and see if it makes any difference in meaning.

> Not: We will take action *if and when* we get your reply.
> But: We will take action *if* we get your reply.
> Or: We will take action *when* we get your reply. (if you are reasonably sure that it will be sent)

If, whether. Writers often use these two words interchangeably in introducing clauses that refer to alternatives. Grammarians disagree about the wisdom of making a distinction between them. Some hold firmly to the belief that ambiguity *can* result when *if* is used in such sentences as these—

> Let me know *if* you can attend the conference.
> Let me know *whether* you can attend the conference.

They maintain that the first sentence tells the reader that he is to let us know *only if he can* attend, not if he cannot—but that the second sentence makes it unmistakably clear that he is to let us know either way, whether he can attend or whether he cannot.

Other grammarians, equally eminent, say that this notion that there is a distinction is a very recent one and that venerable grammarians saw no such distinction.

The Revenue writer must, of course, reach his own conclusion. We suggest, however, that in formal writing and in printed publications the distinction be made.

Imply, infer. These words, used very frequently in our writing, are often misused. They need not be, for the difference between them can be made very clear. They are as unlike as *throw* and *catch*.

Imply means to signal or to hint at a meaning; *infer* means to deduce something from the signal or the hint.

It is always the writer or the speaker who *implies* something—he *throws* the hint out for the reader or the listener to catch. It is always the reader or the listener who *infers*; he *catches* the signal or hint.

> The Director *implied* that he was dissatisfied with production records.
> The staff *inferred* that he wanted them to do something about the matter.

In the last analysis. An outmoded expression.

I wish to state (May I state that). Windups that make writing verbose. If you wish to state something, just go ahead with it.

> Not: *I wish to state that* it is the consensus of the committee that he be accepted as a candidate.
> But: It is the consensus of the committee that he be accepted as a candidate.

Inasmuch as. Whenever possible, substitute *since* or *because*.

Initiate, begin, commence. Although these words are quite similar in meaning, they are not exact synonyms; and the careful writer will find it profitable to refer to a dictionary of synonyms or of current American usage for the shades of meaning between them.

Many writing consultants urge us to substitute *begin* for *initiate* in Government writing; and in letters to taxpayers, we would do well to follow this advice. One reason is that *initiate* is properly used in referring to taking a first step in a rather important matter. We may *begin* an investigation, *begin* an interview, *begin* a conversation. But we *initiate* a series of high-level conferences between persons of great importance; we *initiate* a major, significant program.

You can see, then, why the use of *initiate* in speaking of a simple routine matter—to *initiate* the movement of furniture from one place to another—is pompous and even somewhat ludicrous. It is what today's teenager calls "making a big production of something."

Prefer *begin* in most letters; reserve *commence* and *initiate* for more formal matters.

In the course of. Often a wordy way of saying *during*.

> We found *in the course of* our examination. . . . (*during* our examination)

It . . . it. Avoid the use of both the expletive *it* and the personal pronoun *it* in the same sentence.

> Not: *It* is our opinion that *it* is a matter that requires additional study.
> But: It is our opinion that this matter requires additional study.
> Or: In our opinion, *it* is a matter that requires additional study.

Its, it's. Avoid the careless error of using an apostrophe to indicate the possessive case of the pronoun.

> *Its* is the possessive form—Each letter is in *its* folder.
> *It's* is the contraction of *it is*—We believe *it's* clear to everyone.

Kind, kindly. Greatly overworked words; should be omitted from most letters. Substitute "please" or "won't you" or "we shall appreciate" and give your letters more vigor.

> Not: *Kindly* let us have this information by May 10.
> But: *Please* send us this information by May 10.
> Or: *We should appreciate* your sending this information by May 10.

Kind (this). Most careful writers and most discriminating readers prefer *this kind* and *these kinds,* even though some writing consultants express little concern when the plural *these* is used with the singular *kind.*

    Say: We do not have *these kinds* of binders.
    Or: We do not have *this kind* of binder.
    Not: We do not have *these kind* of binders.

Later, latest; latter, last. *Later* and *latest* pertain only to time. *Latter* and *last* pertain to succession or order of arrangement.

    The conference was postponed to a *later* date.
    This is the *latest* report on their progress.
        (Not the *last* report they will make, simply the *latest* one)
    Both the letter and the form have been received, but the *latter* is incomplete.
        (Used to refer to the second of two items)
    This is the *last* report prepared by the agent before he retired.

Lay, laid, laid. Do not confuse with the principal parts of *lie—lie, lay, lain.* *Lay,* meaning to place, must have an object. *Lie,* meaning to rest or recline, does not take an object. We *lay* something down—a tool, a law, a paper. But we ourselves *lie* down.

    I will *lay* it on the desk for you. (put it there)
    Yesterday I *laid* a fountain pen on the desk. (put it there)
    Every day this week I *have laid* a Daily Progress Report on his desk.

    I *lie* on the couch every day after lunch.
    Yesterday I *lay* there for 2 hours.
    I *have lain* there for hours without falling asleep.

Liberty (take the liberty of). The expression "*I have taken the liberty of* referring your letter to the Regional Commissioner at Main City" is considered old fashioned and hackneyed. Try a more direct and natural style.

    Instead of: We *have taken the liberty of* forwarding your letter of May 17 to the Regional Commissioner at Main City for appropriate action.
    Substitute: We have *sent* your letter of May 17 to the Regional Commissioner at Main City. I am sure you will hear from him soon.
    Or: Your letter of May 17 has been referred to the Regional Commissioner at Main City . . . .
    Or: We have asked our Regional Commissioner at Main City to answer your letter of May 17.

Likely, liable. Often confused in speaking; less often in writing. *Likely* is used to express high probability—it is *likely* that he will get the promotion. *Liable,* when used in a legal sense, to mean bound by law or legally answerable for some action, causes little trouble—"He is *liable* for damages sustained in the accident" or "He is *liable* for

Writer's Guide to Current Usage

taxes on . . . ." Careful speakers and writers avoid the use of *liable* as a synonym for *likely*.

> Not: He is *liable* to be in travel status during August.
> But: He is *likely* to be in travel status during August.

Line, along this line. Here are favorites of the writer who prefers gobbledygook to plain English. *Line*, even though correctly used in the sense of procedure, is grossly overworked.

> Instead of: His experience *in this line* is considerable. (Vague)
> Substitute: His experience *in management training* is considerable. (Specific)

Loan, lend. Here is another matter of controversy—whether *loan* may be properly used as a verb. Its use as a noun is, of course, unquestioned—"He received a *loan* of $50." But grammarians have for years maintained that *lend* is the proper verb in such a sentence as "He will *lend* me the money to buy the stocks." In official writing, the conservative use of *lend* as a verb form seems wise; in informal speech, one can be less precise.

> Not: It is a matter of record that the taxpayer's father *loaned* him the money to buy the business property.
> But: It is a matter of record that the taxpayer's father *lent* him the money to buy the business property.

It is only fair to call your attention to the statement of several authorities on language that *loan* as a verb is quite respectable and is being used by many banking and financial experts.

You may therefore, in your personal business correspondence, want to use the term; our counsel for the use of *lend* is based on the belief that Revenue writing should meet the standards of the most conservative, as well as the most liberal, readers.

Major. Do not overwork this word when you may substitute *main*, *important*, *chief*, *principal*, *significant* or similar word.

Majority vs. most. Use *majority* on those occasions when you are contrasting the *majority* with the *minority*.

> The *majority* favors the passage of the bill; the *minority* views the passage of the bill with alarm.

Most authorities recommend that *majority* not be used when *most* will do as well:

> Preferred: *Most* of the agents prefer the new method.
> Not: The *majority* of the agents prefer the new method.

May, might. *May* indicates either permission or possibility. *Might* implies possibility.

> You *may* go if you wish. (permission)
> We *may* go to the Convention; we haven't decided yet. (possibility)
> We *might* go to the meeting if it is held on Friday. (possibility)

Might is used in subordinate clauses when the verb in the main clause is in some tense indicating past time. *May* is used in the subordinate clause when the verb in the main clause is in the present or future tense.

> He *said* that I *might* borrow his Handbook for a day or two.
> He *says* that I *may* borrow his Handbook for a day or two.

Meet with your approval. This expression is limp from overuse.

> Instead of: We hope our actions *will meet with your approval.*
> Substitute: We hope you will *approve* our actions.

Memorandums, memoranda. Both are acceptable plural forms of the word *memorandum.* Current usage, however, seems to favor *memorandums.*

Menial. Avoid the use of this word when you mean *unskilled.* Menial has an unpleasant connotation; it implies that one is taking a contemptuous view of the task or even of the person performing it.

Minimize. A perfectly good word—but don't overwork it. Substitute *underestimate, disparage,* or *belittle* for variety.

No expense has been spared. Grossly overused. All it says to most readers is that evidently a lot of money has been spent. Avoid this hackneyed expression. (Fortunately, it is not used so frequently in Government writing as in business writing.)

Note. When used in such expressions as "We *note* that you have not received the announcement," it is considered pompous; some authorities label it "supercilious," though writers seldom realize that readers have this reaction.

> Instead of: We *note* that not all the supplies were received on time.
> Substitute: We are sorry that you did not receive all the supplies on time.
> Instead of: You *will note* that evaluation questionnaires are to be forwarded to this office when completed.
> Substitute: Please send the completed evaluation questionnaires to this office.

None. When *none* is followed by a prepositional phrase which contains a plural object, writers sometimes have trouble with the verb. *None* may properly take either a singular verb or a plural verb (if the noun in the prepositional phrase is plural).

>Either: *None* of the *agents* IS ready to submit a report.
>Or: *None* of the *agents* ARE ready to submit a report.

If you want to emphasize that *not one* of them is ready, say so:

>*Not one* of the *agents* IS ready to submit a report.

Number. Though considered plural, the word *number* takes a plural verb when preceded by "a" and a singular when preceded by "the."

>A *number* of returns *have been* audited.
>THE *number* of returns audited *is* smaller this year than last.

"A number" implies consideration of the individual units; "the number" implies consideration of the total—collective use.

Only. Has the habit of getting out of its proper place. Be sure to place it as close as possible to the word it modifies, so that there is no danger of its being a squinting modifier. Remember, the reader depends on the *placement of modifiers* to determine which word is being modified.

>This confusion can *only* be alleviated by a change of policy.

This can be interpreted in two ways:

>This confusion can *only be alleviated*—it cannot be corrected entirely, simply "alleviated."
>
>*or*
>
>This confusion can be alleviated *only* by a change of policy.
>(It *can be* alleviated, but only a change of policy can do it; nothing else can.)

Even though some efforts to put *only* close to the word it modifies may seem to be "nit-picking," any effort put forth to clarify the meaning of the *example* given here would be well worth the time devoted to it.

Check the *only*'s in your sentences; be sure they are placed so that there will be no ambiguity.

Overall. Used as an adjective, this word has muscled its way into almost every letter, memorandum, and report written in Government. Sometimes it is a blessing to us, for we can think of no other *one* word that carries so much meaning. But often it is a curse, for it seduces us into settling for a vague, general *"overall"* meaning instead of searching for a specific meaning which another word might convey.

The next time you reach for the word *overall*, consider such substitutes as *total, aggregate, average, comprehensive, whole,* or *complete*.

> He has called my attention to the *overall* requirements of this Division for next year. (*total*)
>
> Compared with June of last year, *overall* collections showed an increase of more than $4 million. (*aggregate*)
>
> The training guides in the library have an *overall* length of 30 pages. (*average*)
>
> An *overall* plan for basic supervisory training is being developed. (*comprehensive*)
>
> The supervisor feared that the employees would not be willing to look at the *overall* picture. (*whole*)
>
> One series of training conferences was conducted, but the *overall* training program was never finished. (*complete*)

Our. Avoid being too possessive about the employees under your supervision. The use of OUR Mr. Smith is considered both old fashioned and hackneyed.

> Not: *Our* Mr. Smith will visit your office next week.
>
> But: Mr. Smith of our office will visit you next week.
>
> Or: Mr. Smith, one of the Regional Analysts, will visit your office next week.

Party. Except in legal documents, no *person* should be referred to as a *party*.

Per. A Latin word meaning *through* or *by*. It is used most often in Latin expressions such as *per annum* and *per diem* and causes no trouble in these constructions. It is also used without problem in certain standard terms such as *miles per hour* and *words per minute*, although there is a trend toward the preferred use of *miles an hour* and *words a minute*.

Avoid the use of *per* with English words to form phrases like *per your request* and *per your letter of* (or, *as per your letter*).

These guidelines may help you:

1. *Per* is correct and preferred before other Latin words.
2. *A* or *an* is correct and preferred before English words.
3. *Per* is incorrectly used in expressions that mean *in accordance with* (such as *per your request* when you mean *in accordance with your request* or *as you requested*).

Per cent, percent. The Government Printing Office Style Manual and other recognized handbooks give *percent* as the preferred form.

Percentage, proportion, some. Avoid the loose use of *percentage* or *proportion* when you really mean *some* or *many* or *few*. It is quite correct to say—

> *In a high percentage* of tax cases, the revenue agent will find little evidence of fraud.
> Only *a small proportion* of the sum collected was used for administrative expenses.

But this use shows the relation of one thing to another. Do *not* use *percentage* or *proportion*, instead of the simple words *some*, *many*, and *few* when you are expressing an exact number.

> Not: This method has proved of much value *in a percentage* of training classes.
> But: This method has proved of value in *many (some, a few)* training classes.
> Or: This method has proved of value *in a large percentage of (in a great many)* training classes.

Period, for a period of. In some Revenue writing, it is essential that we say that something was done *for a period of* two years. But we seem to have fallen into the habit of using the term when it adds nothing but verbiage. Avoid overusing it.

> Instead of: He kept a daily record of telephone inquiries *for a period of* 2 months.
> Substitute: He kept a daily record of telephone inquiries *for 2 months*.
> Or, better: *For 2 months*, he kept a daily record of telephone inquiries.

Peruse, perusal. Considered pompous and stilted in daily correspondence. Substitute simpler, more natural words.

> Instead of: After a careful *perusal* of your proposal, we have concluded that we cannot agree to it.
> Substitute: After a careful *study (reading)* of your proposal, we have concluded that we cannot agree to it.

> Instead of: *Peruse* this request carefully; then let me know whether you think we should grant it.
> Substitute: *Read (check over)* this request carefully, then . . . .

Position (in a position to). Whenever possible, avoid the use of *in a position to* in daily correspondence; it often leads to verbosity and to stilted writing.

> Instead of: We regret that we are not *in a position to* send you copies of the Taxpayers Guide.
> (What *position* do we have to be in?)
> Substitute: We are sorry that we *cannot* send you copies of the Taxpayers Guide. (Or, that we are *unable to* send you copies . . . .)

Presently, now. One of the "pet peeves" of many careful writers is the frequent use of *presently* when *now* is meant. *Presently* is used by most careful writers to mean *forthwith* or *soon*; do not water it down to mean *now* or *at present*.

>Not: We are *presently* engaged in the preparation of a handbook for revenue officers.
>But: We are *now* preparing a handbook for revenue officers.
>Or: We *are preparing* a handbook for revenue officers. (This form of the verb indicates *the present time*.)

Preventive. Authorities agree that *preventive* is preferable to *preventative*.

>Not: *Preventative* measures should be taken.
>But: *Preventive* measures should be taken.

Principal, principle. The confusion caused by these words is mostly the way they are spelled. *Principal* has many meanings: *Main* (the *principal* city—the *main* city); the *principal* of a school; the *principal* and his agent—a legal use; the *principal* and interest—financial term. *Principle* has only *one* main meaning—it means a primary truth or rule.

Use this mnemonic device to remember the difference in spelling:

>Princip<small>LE</small>
>R<small>u</small><small>LE</small>   Both end in <small>LE</small>

If you are sure of the spelling and use of *principle*, you can remember that *in all other instances*, the word is *principal*.

Proved, proven. Except when used as an adjective, a *proven* treatment, *proven* should be discarded in favor of *proved*.

>Not: The effectiveness of this method of computing tax was *proven*. (Archaic use)
>But: The effectiveness of this method was *proved*.

Provided, providing. For years, grammarians and precise writers insisted that only *provided* could properly be used as a conjunction—that *providing* could be used only as part of the verb form. And many careful writers and conservative readers still hold this view. However, current usage accepts the use of *providing* as a conjunction, as many up-to-date handbooks and dictionaries show.

Conservative writers prefer:

>You may use this method of computing tax, *provided* (<small>NOT</small>, *providing*) you itemize your deductions.
>Regulations *providing* for the proper listing of these items may be found on page 17.

Current usage permits:

>You may use this method of computing tax, *provided* <small>OR</small> *providing* you itemize your deductions.

Writer's Guide to Current Usage

Pursuant. Avoid the use of this formal, somewhat technical term except in formal Revenue writing and letters to professional taxpayers.

> Not: *Pursuant* to your request of May 30, we are sending ten copies of Your Federal Income Tax.
>
> But: *As you requested* in your letter of May 30, we are sending ten copies of Your Federal Income Tax.

Re, in re. Both *re* and *in re* are, fortunately, being used less often in Revenue letters. They should be reserved for use in legal documents. Some authorities say that *re* is an abbreviation whose meaning has been lost, or at least has been misplaced, so that few writers know for sure what *re* actually means. Whether this is true or not, the use of *re* or *in re* in Revenue letters makes them seem stilted and overformal.

> Instead of: *In re* your letter of October 10, we wish to advise that the claim mentioned therein is being processed and that . . . .
>
> Substitute: The claim you referred to in your letter of October 10 is being processed and . . . .

Received, in receipt of. The habit-forming phrase *in receipt of* tempts the writer to bog down in the first paragraph of his letter and to devote a whole sentence, or more, to telling the taxpayer nothing more than that the Post Office Department has done its usual dependable job of delivering the mail and that we have, in fact, *received* the letter we are answering.

Whenever possible, avoid the use of *in receipt of* in your daily correspondence.

> Instead of: We are *in receipt of* your letter of June 15, in which you request to be advised as to whether or not . . . .
>
> Substitute: Thank you for your letter of June 15, asking whether . . . .
>
> Or, better: The claim for refund, about which you asked in your letter of June 15, is being processed and . . . .

Recurrence. Referring to the careless mispronunciation and misspelling of this word may be carrying coals to Newcastle, but we think it is misused often enough to justify this brief comment.

Very often, speakers are careless in their pronunciation of *recurrence*, pronouncing it as if it were *re–oc–cur–rence*. Much less often, it is misspelled in letters. Be on your guard against this illiterate usage.

Remain (we remain, I remain, I am). Fortunately, these old-fashioned closing phrases are seldom seen in Revenue letters. They are considered by many authorities to be not only old fashioned but weak and spineless.

Avoid the participial ending that invites them:

> Trusting that this meets with your approval, *I remain* (I *am*)
> Hoping that this gives you the information you need, *we remain* (we *are*)

Be modern and direct in your closing sentences.

Replying to your letter of, referring to your letter of. All participial openings are considered weak and somewhat stilted. They are dangerous, too. For they lead to the *dangling constructions* that were discussed in Text 6 on modifiers and in Text 10 on the effective sentence.

> Not: *Replying to your letter of* June 10, the report about which you asked is being typed and will reach you not later than June 15.
> (It seems that the *report is replying to your letter*, doesn't it?)
> But: The report you asked about in your letter of June 10 is being typed and will reach you by June 15.

To avoid the weak participial opening (or closing), either change it to a complete clause (or sentence) or eliminate it.

Same. Quite properly used to mean *identical*. "This is the *same* approach that I took"; "She is the *same* person I had in mind for the job." It may also be properly used in such constructions as "We agreed to pay him $9 a day, and we shall pay you the *same*."

But the use of *same* to mean the identical thing discussed earlier is considered archaic by most authorities; they recommend substituting a suitable pronoun.

> Not: We therefore recommend that you complete *same* by the end of the fiscal year.
> But: We therefore recommend that you complete *it* (or *them*—or, perhaps more specifically, *the case*) by the end of the fiscal year.

Same identical. A redundancy; *same* means *identical*.

Say, state. Writers are often counseled to substitute *say* for *state* to avoid writing that is overformal and stilted. And this counsel can (and should) be followed whenever possible. But writers need to know the distinction between the two words, so that when formal writing requires the meaning which ONLY *state* can express, they can use it with assurance.

Say means simply to tell, to relay information, to relate:

> He *said* that he filed a joint return.
> The Director *said* that he preferred a direct, natural writing style in letters to taxpayers.

State, however, means to set forth (formally), to make a specific, definite declaration.

Writer's Guide to Current Usage 241

>The lawyer *stated* the assumptions upon which he had based his arguments. The objectives of the program are clearly *stated* in the Commissioner's introductory comments.
>
>He *stated* the provisions that must be met.

Using *state* when a simple *say* will suffice will quite naturally result in stiff, overformal writing. But using *say* or *said* loosely as alternatives for *state* or *stated* may weaken and minimize the effect of a formal report or other document.

Scan (skim). Many writers are surprised when their readers misinterpret an instruction in which the word *scan* has been used. But *scan* has become a dangerous word because it carries *two totally different* meanings.

Used originally to refer to analyzing poetry—to *scan* poetry or verse, it now means *to examine carefully, to scrutinize, to read painstakingly and analytically.* Thus, to *scan* a report means to read it very carefully, to scrutinize it, to analyze it.

This is ONE meaning—and the only one that many authorities and many conservative writers will recognize and endorse. But usage in America is forcing a SECOND meaning to the front: *To glance hurriedly over, to skim through, to look at somewhat superficially.*

To those who interpret *scan* to have this second meaning, the instruction to *"scan* a report" would mean that they were simply to give it a *"once over lightly"* and get the gist of it.

You can see the need for caution, with two such conflicting meanings within easy reach of your reader. Be sure you make your meaning clear!

Spouse. Has a special legal meaning which is quite familiar to the Revenue writer. Its use in legal documents, in Regulations, and in similar matter is appropriate. In fact, it is essential, for there is no other ONE word that refers equally to either the husband or the wife of a taxpayer.

But its use in letters is unnecessary and undesirable—*unnecessary* because, since we are writing to a particular taxpayer, we *know* whether we are referring to the husband or the wife and need not use the covering word "spouse"; *undesirable* because it destroys the directness and naturalness we want in letters to the public.

>Not: You request to be advised as to whether or not you may file a joint return. In this connection your attention is invited to the fact that the taxpayer and his spouse may, under the provisions of section 123 of Regulations . . . .
>
>But: You and *your wife* may file a joint return, provided (OR *if*) you . . . .

Shall, will. Grammarians and conservative writers have fought the good fight in trying to make the distinction between these two words unmistakably clear. In speaking and in informal writing, most people make little distinction between them (however unfortunate you may, or may not, consider this to be). In formal writing—and especially in directives, manuals, policy statements, and similar matter—a clear distinction is made.

Both words express the future; the difference lies in which one is to be used to express a simple future action; willingness to perform an act; obligation or compulsion (mandatory action).

Precise, conservative use requires writers to—

(1) Use *shall* with the first person *I* and *we* to express a simple future action (simple futurity) or willingness.

> I *shall* discuss the matter with the Group Supervisor. (a simple statement of future action planned)
> We *shall* be glad to answer his letter.

(2) Use *will* with the second person (*you*) and with the third person.

> You (he, it, they) *will* be chosen for the position.
> He (they) *will* be glad to take care of the adjustment.

(3) Reverse the order to show determination, obligation, or compulsion.

> I (we) *will* have this ready for you by the deadline date. (It's a *promise;* we *will* do it by then)
> You (he, they) *shall* submit a progress report each day. (It's an *order;* it's mandatory)
> It *shall* be our policy to take action on delinquent accounts by . . . .

NOTE: Careful writers and discriminating readers still expect this use of *shall* and *will*. Current usage, however, accepts the use of *will* with ALL PERSONS to mean simple future action—thus making respectable such sentences as—

> I (We) *will* (not the precise *shall*) be glad to answer the inquiry.
> I (We) *will* (not meaning determination, but simple futurity) report the matter to him.

But commands, orders, policies, and regulations are still carefully written using *shall* with the second and third persons to show compulsion:

> It *shall* be submitted within 90 days.
> You *shall* be responsible for the project.
> He *shall* submit a report each month.
> The X Function *shall* be responsible for . . . .

Writer's Guide to Current Usage 243

Should, would. These two are explained in Text 4, but here are a few additional uses that writers should be familiar with:

> *Should* is used with all three persons to express—
>> *obligation or duty* (as a synonym for *ought to*):
>>> I know I *should* edit my writing more carefully.
>
>> *a condition:*
>>> If he *should* call, tell him I will be back in the office soon.
>
>> *expectation:*
>>> Our letter *should* have reached the taxpayer by now.
>
> *Would* is used with all three persons to express—
>> *habitual or customary action:*
>>> Each morning the clerk *would* follow the same ritual of dusting office furniture, watering plants, and sharpening pencils.
>
>> *insistence:*
>>> He *would* delay making decisions, even though his superiors advised him to overcome this personal weakness.

Subsequent to. Correct in legal documents, but stilted and verbose in routine correspondence. Substitute the word *after*, which has a simple dignity of its own.

> Not: *Subsequent to* our conference with you, we learned that you had additional information . . . .
>
> But: *After* (or *following*) our conference with you, we learned that you had additional information . . . .

Self-addressed. Many authorities have fun discussing the fact that there is no such thing as a "*self-addressed,* stamped envelope." What the writer means is "an addressed, stamped envelope."

Such. Often overworked; try substituting *these* or similar words. Especially in a phrase like "such time as," it can often be omitted.

> Not: Until *such* action can be taken.
> But: Until *this* action can be taken.
>
> Not: Until *such* time as you are free to discuss the matter . . . .
> But: Until you are free to discuss the matter . . . .

Thanking you in advance. Though often used to add to the tone of the letter, this phrase is considered by most readers to be presumptuous, if not insulting. To "thank" a person "in advance" is to put him under obligation to grant you the favor you are asking.

This is to inform you that. A windup that helps to make letters verbose and certainly to make them more frigid and pompous.

> Not: *This is to inform you that* we shall forward the training materials early next week.
> But: We shall forward the training materials early next week.
> Not: *This is to inform you that* we are presently engaged in gathering data that you can use in your study of trends in taxation.
> But: We are now gathering data that you can use in your study of trends in taxation.

Toward, towards. Both are correct. *Toward* seems to be preferred, however, by most writers.

Undersigned. Fortunately, the use of *the undersigned*—meaning the person who wrote the letter or the memorandum—is dying out of Revenue writing. Authorities condemn its use because it seems to represent the writer's studied effort at modesty and because it results in stilted, pompous writing. We think that many Revenue writers gladly abandoned it when the ban was taken off the use of personal pronouns.

The writer. This expression, like *the undersigned,* is being used less often in Revenue writing now that the direct, natural writing style is considered desirable for most of our writing. Substitute *"I,"* or recast the sentence if the personal pronoun cannot be used.

PART B—PREPOSITIONAL IDIOMS

abatement *of*	The taxpayer was told about the *abatement of* his tax.
accede *to*	We cannot *accede to* the taxpayer's request for an extension of time.
accessory *of*	He was an *accessory of* the criminal.
accessory *to*	He was an *accessory to* the act.
accommodate *to*	He finds it hard to *accommodate* himself *to* new situations. (changed conditions)
accommodate *with*	We *accommodated* him *with* a loan of five dollars.
accompany *by*	He was *accompanied by* a counsel. (a person)
accompany *with*	The letter was *accompanied with* an affidavit. (a thing)
accord *in*	The committee members *accord in* their decisions.
accord *to*	There shall be *accorded to* each man what he earns.
accord *with*	I am in *accord with* the findings.

Writer's Guide to Current Usage

accountable *for*	The Division Chief is *accountable for* his actions.
accountable *to*	I am *accountable to* the Chief for my actions.
accused *by*	He was *accused by* the plaintiff of having filed a false statement.
accused *of*	He was *accused of* perjury.
acquiesce *in*	The Commissioner has *acquiesced in* the decision.
acquit *of*	He was *acquitted of* the crime.
acquit *with*	He *acquitted* himself *with* honor.
adapted *for*	The work simplification guide was *adapted for* our use.
adapted *from*	The movie was *adapted from* the book.
adapted *to*	He finds it difficult to *adapt to* new procedures.
adequate *for*	His salary was not *adequate for* his needs.
adequate *to*	His ability was *adequate to* the job.
adverse *to*	The counsel was not *adverse to* discussing the compromise.
averse *to*	He was not *averse to* hard work.
advise *of*	The employees were *advised of* the new regulations.
affix *to*	A revenue stamp was *affixed to* the container.
agree *in*	We *agree in* principle with those who favor the plan.
agree *on*	They cannot *agree on* the delegation order.
agree *to*	They state that they *agree to* the compromise.
agree *with*	The taxpayer and his counsel *agree with* us that . . . .
amenable *to*	He was *amenable to* our argument.
analogous *to*	This situation is *analogous to* the one we faced last year.
annoy *by*	The clerk was *annoyed by* the frequent interruptions.
annoy *with*	The supervisor showed that he was *annoyed with* the recalcitrant employee.
apparent *in*	His attitude is *apparent in* his actions.
apparent *to*	The trouble is *apparent to* everyone in the office.
append *to*	A rider was *appended to* the bill.

appreciation *for*	The student had a real *appreciation for* the arts.
appreciation *of*	He expressed *appreciation of* their hard work.
appreciative *of*	We are *appreciative of* their efforts.
authority *in*	Dr. X is an *authority in* his field.
authority *on*	Mr. X is an *authority on* linear programming.
authority *to*	He has *authority to* sign this document.
basis *for*	The agent said they had a sound *basis for* agreement.
basis *in*	His argument has no *basis in* fact.
commensurate *with*	His salary was *commensurate with* his abilities.
comply *with*	We must *comply with* the Chief's request.
concur *in*	We *concur in* the decision of the survey committee.
concur *with*	One member did not *concur with* the others.
conform *to*	All agents must *conform to* the regulations.
consist *in*	His value *consists in* his ability to work with others.
consist *of*	The handbook *consists of* principles of supervision.
consistent *in*	We should be *consistent in* applying the law.
consistent *with*	His actions are not *consistent with* his statements.
correspond *to*	His description of the incident *corresponds to* what we believe to be the case.
correspond *with*	We have been *corresponding with* his counsel.
demand *from*	What did he *demand from* them in payment?
demand *of*	They have *demanded* an accounting *of* the company funds.
differ *from*	My estimate of the total tax due *differs from* his.
differ *in*	We *differ in* our opinions on the matter.
differ *on*	They *differed on* the amount to be assessed.
differ *with*	I *differ with* him about the evaluation method to be used.
discrepancy *between*	There is a *discrepancy between* the two accounts.
discrepancy *in*	There is a *discrepancy in* his account.
displeased *at*	The supervisor was *displeased at* the employee's conduct.
displeased *with*	The supervisor was *displeased with* the employee.

Writer's Guide to Current Usage 247

eligible *for*	He is *eligible for* the job.
eligible *to*	Everyone is *eligible to* apply for the job.
equivalent *in*	His office and mine are *equivalent in* size.
equivalent *of*	This is the *equivalent of* a full payment.
equivalent *to*	Each payment is *equivalent to* a week's salary.
excepted *from*	He was *excepted from* further responsibility.
excluded *from*	This item may be *excluded from* gross income.
exempt *from*	This type of income is *exempt from* tax.
expect *from*	What return do you *expect from* your investment?
expect *of*	What does the Chief *expect of* his assistant?
familiar *to*	The taxpayer's name is *familiar to* me.
familiar *with*	He is quite *familiar with* the proceedings.
find *for*	The jury *found for* the defendant.
furnish *to*	Adequate supplies were *furnished to* them.
furnish *with*	Please *furnish* us *with* background information on this matter.
habit *of*	He made a *habit of* waiting until the report was due before he began writing it.
identical *with*	That case is *identical with* the one I am working on.
identify *by*	The witness was *identified by* the tattoo on his arm.
identify *to*	The witness *identified* the suspect *to* this office.
identify *with*	He was *identified with* the opposing members.
ignorant *of*	He was *ignorant of* his rights.
improvement *in*	The *improvement in* his writing was soon noted.
improvement *on*	His second draft was an *improvement on* the first.
inconsistent *in*	He was *inconsistent in* his review.
inconsistent *with*	This is *inconsistent with* established policy.
infer *from*	We *infer from* his statement that he plans to discuss the adjustment further.
influence *for*	His *influence* was always *for* harmony.
influence *by*	We were all *influenced by* the Director's statements.

influence **on** (**upon**)	The rumor of an organizational change had an *influence on* (*upon*) production.
influence **over**	The supervisor had a strong *influence over* his staff.
influence **with**	He referred frequently to his *influence with* those in authority.
inform **of**	Supervisors should keep their subordinates *informed of* any changes in procedure.
inherent **in**	A capacity for growth is *inherent in* all people.
insert **in**	This phrase should be *inserted in* the draft.
intercede **for**	My lawyer *interceded for* me.
intercede **with**	He *interceded with* the board in my behalf.
invest **in**	The taxpayer said he had *invested* the money *in* stocks.
invest **with**	He was *invested with* full power to act.
irrelevant **to**	This statement is *irrelevant to* the matter under discussion.
irrespective **of**	They decided to appoint him *irrespective of* the criticism that might result.
liable **for**	He is *liable for* damages.
liable **to**	The employee is *liable to* his employer.
liberal **in**	He was very *liberal in* his views.
liberal **with**	He was *liberal with* praise.
necessity **for**	There is no *necessity for* a reduction in force.
necessity **of**	We are faced with the *necessity of* reducing travel expenses.
oblivious **of**	He was *oblivious of* the effect that his remote manner had on his employees.
precedent **for**	Is there a *precedent for* this action?
precedent **in**	His decision established a *precedent in* law.
recompense **for**	He was fully *recompensed for* the time he spent on the work.
reconcile **to**	We have become *reconciled to* our fate.
reconcile **with**	Our views cannot be *reconciled with* his.

Writer's Guide to Current Usage

similarity *in*	I agree that there is much *similarity in* their appearance.
similarity *of*	The *similarity of* the cases caused confusion.
similarity *to*	This time-saving device shows a *similarity to* one I have.
talk *of*	The traveler *talked* long *of* his experiences.
talk *to*	The lecturer *talked to* a large audience.
talk *with*	The lawyer *talked with* his client.
transfer *from*	He has been *transferred from* his former position.
transfer *to*	They *transferred* him *to* another department.
unequal *in*	The contestants were *unequal in* strength.
unequal *to*	She was *unequal to* the demands placed on her.
use *for*	He had no *use for* the extra table.
use *of*	She made good *use of* her opportunity.
wait *at*	I will *wait at* the back of the conference room until I can talk with the conference leader.
wait *for*	He seemed to be *waiting for* someone.
wait *on* (*upon*)	This matter must *wait on* (*upon*) my leisure.

INDEX

NOTE.—This index does not include an alphabetical listing of the words and phrases in the Writer's Guide to Current Usage.

A

Abbreviations
    a or *an* preceding, 38a
    period after, 66a
    plural of, 14f
Absolute
    case of subject, 12f
    defined, 44
    punctuation of, 64d
Abstract words
    contrasted with concrete, 72
    defined, 10e
    overuse in "gobbledygook," 85b
accompanied by
    not affecting number of subject, 18b
Accusative case (see Objective case)
Active voice
    defined, 33
    desirability of, 3c, 85c
    uses of, 34
Adjective
    a, an, 38a
    clause, 5, 46a
    comparison of, 42, 43
    compound, 41
    coordinate, punctuation of, 65
    defined, 4d, 7d, 34c
    demonstrative, 38
    dependent clause as, 5, 46a
    descriptive, 38
    distinguished from adverb, 40
    hyphenated, 41
    infinitive as, 44a
    infinitive phrase as, 44b
    interrogative, 38
    limiting, 38
    multiple, 47c
    overuse of, 79
    predicate adjective, 7a, 40d
    pronominal, 38
    participial phrase as, 44d
    participle as, 44c

Adjective—Continued
    placement of, 47
    possessive, 38
    possessive compounds, 14d
    prepositional phrase as, 45
    types, 38
    value of, 37a
Adjective clause (see Clauses)
    defined, 5
    nonrestrictive, 46a, 62
    restrictive, 46a, 62
    use of, 46a
Adjective phrase (see Phrases)
    infinitive, 5a, 44b
    participial, 5a, 44d
    placement of, 47e
    prepositional, 5a, 45
    prepositional-gerund, 44e
Adverb
    comparison, 42, 43
    conjunctive, 56d, 61c, 84a
    defined, 4e, 37c
    dependent clause as, 46b
    distinguished from adjective, 40
    distinguished from predicate adjective, 40d
    infinitive as, 44a
    infinitive phrase as, 44b
    interrupter, punctuation of, 63a
    overuse of, 79
    placement of, 47
    prepositional phrase as, 45
    relative, 7e, 40a, 57d
    types, 39
    used to connect coordinate clauses, 56d
    used to introduce subordinate clause, 57b
Adverb clause (see Clauses)
    defined, 5, 46b
    interruptive, punctuation of, 63a
    introductory, punctuation of, 63a

Adverb clause—Continued
    placement for emphasis, 47h
    nonrestrictive at end of sentence, punctuation of, 66d
    subordinating conjunctions used to introduce, 57b
Adverb phrase (see Phrases)
    infinitive, 5a, 44b
    prepositional, 5a, 45
    prepositional-gerund, 44e
Agreement
    defined, 15
    consistency in, 15c, 17
    of collective noun with verb, 16a
    of pronoun and antecedent, 15b
    of subject and verb, 15a
all, 16a
allege, danger of use, 77
among, between, 49d
and
    as conducive to wordiness, 84b
    as signal that elements are coordinate, 56b, 84a
    loosely used as a connective, 86b
    to begin a sentence, 58f
    too many *and*'s, 58d
    vs. *also*, 58a
    vs. *but*, 58e
and etc., 58b
and/or, number of subjects joined by, 16h
and which, and who, but which, 58c
Antecedent of pronoun
    agreement of pronoun with, 15b
    ambiguous, 19a, 84i
    defined, 15b
    implied, 19c
    in subordinate construction, 19b
    possessive wrongly used as antecedent, 19b
Anticlimax
    placement of clauses, for emphasis, 87d
any, 16a
anyone, anybody, number of, 16d
Apostrophe
    to form possessive case, 14f
Appositive
    case of, 12, 13, 14d
    defined, 12
    punctuation of, 62, 62c, 66d
Articles
    defined, 38a
    use, 38a
    with abbreviations, 38a

as
    case after, 12c
    misused for *that* or *whether*, 58h
    since or *because* in place of, 58g
as if, subjunctive after, 30f
as though, subjunctive after, 30f
as well as
    not affecting number of subject, 18b
assert, claim, maintain, 77
at, in, 49c
Auxiliary verbs, 7b

B

because
    use to show subordination, 57b
    use instead of *since, as*, 58g
below, beneath, down, under, underneath, 49e
between, among, 49d
both . . . and
    to show coordination (parallelism), 7e, 56c, 84a
but
    meaning *except*, 13c
    to begin a sentence, 58f
    used to signal coordination, 55, 56b, 84a
    punctuation before, 61a

C

Case
    defined, 3a, 12
    following forms of *to be*, 12d, 13e
    following infinitives, 12d, 13e
    following *than* or *as*, 12c
    nominative case, 12
    objective case, 13
    of appositives, 12, 13, 14d
    of words linked by *and* or *or*, 12, 13, 14d, 16f, 16g
    of interrogative pronouns, 12a
    of relative pronouns, 12b
    of subjects of "ing" words, 13f, 14h
    of subjects of infinitives, 13d
    possessive case, 14
    of *who* and *whoever*, 12b
Choice of words, 67–79
    (See also Words)
Clarity
    by choice of words, 70–76
    by sentence construction, 84
    by use of readability factors, 85
    essential for effective sentence, 83

Index

Clauses
  adjective clause
    defined, 5
    placement of, 47f, 84e
    restrictive and nonrestrictive
      defined, 46a
      punctuation of, 46a, 62, 62a, 66d
      use of *that* or *which* to introduce, 46d
      words used to introduce, 46a
  adverb clause
    defined, 5
    placement of, 47b, 84e
    introductory, punctuation of, 63a, 66d
    words used to introduce, 46b
  defined, 5
  dependent clause
    defined, 5
    functions of, 46
    used to subordinate, 84b
    words used to introduce, 46
  elliptical clause
    dangling, 46c, 84d
    defined, 46c
  independent clause
    defined, 5, 61
    punctuation of, 61, 66d, 66e
    words used to connect, 7e, 56, 84a
Collective noun
  defined, 10c
Collective words
  abstract, 16a(2)
  common, 16a
  company names, 16a
  short collectives 16a(1)
  special collectives 16a(2)
Colon
  between main clauses, 61d, 66f
  placement inside or outside quotation marks, 66i
  to introduce a list, 66f
  to introduce a long quotation, 66f
Comma
  conventional rules governing, 66
  functional rules governing, 61–65
  importance of, 60
  in echo questions, 61d, 66d
  with addresses, dates, titles, 64c, 66d
  with coordinate items in series, 65, 66d

Comma—Continued
  with interrupting expressions identifying source, 64b, 66d
  with interrupting transitional expressions, 64a, 66d
  with introductory adverbial modifiers, 63a, 66d
  with introductory prepositional phrases, 63b, 66d
  with introductory transitional expressions, 63c, 66d
  with main clauses joined by coordinate conjunctions, 61a, 66d
  with nominative absolute, 64d, 66d
  with nonrestrictive adjective modifiers, 62, 62a, 66d
  with nonrestrictive adverbial modifiers, 62b, 66d
  with nonrestrictive appositives, 62c, 66d
  with quotation marks, 66i
  with short, parallel main clauses, 61d, 66d
Comma splice, 61, 84c
Command language
  imperative mood, 28
Comparative degree, 42a
Comparison
  adjectives and adverbs that cannot be compared, 43a
  degrees of, 42a
  incomplete comparison, 43c, 84f
  irregular, 42c
  of adjectives and adverbs, 42
  with *other* or *else*, 43b
Complement
  defined, 7c
  direct object, 7c
  indirect object, 7c
  of linking verb, 7c
  predicate adjective, 7c, 40d
  predicate noun, 7c, 12d
Complex sentence, 6c
Compound
  adjectives
    defined, 41a
    following noun, 41b
    hyphenation of, 41c, 41e
    preceding noun, 41a
    proper, 41d
  nouns
    forming possessive of, 14d
  object
    defined, 13

Compound—Continued
   sentence
      defined, 41a
      punctuation of, 61, 66d, 66e
   subject
      case of, 12, 16f
      defined, 16f
      number of, 16f
Compound-complex sentence, 6d
Concrete noun
   use of, 72
Condition contrary to fact
   subjunctive used to express, 30d
Conjunction, 4g
Conjunctive adverb
   defined, 7e
   lists of, 7e, 56d, 84a
   punctuation of main clauses connected by, 56d, 66e
   to begin a sentence, 58f
   use of 56d, 84a (See Connectives)
Connectives
   categories of, 7e
   conjunctive adverbs, 7e, 55, 56, 84a
   coordinating conjunctions, 7e, 55, 56, 84a
   correlative conjunctions, 7e, 56c, 84a, 85c
   defined, 7e
   prepositions, 7e, 48–53
   relative adverbs, 7e, 46a, 57d
   relative pronoun, 7e, 46a, 46d, 55, 57c
   subordinating conjunctions, 7e, 57b, 84b
   importance as signals to reader, 84a
   joining elements of equal rank, 7e, 55, 56, 84a
   joining elements of unequal rank, 7e, 55, 57, 84b
Connotation
   contrasted with *denotation*, 59c
   defined, 59c
Coordinating conjunctions
   defined, 7e, 56b, 84a
   punctuation between clauses joined by, 61a, 66d
   to begin a sentence, 58f
   use to show parallelism, 56b, 84a
Coordination
   how to show, 56a
   shown by conjunctive adverbs, 56d, 84a

Coordination—Continued
   shown by coordinate conjunctions, 56b, 83a
   shown by correlative conjunctions, 56c, 84a
   shown by punctuation, 56e, 61
Correlative conjunctions
   definition and use, 7e, 56c, 84a
   placement of, 56c, 84a
   use in parallel constructions, 56c, 85c

D

Dangling modifiers
   contrasted with nominative absolute, 44g
   described, 3d, 44f, 84d
   elliptical clause, 46c
   gerund phrase, 44f
   infinitive phrase, 44f
   participial phrase, 44f
   prepositional phrase, 45a
Dash
   to set off nonrestrictive appositive, 62, 66g
   to set off nonrestrictive modifier, 62, 66g
   with main clauses, 61d, 66g
data, singular or plural, 16c
Dates, punctuation of, 46c, 66d
Degrees of comparison, 42a
Demonstrative adjectives
   type of pronominal adjective, 38
Demonstrative pronoun
   defined, 11e (See Pronouns)
   possessive of, 14h
Denotation, 69c
Dependent clause
   defined, (See Clauses)
Direct address
   case of, 12e
   punctuation, 64e, 66d
Direct object, 7c
   case of, 13a
Direct quotation
   punctuation of, 66i
Doublets, 75

E

each
   number of, 16d
Economy
   of expression, 86a
   with words, 75

Index

either
    number of, 16d
either . . . or, 56c, 84a
    (See Correlative conjunctions)
Elliptical clauses
    dangling, 46c, 84d
    defined, 46c
else
    possessive case, 14a
Emphasis in the sentence
    by periodic structure, 87d
    by position in, 87d
    by use of active voice, 35, 85e
every
    number of subject modified by, 16d
everyone, everybody
    number of, 16d
Expletives
    described, 18a
    it
        not to be used in same sentence with personal pronoun *it,* 18a
        number of verb following, 18a
    there
        number of verb following, 18a
        overuse of, 86a

F

Faulty parallelism, 56c, 85c
few
    number of, 16d
Fractions
    number of, 16b
Future perfect tense
    defined, 22f
    uses, 22f
Future tense
    shall-will and *should-would* with, 22e
    uses, 22e

G

Gender
    defined, 9a
Gerund
    defined, 7f
    distinguished from participle, 13f
    possessive with, 14h
    tense of, 24a
    tense sequence, 25c
Gerund phrase
    as modifier, 44e
    defined, 5a, 7f
    in prepositional phrase, 44e, 84d

Gobbledygook
    characteristics of, 75, 85b

H

here
    introducing a sentence, 18a
    number of verb with, 18a
Hyphen
    forming possessive of hyphenated compound, 14d
    in compound modifiers, 41
        in modifiers preceding noun, 41a
        in modifiers following noun, 41b
    suspending hypens, 41c

I

ics
    nouns ending in, number of, 16c
Idiom (see "Writer's Guide")
    defined, 49a, 76
    use, 76
if
    clauses, mood of verb in, 31
    vs. *whether,* 58i
Imperative mood (see Mood)
    definition and uses, 28
    in procedure writing, 28
Impersonal use of *it, they, you* contributing to wordiness, 19d
in, at, 49c
in addition to
    phrase introduced by, not affecting number of subject, 18b
including
    phrase introduced by, not affecting number of subject, 18b
Incomplete comparisons, 43c, 84f
    (See Comparison)
Indefinite pronoun
    gender, 16d
    list of, 4b
    number and person of, 16d
    possessive of, 14a
Independent clause, 5a (see Clauses)
Indicative mood (see Mood)
    definition and use of, 27
Indirect discourse
    defined, 23b(4)
    Revenue use of, 23b(4)
Indirect object
    case, 13b
    defined, 7c

Indirect quotation
    punctuation of, 66i
Infinitive
    as modifier, 44a
    case with, 12d, 13d, 13e
    defined, 7f
    split, 44a
    subject of, 13d
    tense of, 24c
    tense sequence of, 25b
    to as part of, 44a
Infinitive phrase
    as adjective, 5a, 44b
    as adverb, 6d, 44b
    as noun, 5a
    dangling, 6d, 44f, 84d
Intensive pronouns (see Pronouns)
    defined, 11f
    list of, 11f
    no comma with, 11f
Interrogative adjective
    illustrated, 38
Interrogative pronouns (see Pronouns)
    case of, 12a
    defined, 11c
    number of verb with, 18a
is when
    misuse of in definition, 58n
is where
    misuse of in definition, 58o
it
    impersonal use, 19d
    not to be used in same sentence with personal pronoun *it*, 18a
    number of verb with, 18a
Itemization, 85d
its and *it's* distinguished, 14a

J

Jargon, 70

L

Length
    variety in sentence length, 87c
Level of usage, 69c
Linking verb
    defined and described, 7b
    followed by predicate adjective, 7c, 40d
Loose sentence (see Sentence)
    contrasted with *periodic*, 87d

M

Main clauses (see Clauses)
many a, number of, 16d
Measure, units of
    number of, 16b
memorandum
    plural of, 16c
Modifiers
    adjectives, 4d, 7d, 37c, 40
    adverbs, 4e, 7d, 37c, 40
    compound, 41
    dangling, 3d, 7d, 44f, 45a, 84d
    defined, 7d
    dependent clause as, 46
    importance of, 37a
    misplaced, 47, 84c
    nonrestrictive, 46a, 62, 66d
    overuse of, 79
    placement of, 47, 84c
    prepositional phrase as, 6a, 45, 54a
    restrictive, 46a, 62
    squinting, 47g, 84e
    verbals as, 7f, 44
Mood
    defined, 26
    imperative, 28
    indicative, 27
    shift in, 32
    subjunctive, 27, 29, 30, 31
more, 16a(1), 42b
most
    number of verb following, 16a(1)
    vs.-*est*, 42b
Multiple
    modifiers, placement of, 47c
    words with multiple meanings, 74 (see Words)

N

neither
    number of, 16d
neither . . . nor
    defined as correlatives, 56c, 84a
    use to show parallelism, 56c, 84a
Nominative absolute (see Absolute)
Nominative case (see Case)
nobody, no one
    number of, 16d
none
    number of verb following, 16a(1)
note
Nonrestrictive modifier (see Modifiers)

Index 257

nor
    number of compound subject joined by, 16g
    principal clauses joined by, punctuation of, 61a
not only . . . but also
    defined as correlatives, 56c, 84a
    use to show parallelism, 56c, 84a
Noun clauses (see Clauses)
Noun phrases (see Phrases)
Nouns
    abstract, 10c
    case, 9b
    characteristics, 9
    collective, 10c
    common, 10b
    concrete, 10d
    confusing singular and plural forms of, 16c
    defined, 4a, 10
    functions, 8
    gender, 9a
    number, 9c
    proper, 10a
    possessive of, 14
Number
    confusing singular and plural forms, 16c
    defined, 9c
    not affected by intervening phrase, 18b
    of collective nouns, 16a
    of pronoun and antecedent, agreement, 15b
    of pronouns with antecedents, 19
    of subject and verb, agreement, 15a
    of subjects joined by *and*, 16f
    of subjects joined by *or* or *nor*, 16g
    preceded by *a*, 17
    preceded by *the*, 17
    shift in, 15c, 17

O

Object (see Complement)
    defined, 7c
    direct, 7c, 13a
    indirect, 7c, 13b
    of a preposition, 13c
Objective case, 13–13f
    (See Case)
Obsolete words, 73
    (See Words)

Omission
    denoted by periods, 66a
    faulty
        of antecedent, 19c
        of auxiliary verb, 17
        of signal for parallelism, 85c
        of *that*, 58k
        of prepositions in idioms, 53
    proper
        of *that* after *saying, thinking*, etc. 58l
one
    as antecedent, 16e
    as subject, 17
only
    placement of, 47d
only one of the
    number of verb with, 16e
or
    number of compound subject joined by, 16g

P

Paragraphing
    introduction to, 89
Parallelism
    as aid to clear writing, 85c
    by use of conjunctive adverbs, 56d
    by use of coordinate conjunctions, 56b
    by use of correlative conjunctions, 56c
    defined, 56a
    faulty omission of second signal, 53, 85c
    faulty parallelism, 56c
    itemization, 85d
    punctuation, 56e
    repetition of words to signal, 85c
Parentheses
    with nonrestrictive modifiers, 62, 66h
    with other punctuation marks, 66h
Parenthetical elements
    defined, 64
    punctuation of, 64, 66d
Participial phrase
    as modifier, 44d
    dangling, 7d, 44f, 84d
    defined, 6b, 7f
    restrictive or nonrestrictive, 6b
Participle
    as modifier, 44c
    distinguished from gerund, 13f
    illustrated, 7f

Participle—Continued
    in dangling constructions, 6b, 44f, 84d
    subject of, 13f
    tense of, 24b
    tense sequence of, 25a
Passive voice
    defined, 33
    overuse, 85e
    personal pronoun and, 35
    proper use, 85e
    uses, 34
Past perfect tense (see Tense)
Past tense (see Tense)
Period
    after abbreviations, 66a
    position inside quotation marks, 66i
    to emphasize individual clauses, 61b
    to mark the end of a sentence or sentence fragment, 66a
    to show omissions from quoted matter, 66a
Periodic sentence (see Sentence)
    contrasted with loose sentence, 87d
    for emphasis, 87d
Person
    property of verb, defined, 7b
    shift in, 17, 84g
Personal pronoun (see Pronouns)
    case of, 12, 13, 14
    compound, 11f
    defined, 11a
    possessive of, 14a
Phrases
    absolute, 44g
    as modifiers, 44, 45
    defined, 5a
    gerund phrase, 7f, 44e
    infinitive phrase, 5a, 7f, 44b
    noun phrase, 5a, 44e
    participial phrase, 5a, 7f, 44d
    prepositional-gerund phrase, 44e
    prepositional phrase, 5a, 45, 54
Placement of modifiers, 47, 84e
    adverb clauses, 47h
    between subject and verb, 47a
    groups of adjectives, 47c
    long modifying phrases, 47i
    phrases and clauses, 47e
    relative clauses, 47f
    single adjectives, 47b
    single adverbs, 47d
    squinting constructions, 47g

Planning and organizing
    importance of to effective writing, 1, 82
Point of-view
    unnecessary shift in, 84g
    shift in number or person, 17
    shift in subject or voice, 17, 36
    shift in tense or mood, 23a, 32
Positive degree, 42a
Possessive case, 14
    defined, 14
    of abbreviations, 14f
    use of "of" phrase to form, 14c
    with compound words, 14d
    with gerund, 14h
Predicate
    adjective, 7c
        distinguished from adverb, 40d
    nominative, 7c
        case, 12d
        number differs from that of subject, 18c
    complement
        defined, 7c
Preposition
    choice of, 49
    compound, 48b
    defined, 4f, 7e, 48
    faulty omission of, 53
    idiomatic use of, 49a
    in parallelism, 53a, 85c
    in phrase, 6a, 45
    object of, case, 13c
    phrasal, 48c, 50, 75
    placement of, 54
    simple, 48a
    superfluous, 51
Prepositional-gerund phrase, 44e, 84d
Prepositional phrase
    as adjective, 45, 62
    as adverb, 5a
    as noun, 5a
    dangling, 45a, 84d
    defined, 5a, 54
    overuse of, 54
Principal clause (see Clauses)
part of
    followed by plural nouns, number of, 16b
percent of
    followed by plural nouns, number of, 16b

Index

Plurals
    confusing singular and plural forms, 16c
Present perfect tense, 22b
Present tense
    defined, 22a
    emphatic present, 22a
    habitual action, 22a
    historical present, 22a
    universal truth, 22a
    uses, 22a
Pronouns
    agreement, 15–18
    characteristics, 9
    defined, 4b, 11
    demonstrative, 11e
    functions, 8
    indefinite, 11d
    interrogative, 11c, 18a
    personal, 11a
    reference of, 19–19d, 84i
    reflexive, 11f
    relative, 11b, 46d, 55, 57c
    special problems with, 19
Proper noun, 10a
Punctuation
    after introductory expressions, 61d, 63, 66d
    before conjunctive adverbs, 61b, 66e
    colon, 66f
    comma, 61–65, 66d
    conventional, defined, 60
    dash, 61d, 62, 66g
    enclosing appositives, 62, 66d, 66g, 66h
    enclosing modifiers, 62, 66d, 66g, 66h
    enclosing parenthetical expressions, 64, 66d, 66g, 66h
    exclamation mark, 66c
    importance of, 3f, 59b
    parentheses, 66h
    period, 61b, 66a, 66i
    question mark, 66b, 66i
    quotation marks, 66i
        placement of other marks inside or outside, 66i
    semicolon, 61c, 61d, 66d
    to distinguish between question and request, 66a, 66b
    to separate items in series, 65, 66d, 66e
    to separate main clauses, 61, 66a, 66c, 66d

Punctuation—Continued
    to set off nonrestrictive elements, 46a, 62, 66d
    to show coordination, 56c

Q

Question mark
    after direct question, 66b
    faulty use following request, 66a, 66b
    in interrogatory series, 66b
    position with quotation marks, 66i
    to indicate doubt about correctness of statement, 66b
Quotation marks
    before each quoted paragraph, 66i
    colon precedes, 66i
    comma precedes, 66i
    for direct quotation, 66i
    placement of punctuation marks inside or outside, 66i
    with titles, 66i

R

Readability factors, 85
Reference of pronouns, 19–19d, 84i
Reflexive pronoun (see Pronouns)
    as substitute for personal pronoun, 11f
    defined, 11f
Relative adverb, 7e, 40a, 57d
Relative clause (see Clauses)
    placement of, 47f
    subject of, case, 12b
Relative pronoun (see Pronouns)
    antecedent of, 16e
    as connective, 7e, 46a, 46d, 55, 57c
    case of, 12b
    defined, 11b
    number and person of, 16e
    possessive of, 14a
Restrictive modifier
    adjective clause, 46a
    punctuation of, 62
    that, which to introduce clause, 46d
remainder of
    followed by noun, number of, 16b
rest of
    followed by noun, number of, 16b

S

Semicolon
    position outside quotation marks, 66i
    to separate items in series, 66e
    to separate main clauses, 61c, 66e

Sentence
    appropriate style of, 87
    classification of, 6
        simple, 6a
        complex, 6c
        compound, 6b
        compound-complex, 6a
    connectives, 7e
    emphatic positions in, 87d
    formal and informal style in, 87a
    fragments, 24d, 66a
    identification table, 88
    loose, 87d
    modifiers, 7d, 37–47
    periodic, 87d
    planned, 82
    qualities of effective sentence, 81
    too-full, 86b
    variety, 87b, 87c
    what makes it clear, 83, 84
    what makes it concise, 86
Sequence in tense, 23 (see Tense)
shall, will, 22e
Shifts
    in mood, 32
    in number and person, 17
    in subject, 84g
    in tense, 84g
    in voice, 36, 84g
should, would, 22e
Slanted writing, 27, 79
some, 16a(1)
Split construction, 53b, 84h
Split infinitive, 44a
Squinting modifier, 47g, 84e
Style, 87
Subject
    clauses as, 5
    defined, 7a
    joined by *and,* number of, 16f
    joined by *and/or,* number of, 16h
    joined by *or* or *nor,* number of, 16g
    parts of speech used as, 7a
    phrases as, 7a
Subjunctive mood (see Mood)
    defined, 29
    forms, 29a
    uses, 30
Subordinate conjunctions, 7e, 57b
Subordination
    how to show, 57a, 84b
    with relative adverb, 57d
    with relative pronoun, 57c
    with subordinate conjunctions, 57b

Substantive, 7a
Superlative degree, 42a
Suspending
    constructions, 53b
    hyphens, 41c

T

Technical and legal terms, 70
    multiple meanings, 74
    words of foreign origin, 70
Tense
    defined, 21a
    future perfect, 22f
    future, 22e
    past perfect, 22d
    past, 22c
    present perfect, 22b
    present, 22a
    progressive form, 21b
    sequence of, 23
    tenses of verbals, 24
than and *as,* case of pronoun after, 12c
that
    faulty repetition of, 58m
    introducing clauses, 46d
    introducing parallel clauses, 58k
    proper omission of, 58l
there, introducing sentence, 18a, 86a
Time table, 25d
Tone, 77

U

Units of measure, number of, 16b
Usage, levels of, 69c

V

Variety
    in sentence length, 87c
    in sentence types, 87b
Verbals
    as modifiers, 44
    defined, 7f
    in sentence fragments, 24d
    tense, 24
    tense sequence, 25
Verbs
    agreement with subject, 15a
    defined, 4c, 7b
    irregular, 21c
    linking, 7b, 40d
    mood, 26–31
    principal parts, 21c

Index

Verbs—Continued
    properties, 7b
    regular, 21c
    tense, 21
    time table, 25d
    voice, 33, 34
Voice
    active, 33, 85e
    defined, 33
    passive, 33, 85e
    uses, 34

W

when, 58n
when vs. *while*, 58p
where, 58o
whether vs. *if*, 58i
whether vs. *whether or not*, 58j
which, introducing clauses, 46d

while
    vs. *although, though, and, but*, 58q
    vs. *when*, 58p
who
    agreement, 16e(2)
    case of, 12b
    introducing clauses, 46d
whose vs. *who's*, 14a
Windups, 75
Words
    characteristics of, 69
    concrete, 72
    current usage, 73
    economy, 75
    impersonal, 78
    importance of, 68
    simple, 71
    technical and legal terms, 70
    that antagonize, 77
    that please, 77
    with multiple meanings, 74